BEYOND

AN ABSENCE OF

FAITH

Stories About the Loss of Faith
And the Discovery of Self

Edited by

Jonathan MS Pearce

Tristan Vick

Foreword by Jeremy Beahan

Beyond An Absence of Faith: Stories About the Loss of Faith
And the Discovery of Self
Edited by Jonathan MS Pearce and Tristan Vick
Copyright © 2014 Onus Books

Published by *Onus Books*

First Edition, May 1 2014

Cover design: Tristan Vick

Image credit: X-ray: NASA/CXC/U.Mich./S.Oey, IR: NASA/JPL, Optical:
ESO/WFI/2.2-m

Printed by Lightning Source International

Trade paperback ISBN: 978-0-9926000-0-6

OB 06/10

PRAISE FOR *BEYOND AN ABSENCE OF FAITH*

Pearce and Vick have brought together a diverse group of voices with one thing in common—they have moved beyond being "former believers" into being active participants in humanity. Each of the stories shared is unique, but former believers will find something they can identify with in every one. From the pain of separation from friends and family, to the joy of being liberated from a sexist mindset, to the harsh reality of having to find a new career in the middle of your life because you have embraced reason, these personal stories help to reinforce for the non-believer that you are not alone in your journey. Instead, you are walking a path many have gone down before, and you can take solace in knowing that these authors have been there as well.

Dr Caleb Lack, author of several books on psychology, skeptical blogger at *Great Plains Skeptic*

Religion is a thorny tree with roots that coil and twist to the very bedrock of how people are able to make sense of their lives and the world, and a mind so ensnared is in a perilous trap. The way out is hard to find, and if discovered is fraught with difficulties that all point back inside. *Am I alone? Will my friends and family reject me? How can I make sense of the world, my life, and myself?* The story of a religion lost and a mind set free is a compelling chronicle of the human spirit triumphant, a necessary connection with the humanity of those with the courage to think freely, be honest with themselves and others, and face what comes. *Beyond an Absence of Faith* is a beautiful and highly recommended collection of very moving accounts that will connect the reader with what it means--and what it takes--to be a human unencumbered by the toxic grip of faith.

James A. Lindsay, author of *Dot, Dot, Dot: Infinity Plus God Equals Folly*

Being a non-believer has its challenges and rewards. However, it is the becoming that can be the most challenging, the most harrowing, the most frightening, and then perhaps the most rewarding of experiences. From fear to elation, the journey from faith can be just as emotional as any journey to it. And like any journey, it's good to have people along for the ride. In *"Beyond an Absence of Faith"*, the stories of others who have made the transition can provide solace for those with doubts but are afraid to go down the path. Let's face it, we need reasons as much as stories to help us grow, and the personal stories in this book can provide the empathy and courage to believe only in things with good reasons.

Aaron Adair, author of *The Star of Bethlehem: A Skeptical View*

Beyond an Absence of Faith is an extremely important book. I say this because as a species, we are inherently social creatures and as such, we respond more readily to social influence than we do to reasoned, logical and other forms of argumentation. Whilst this book does contain brilliantly reasoned and logical arguments against faith and theism, its true power rests within its appeal to social influence. For this reason, Beyond an Absence of Faith has the potential to reach those powerful social dimensions of the believer's mind, while at the same time comforting those who have recently suffered the social and psychological agony of leaving their religions.

Michael Sherlock, author of *I Am Christ: The Crucifixion–Painful Truths*. and *The Gospel of Atheism & Freethought–According to Sherlock*.

We dedicate this book to the atheists, agnostics, nonbelievers, skeptical and eternally curious people, both past and present, whose voices have for too long gone virtually unheard. May this work be tribute to the fact that you are not alone; and together—we have a voice.

Acknowledgements:

This book would not have been completed without the significant help of several others. First and foremost, the writers themselves should be thanked for putting their lives in these pages. Not an easy task, especially considering everyone has had different experiences with writing, making their effort that much more remarkable. We are also heavily indebted to Rebecca Bradley for her invaluable editorial and proofing assistance. All remaining mistakes are, of course, fully our own doing. Thanks must also go out to Edward T. Babinski for some great assistance and feedback in the early stages of the manuscript. Thanks to Jeremy Beahan for stepping up to help us right when we needed it and for his most excellent foreword. We advise checking out the superb podcast, *Reasonable Doubts*, that he and his team produce when you get the opportunity. Finally, we would like to thank our families who, with great patience, allow us to hide away behind the glowing screens and clacking keys of our computers collating, editing and preparing collections like this one. We are sincerely grateful.

CONTENTS

FOREWORD

JEREMY BEAHAN

What you hold in your hand is no ordinary book on Atheism. Over the past decade a number of excellent books have been published on the subject of non-belief. Drawing both from ancient traditions and the cutting edge of contemporary philosophy and science these books attempt to refute the claims of religious apologists while offering a rational case against belief in a God. But human beings are not, and have never been, purely rational animals. We adopt beliefs and reject them for reasons that are relevant to our own circumstances—reasons that are deeply emotional and experiential as well as intellectual. Many popular books on atheism lack this personal dimension. Thankfully, this book is not one of them. In the pages that follow you will encounter more than abstract arguments against religious propositions. You will meet real people who were once devout but have discovered a new life awaiting them beyond faith. Immerse yourself in their stories and a richer picture will develop as to why so many people today have become dissatisfied with religious answers to life's questions. You will

i

also find an inspiring vision of what life can be like after religion. Believers will find valuable insights into the mind of apostates and hopefully will feel sympathy upon understanding the struggles they must endure. Doubters may find relief and guidance knowing that others have walked this path before and emerged stronger than they began. Lifelong atheists may come to appreciate their formerly-devout friends and will better understand how to enter into meaningful, constructive dialogue with religious peers. There is much wisdom waiting in these pages for anyone who takes the time to read them.

Stories of the kind you are about to read are sometimes called "*deconversion* accounts"—the atheist's counterpart to religious testimonials of faith. As one who has heard many such stories I can tell you they are often as unique as the people telling them. Some deconverts hated their religious upbringing. They recall feeling traumatized by stories of demons, hellfire and the tortures that await the damned. Withering under oppressive rules their natural curiosity and self-respect was nearly smothered by decades of indoctrination into the tenets of their faith. Some counted the days until they were old enough to escape the totalitarian grip of their religion. For others, their religious upbringing was by-and-large a positive experience. Raised in loving households and nurtured by their congregations, religion provided them a clear sense of themselves and a feeling of belonging. People raised in contexts like this have little to rebel against and their deconversion tends to happen mostly for intellectual reasons. When their private doubts become public they often feel a profound sense of loss, having been cast away from the only supportive community they have ever known.

For those who have lived their whole lives in a religious context, leaving the faith may present serious challenges to their health and wellbeing. Raised under an authoritarian parenting style, taught to believe that morality consists of blind obedience to inflexible rules of conduct, some believers never learn to reason their way through difficult moral situations. Self-control is maintained by the threat of divine punishment or fear of judgment from religious peers. Upon realizing they are not under the watchful eye of an angry God these apostates can be especially vulnerable to substance abuse, addiction and other forms of self-destructive behavior. Similarly, some find themselves unprepared to cope with the intellectual complexities of life outside the faith. Beliefs can change quickly. Habits of thought, however, tend to be more entrenched. As oppressive as a dogmatic faith can be, it does offer the believer the comfort of convictions that need not be questioned. A recent deconvert may miss the psychological security of religion and seek out such dogmatic assurances elsewhere. In some cases, inadequate religious schooling may have left them far behind their more secular peers or without the skills necessary to find well-paying jobs in the workforce. Such problems are most common for individuals leaving severely authoritarian religious backgrounds. The vast majority of apostates leave the faith with both their "moral compass" and critical thinking skills not only intact, but functioning better than ever. Nevertheless, there are other challenges deconverts face that are more universal.

Nearly all deconverts will face challenges in their family life. By rejecting religion, one may risk being disowned by one's parents, children, spouses or friends. Even when the consequences are not so drastic, a major change of worldview can destabilize relationships that were originally forged or strengthened through shared conviction. If new ways of nurturing those bonds cannot be discovered, relationships will suffer. Recognizing this, many apostates feel pressure to keep their doubts hidden. Even those who refuse to hide their doubt often stress over how and when they should "come out" as an atheist to their family and friends. One's livelihood can also be threatened by leaving the faith. It is hard to quantify just how much discrimination non-theists face in the work place but stories abound of those who lost clients, were passed by for promotions or whose jobs were terminated when their atheism became known.

Less tangible, but just as important, are the emotional & existential challenges faced by apostates after leaving the fold. While some formerly religious people claim to have never really believed, a great many more believed with conviction. Religion once defined the boundaries of their reality. It gave the world a sense of meaning and purpose. Even during the hardest trials of life, faith could be turned to as a refuge. But after religion, the apostate finds themselves in a universe that looks the same but is frighteningly unfamiliar in character. Having rejected the false consolations of religion, the deconvert must confront the reality of their own fragile and fleeting existence. Lost loved ones are now lost forever. Gone too are all assurances that suffering happens for a reason or that injustices here on earth will be made right in the world to come. Some grieve the loss of their deity the way one would a father or trusted companion. Others must cope with the feeling of being betrayed, misled or even abused spiritually by their religious mentors. It is not uncommon for a deconvert to feel "lost" as the moral and metaphysical clarity they once enjoyed evaporates leaving a dizzying sea of perspectives in its place.

Despite the hardships of losing faith, many also find this time to be exhilarating. Even the most familiar experiences can take on a new sense of wonder as the deconvert rediscovers themselves and the universe they inhabit. For many this is first time they've had the freedom to entertain ideas without securing the approval of a creed or holy text. Reveling in this newfound autonomy, many cast their intellectual nets far and wide, capturing as much knowledge as they can. At first they may change their views as often as they change their clothes, but this is not a reason for embarrassment. Realizing one is wrong is simply an opportunity for getting things right. As their knowledge and skill in thinking develop, so too does their confidence in their own reason and judgment. Questions about the nature of existence remain but do not provoke the same anxiety as before. If supported by strong evidence, even propositions held tentatively will seem more trustworthy than the fragile yet hyperbolic "certainties" of a faith maintained through ignorance. The unknown, once frightening, now presents itself as a delightful invitation to inquiry, an opportunity to exercise one's curiosity and further hone the set of intellectual tools they've acquired.

For those who came from more oppressive communities, deconversion has also provided them a second chance to seek out fulfillment in experiences once forbidden. This may mean finally being able to dance or to wear the clothing, eat the food, watch the films, and listen to the music they've always wanted to. Simple amusements, perhaps, but nonetheless valuable to one who has never enjoyed those freedoms. This newfound liberty can also lead to personal transformations that are lasting and profound. Some find the courage to escape abusive relationships. Others embark on new personal projects or find fellowship once again in communities that share their newfound values. Many begin to recover from years of shame and guilt attached to sexuality. Making peace with their bodies and desires, they now have the space to explore attraction in healthy ways. For some it may even be the first time they've been able to truly love the kind of person they would choose to love. Far from a loss, leaving religion can be liberating. The same people who before could not even imagine living without faith often look back wondering why they hadn't left earlier. Despite all hardships endured, losing God, it turns out, is just the first step in finding oneself again—this time in a strange but beautiful cosmos rich with wonder and possibility.

Jeremy Beahan, Grand Rapids, 2014

INTRODUCTION

JONATHAN MS PEARCE

AS A PHILOSOPHER WHO DEALS PREDOMINANTLY WITH THE abstract ideas concerning religion, such as Cosmological Arguments or Ontological Arguments, I am guilty of being one step removed from the reality of religion; that is, the act of having faith and believing in something on a daily basis which molds my every action and character. Indeed, it often seems as though I live in an abstract world of endless argument in a predominantly online life where emotions and invective are easy to come by, but easy enough to walk away from, coming, as they do, from far off corners of the web-connected world.

Belief is, arguably, mainly a psychological affair. That is to say, if one is arguing about *whether* to believe, one is rationally engaging with arguments and evidence. However, *in* believing, one is committing one's mind to a faith and a set of directives in a deeply personal manner, handling evidence and non-believers in a truly psychological and emotive way. When one's family member is a non-believer and one sincerely imagines them serving an eternity of torment in hell, then one's rationality is fundamentally tainted with emotion, which in turn can mean one then acts in a highly emotional manner.

As well as being psychological and social in nature, belief is often experiential insofar as believers can be impervious to philosophical and rational arguments because they are trumped by the notion that the believer has experienced God, communicated with their Creator, interacted with, and had things revealed by, the entity in which they have faith. This presents further problems for the person who then deconverts. What, then, explains these phenomena? Has the believer been lying to themselves, or mistakenly deluding themselves over a long period of time? Is it the influence of important others which lends itself to aiding the delusion? Will there be an emptiness in place of this kind of experience and, possibly, comfort? All these aspects of belief can play merry hell with the believer who starts on that long and often lonely journey into disbelief.

This theme of loneliness, of having to pit oneself against the will and determination of significant others in families and communities, is commonplace in the deconversion paradigm. However, as the nontheist community grows in size and voice, so there is more comfort and support for the person leaving a religious faith. The internet, for example, with its plethora of social media and bespoke online communities offers sounding boards and support networks where once there were none. The road need no longer be lonely, though it is far too often immensely painful.

This scenario is admittedly alien to me. And that is why this collection of accounts is so fascinating. Everyone is an armchair psychologist, if one is to be honest enough. But unless you have been through the difficult, painful, life-changing process of leaving an all-pervasive faith, then this is the next best thing to understanding the challenges facing people who undergo such transformations.

So the reason for this book is twofold. Firstly, it is a cathartic process for the authors involved; a final piece of closure, perhaps, for a long and arduous journey; a final purge, if you will. Secondly, it has been written as a source of comfort and support to those others who are going through, and will go through, this difficult process. You are not alone. Not anymore, in this global and progressive community, where there are people like you, brave and willing to break out of conforming to the religious orthodoxy of whatever community they, and you, live in.

Jonathan MS Pearce, 29 March 2013

"Nothing is so difficult as not deceiving oneself."

—Ludwig Wittgenstein (*Culture and Value*)

1

SARAH SABELLA

Sarah's Journey: Coping with "Residual Christianity"

I WAS BROUGHT UP IN WHAT I NOW REFER TO AS THE "FUNDIE bubble", where I was raised to be completely unaware of how the real world worked. All I really knew for sure was that there were evil forces out there, seeking to lure me into their clutches. For example, I recall the cover of a religious booklet from our magazine rack which depicted some of the "evil" my parents had in mind. On it was a ninja turtle (yes, seriously), a college professor, a hippie (I assume), an immodestly dressed woman, and Satan himself playing what seemed to be a game of tug-of-war against a mother and father, using their child as the rope. This image sums up my parents' mindset well. Their prime objective was to keep the world out of our home.

When my brothers and I were younger, this was done by banning all secular entertainment and encouraging close friendships with only members of our church, or friends we'd made at Christian camps, Vacation Bible School, and mission trips. A very kind yet non-religious aunt of ours was even pushed away for fear that her "strange" opinions (like acceptance of homosexuality) and secular "lifestyle choices" would lead us astray.

Church was a very big part of our lives. We were involved in just about every opportunity for fellowship it offered, whether we wanted it or not. I didn't enjoy all of the activities but was content for the most part. Church was where my friends were, after all, and I didn't know anything outside of it.

When I was a bit older, secular entertainment was restricted but there were some exceptions. There was at the time a 'Christianized' version of the Teen fashion magazines that were popular among girls my age which contained advice on how to be godly without sacrificing style. Towards the back, there were also secular music and movie reviews complete with Christian alternatives to the secular bands and singers deemed too impure for Christian minds. This helped my mother determine what would be acceptable for us and what should be avoided.

Out of all of my siblings, it seemed that my mother was most worried for my spiritual safety. My oldest brother (I'll call him Seth), partially due to being mildly autistic, has always been easy going and content as long as he is able to keep his most comforting routines. My parents mostly catered to that. Seth tended to do whatever he was told, even if only to keep everyone around him calm and quiet. My younger brother, on the other hand (I'll call him Tommy), was headstrong and blatantly rebellious, but these traits seemed to anger my mother much more than worry her. I have always been inquisitive and strong-willed, but a bit more subtle than Tommy. I believe my mother perceived my "subtlety" as "sneakiness" which, in combination with my age, gender and desire to question, caused her to focus most of her attention on me. Whatever the actual reasons, she made it clear that some of my key personality traits were nothing more than "warning signs" of something terrible.

When I was around thirteen I remember a plaque in the living room with a carving of Philippians 4:8: "Whatever is true, whatever is noble, whatever is right, whatever is pure, whatever is lovely, whatever is admirable—if anything is excellent or praiseworthy—think about such things." It hung above our television set to remind us what we should and should not watch when no one was home to keep us in check. We didn't have cable, which helped keep temptations at bay, but there were still some "questionable" channels, even on basic television. I had (and still have) an overactive conscience, so the plaque-reminder actually worked pretty well. Occasionally, my "sinful impulses" would get the better of me and I would still watch something I knew I shouldn't.

Coincidentally, it was always something sexual in nature. I was a curious teen who knew nothing about sex aside from it being the worst thing ever outside of marriage. Masturbation was never talked about in my home (which I suppose is relatively normal whether one is religious or not) but somehow, I still felt it might be wrong. I actually discovered what I knew as "the feeling" long before I was old enough to really like boys or wonder about sex. It was much later during a youth seminar that I was actually taught that it was "sinful" to pleasure oneself.

At this point, it was something I had been doing habitually, with only a slight feeling of wrongness. Now that I knew it was wrong, the guilt was much more intense. Of course, I couldn't stop and, according to what I'd learned, it was a spiritually dangerous addiction. "Knowing" this did a number on my self-esteem since I deeply and genuinely believed that God was disappointed with me all of the time and I couldn't stop no matter how hard I tried. I asked for forgiveness nightly, but it got to the point where I was even ashamed to mention the subject in prayer.

Nature vs. nurture is complicated, so I can't say for sure what extent religion was responsible for my guilt, but I can recall an incident as far back as kindergarten. I was given a verbal warning during story time for a very minor offense (whispering to a friend, I think), and by the end of the day all I could think about was the trivial bad thing I had done hours before.

I guess I must have been wearing a fearful expression on my face since my teacher bent down to ask me if I was okay as I nervously awaited the hand stamp I was so sure I would not receive (only well-behaved kids got their hand stamped). I remember not being able to look her in the eye, but I nodded, and she stamped my hand anyway. This experience shows that the tendency to obsess over mistakes (sin) and guilt was present early on. As for how much was personality and how much was a result of the "God is always watching" mindset that I was born into, I can't say for sure since I don't remember how religion affected me before the age of five. One thing I can say is that the darker elements of the Christian faith that were present both in my home and in the church certainly fed into personality weaknesses and perpetuated them. Perhaps it's true that some are better suited to religion than others. In my case, it was a rather toxic combination.

From kindergarten to eighth grade, I attended public school. My parents decided to take Seth out of public school to be home-schooled when he was in the seventh grade. I was in fifth at the time. In Seth's case, home-schooling was probably a reasonable option, considering his disability and the way he was being treated by some of the kids there. At some point however, it dawned on my mother that home-schooling was an option not only for Seth, but for me and Tommy as well.

High school was always one of her biggest fears for us since it is often where kids are first exposed to sex and dating and where many Christians are "led astray". There is a film by Dave

Christiano called "Pamela's Prayer" that my mom used to have us watch which sums up the kind of relationship she wanted for us (Pamela didn't date, she "courted" instead, and didn't even kiss her partner until they were married). I think my mom knew that it was mostly wishful thinking, but it was clearly what she hoped for.

Since such virtuous dating was unlikely to happen in a public or even Christian high-school, she took Tommy out before he would have started middle school. I was the most upset about this change while Tommy, being nine or ten at the time, was excited simply because he could learn in his PJ's and eat snacks during class.

My mom agreed to let me at least finish up middle school, since I had one year left. I thought I could use that time to persuade her to let me continue on with my friends to high school, but my efforts were futile. It didn't matter that I was on the honor roll every semester or that I had left a good impression on all of my teachers. Her mind was made up, so the next school year I was home-schooled with my brothers.

We all learned from a Christian curriculum called "School of Tomorrow" under a Baptist umbrella school. This meant that Mr. Broderick, the home-schooling coordinator from the Baptist organization, would take a brief look at our assignments about once a month to make sure everything was in check according to his standards. I now know that even when everything was "in check" according to Mr. Broderick, that it was not actually up to normal standards.

The strongest example was in math, where I was taught from random, mixed math courses (I can recall the word problems specifically being Christianized). I didn't really get sciences either, though I remember creationist propaganda somehow passing for one year of science education. Mr. Broderick and my mother obviously were not too picky about what qualified as science or reading, as long as godly principles were involved.

This particular umbrella school also required a Bible course of some sort. I was basically made to read various Christian books that may have even passed as English. The two books I recall quite well were *Purpose Driven Life* and a book about the evils of Wicca. The point of home-schooling, both my parents' and seemingly the chosen curriculum's, was not to educate and prepare me for life but rather to keep sin, a.k.a. reality, far out of my reach. As a result, when I did actually face the real world, I did so naively and unprepared.

I learned the hard way, a few years later, that even though I was made to believe that I was receiving a better education than most, I was actually pretty behind, academically. As for my brothers, Seth always did just as my mom asked and was able to go on to community college and eventually seminary. Tommy is the worst off because he was home-schooled at such a young age. Fortunately, he seems to be doing well with his computer business and has little interest in going back to school. He's not highly educated but is intelligent enough to have figured a lot out on his own. Unfortunately, he still lives with my parents where they can and do make life stressful for him, especially since he has recently come out as an atheist.

It was during my second year of home-schooling that I met my first boyfriend (I'll call him Daniel) at the only secular environment I was allowed to openly attend: my job. My parents tried, with little success, to nip our relationship in the bud. Sometimes, parents have good reasons for controlling this sort of situation, such as when the person their daughter is dating is controlling or abusive … but in my case, it was simply because I met him at work, a place they had little control over. That and he wasn't "Christian enough" (according to their standards).

My mom in particular had this idea that I'd get together with a guy I'd meet at church someday, or else a nice missionary boy from the Christian camp we attended annually. Meeting a guy at work crushed that dream. As a result of her desperate need to control my life and her belief that there was only one correct path, I was forced to quit my job. Also, to ensure that I wouldn't be able to communicate with Daniel without her consent, my cell phone (that I had bought and paid for) was taken away. Oh yes, and in addition, I was forbidden from dating my own boyfriend.

I managed to work around the matter by inviting Daniel to church and youth group with me, which my mom could do little about. It wasn't that she was being spiteful about it, and I could even see where she was coming from… but while my dad seemed at least sympathetic about it, my mom couldn't even be decent. She couldn't even bear to be in the same room as Daniel. Her mind was made up about him and that was that.

By the time I turned eighteen, my mom began holding college, driving lessons, and various other freedoms and privileges over my head in an even more desperate attempt to force my relationship with Daniel to an end. Her excuse for such tight control was that it was her responsibility as a Christian parent. I'd been looking forward to my eighteenth birthday because I thought it meant I'd finally have some of the normal freedoms that I knew most people my age enjoyed. However, I was no longer a minor but stuck living a life of ultimatums, manipulations, and a total lack of privacy despite my efforts to prove myself responsible.

By the time summer came, I realized that nothing was likely to change. After a heated argument, I couldn't take it anymore. I wrote my mom a letter explaining my feelings, namely that I needed space and time to think, and, in my desperation, I ran away from home to stay with Daniel's family.

I never intended to live there permanently, but after learning that my mom had changed all the locks on me, I couldn't exactly go back.

Living with a boyfriend, of course, was a shady business since it could lead to premarital sex. I honestly did try to save myself for marriage for the first few months of living there, which led to the discovery of some creative loopholes (believe it or not, Sex in Christ dot com[1] pretty accurately sums up my mindset at the time.)

Apparently, living with a boyfriend was also against the rules of church membership. Given that I was pushed to join the church at twelve years old, I was mostly oblivious to such politics. It led to church-court summons being mailed to my house on about a monthly basis, all of which I ignored. According to the final letter, I was to meet before The Session, admit to my sins, repent, and have my membership status determined by the pastor and Session. Until then, I had no idea my church was so "cult-like". At this point, I really began to embrace Daniel's more secular views toward the church and organized religion in general.

On top of what I now consider harassment from the church, I was also dealing with angry letters from my mom about how my "selfishness" and "poorly-chosen lifestyle" were hurting the family. Somehow, the blame was all on me. I even received a "concerned" letter from an uncle, who rarely said a word to me my whole life, in which he explained in great detail that God could very well punish my sinful rebellion with *cancer*.

The fear tactics in that letter were so blatant that it was actually sickening, even for my naive mind. This combined with the new-found freedom to think outside of the bubble is what eventually led me out of religion altogether.

---

[1] See: http://www.sexinchrist.com

Unfortunately, I clung to the love of Jesus for as long as I could. When I finally began to let go of even Jesus, Daniel and I began to drift as well. Our relationship was just short of five years, but I learned more about myself in those years than ever before—and I'll always appreciate his role in that.

It's been about five years since my break-up with Daniel and I've been with my current partner (I'll call him Alan) for about four years now. I met him at my current job where we initially bonded over having both escaped the shackles of the Christian faith.

Luckily, Alan was very knowledgeable, interested in science, and had a love for learning in general which I found to be inspiring in a way I'd really not experienced before.

Our friendship blossomed into something more, and honestly it's the first truly intimate relationship I've ever been in, friendship or otherwise. With him I truly feel like an equal.

I also have him to thank for helping me to believe in myself and in reaching my educational goals. His mother happens to be a high school math teacher, so I've had access to all the materials needed to play catch-up in math. Alan also had, being a college graduate, access to all the information about getting into college that seemed so overwhelming to me before. He showed me what I needed to do to prepare for the SATs (I never took them in home-school).

Now that I'm twenty-five, I am no longer attached to my parent's income. I've worked through Algebra, Geometry, and am now finishing up Algebra 2, so that I can hopefully start applying for undergraduate schools sometime later this year. It's got to be one of the greatest feelings to do all this apart from my mother, who tried to use it as a means of control.

The sad part is that I don't think she is even aware of how awful this kind of manipulation is to a child. Even if this is true, on some unexplored level, she must know that "sinners" like me *can* and *do* succeed.

It's a relief to no longer be affected by such relentless manipulation. On another level, my mind is also liberated. I am free to be honest with myself. I am free to figure out what kind of life suits me. I am free to connect honestly and intimately with others. What I am not yet 100% free of is the guilt.

Some struggles still linger (I call this "residual Christianity"). An example is the tendency to view my own behavior in black and white terms of good or bad. The guilt, I think, is what mostly keeps me from judging others as harshly as myself. I guess once you've learned and embraced viewing yourself as plain ole "sinful" or "dirty" it's a difficult pattern to break.

What I struggle with most now, even recently, is learning how to connect with others without sex. For the longest time, I truly believed that sex was necessary in order to create a genuine bond with someone. This was likely a learned expectation due to feeling the need to hide so much of myself from childhood friends and family and then finally opening up in a sexual relationship with Daniel.

Sexual freedom and freedom from religion are also very much intertwined in my mind, given that the euphoria which accompanied me losing my virginity served as the key to opening up a new world where I was allowed to explore my religious doubts and sexual desires. As a result, I can't seem to feel connected without also feeling some form of sexual attraction simultaneously. I am getting better and learning to separate the two, but I feel crazy for even having to try.

There's no telling what kind of effect repressed sexuality can have on a person. My thoughts are that this burst of hyper-sexuality and confusion is a direct result of having to keep it all under wraps for so long.

I realize now that I may never be free from all of the quirks that result from my upbringing, but I think attainable freedom is simply the ability and willingness to look at yourself and to truly learn to accept yourself for who you are.

I think one of the most depressing things about religion is its ability to rob you of the only freedoms you really have in life. I'm thankful to have finally figured that out for myself, even though it pains me to know that it's still a major problem for others.

2

BUD UZORAS

Three Crises of Faith

AS A CHILD, I WAS PLAGUED WITH RECURRING NIGHTMARES. During the week, my repeated nightmare involved a dragon that swooped down from the clouds at night and consumed me with fire from his mouth. I would usually visit my grandparents' house on the weekends, and there I would have my recurring "giant ants" nightmare. I faced a dragon every night of the week and giant ants on weekends, because I suppose even dragons need a break. Every once in a while, I would have this dream in which I was trapped in an art museum and the paintings came to life and attacked me. I had weird dreams when I was a kid.

I thought about death often when I was a child. My fear of death expressed itself in my nightmares. As I grew older, my dreams moved beyond the recurring images of dragons and giant insects, but I still had nightmares almost every night. Variety is the spice of life they say, though I question whether this applies to nightmares.

Were I to have discovered that those nightmares I had were written and directed by John Carpenter, I wouldn't have been surprised. I was a child afraid of death, afraid of closing my eyes at night in fear that they'd never open again, who dwelled upon death frequently during his waking hours. Sleep was rarely a time of comfort and rest for me as a child.

With the exception of the time I conducted my "Tingling Kneecaps Experiment" (I'll get to that in a bit), I believed in the existence of God the way I believed in the existence of my parents. I accepted the stories I heard at Christmas and Easter, and thanks to the 1977 film "Jesus of Nazareth," I was amazed at how bright Jesus' blue eyes were. Certainly he must have been King of the Jews.

Each night I said my prayers. Each night I had my nightmares. Each day I held fast to my belief in God, trusting him to watch over me and keep me safe, and each day I feared death, dreading its inevitable arrival. I would tell myself that, one day, when I died, I would go to heaven, so I would have nothing to fear. My emotional side was not listening, however. I continued to fear death.

The conflict between my faith in God and my equally strong fear of death planted the first seed of doubt in my mind when I was six years old. I remember lying in bed one night at my grandparents' house, thinking about death. I imagined heaven. As a child, my thoughts of heaven included flying cars and jet packs, because it's heaven and of course stuff like that will be there. I recall thinking that when I got to heaven I'd be able to ask God for a real lightsaber and I would be able to use the Force to move objects with my mind because heaven would be awesome like that. I imagined all my friends and family there, all happy and flying around with their cars and jet packs. Remember, I was only six years old.

Then the thought hit me: what if there is no heaven? What if God doesn't exist, and there's no lightsaber waiting for me when I die? These are pretty deep questions for a six year-old to ask. These are terrifying questions for a six year-old to ask himself alone at night in a pitch-black bedroom. If there was no God, then what would happen when I die? What would become of me?

Horrible images filled my mind. I saw myself dying and entering into eternal blackness, unable to move or see or hear. I imagined myself dead, but still in my body and fully aware of my surroundings. My overactive imagination would not relent, and I saw myself buried, trapped in my coffin in a lifeless body that could never move again. I wonder whether Edgar Allan Poe had such thoughts when he was a child.

I lay in bed, surrounded by the blackness of night, my mind now replacing the silence of a peaceful neighborhood with the shrieks and howls of macabre visions and Lovecraftian images of death and darkness and madness. I buried my head under my pillow, wrapped myself up in my blanket and prayed: "If you're really there, God, and we get to go to heaven when we die, then make my kneecaps tingle so I know you're there."

It was the best I could think of at the time.

Seconds after whispering that prayer I felt a tingling sensation which started from the back of my knees and moved to the front. The feeling in my knees grew so intense that I had to sit up and rub my legs. I could hardly stand it. I felt as though someone were tickling the insides of my kneecaps with feathers. The feeling lasted for about a minute.

Religion was my strongest subject when I attended Catholic school. I have always been intelligent, and I had as solid an understanding of theology as any child could. Still, I do not know how my six year-old mind came up with this prayer, but clearly I was opposed to fideism rather early in my life, long before I knew what the word "fideism" meant.[2] My desire for

---

[2] Fideism, according to the Oxford Dictionary of English, is the doctrine that knowledge depends on faith or revelation.

evidence was placated easily because of my stronger desire for what I believed; that is, I really wanted God and heaven to exist, so I found evidence to make me feel better about believing it, regardless of how strong that evidence was (which I learned later is a problem even most adults have difficulty overcoming). Nevertheless, this was a significant moment in my life. Even as a young boy, I needed a reason to believe.

The kneecap experience may have a psychosomatic explanation, but for a boy, this incident provided sufficient evidence to confirm that what I was told about God and Jesus and heaven was all true. God answered my prayer! Soon after this "tingling kneecap experiment" the lightsabers and jet packs of heaven supplanted the demons and ghouls of my fears. Thoughts of my family and me existing happily in heaven erased the images of my being trapped in a coffin, facing a "Cask of Amontillado" style fate. I slept soundly that night.

I still feared death and I still had nightmares; however, I had this faith in God upon which I leaned whenever my overactive imagination got the best of me. God's existence seemed obvious to me, even in spite of my intense fear. I could not understand how someone could not believe. Everyone I knew believed in God. Even the President of the United States waved and said "God bless America." Without question, I knew there was a god. Little did I know that the seed of doubt planted that night when I was six would lay dormant, only to burgeon into a full-blown crisis a decade later.

Crisis of Faith 1
My Problems Began the Day I Saw Jesus in My Closet

By the time I was sixteen years old, I attended church regularly with my best friend Steve. I was not only a regular fixture at our weekly youth group meetings, but Steve and I were the unofficial leaders of the youth group. I preached my first sermon at age fifteen, and even attended a "Young Preachers Seminar" at Lincoln Christian College, which was designed to help equip the future ministers of the world.

I was one of those "Born Again" types in high school; my wardrobe consisted of a dozen or so Christian t-shirts, each emblazoned with explicitly Christian messages in designs patterned after logos and symbols of pop culture. I wore those shirts with pride, proclaiming to the world like a walking billboard that Jesus was wicked cool and being a Christian was "all that." Many of my friends were the same way. To this day I give my friend Christopher a hard time because of a ridiculous crayon-green shirt he wore in high school that mimicked the Sprite logo, but instead of "Sprite" the shirt said "Spirit." Classic.

I even had an impressive collection of Christian music cassette tapes (Yes, I said *cassette tapes*. That's how we rolled back in my day). During the early 90s, I listened to the best that Christian rock had to offer: bands like *Tourniquet, The Prayer Chain, Dig Hay Zoose, Bride, Believer, The Crucified, Deliverance, One Bad Pig, Scaterd Few, Vengeance Rising, Mortification,* and other bands whose names will live forever in the minds of the Christian metal-heads of my generation. And no one will ever forget *Stryper's* classic anthem, "To Hell with the Devil!"

My first love, however, was hip hop, and needless to say I had quite the collection of Christian rap tapes as well, including such groups as *S.F.C. (Soldiers For Christ)*, *P.I.D. (Preachers In Disguise)*, *Dynamic Twins, Freedom of Soul,* and the legendary *D-Boy,* who was shot and killed in 1990 at age twenty-two, just one week after completing his album "The Lyrical Strength of One Street Poet." In fact, the first CD I ever purchased was D-Boy's "Lyrical Strength" album.

Music has always been a way for me to communicate with others and express how I feel. Music is a way for me to understand how I'm feeling. I use music the way other people use therapeutic massage, counseling sessions, alcohol, or drugs. While I had the same dreams of being a rock star that any teenager has (and a little known fact about me is that I actually have a decent singing voice, though it's only heard when I'm in my car, in the shower, or intoxicated), I'm not a musician, but rather an avid music lover with wildly eclectic tastes who wants to know everything I can about this wonderful creation called music.

Music influences the world, and the world influences music. I learned at an early age that one can learn much about a culture or group of people by examining its music. I used music as a means of communicating with others: "Check out this song. It's like the lyrics were written with my exact thoughts in mind." Music, however, was not merely an instrument at my disposal; it was a constant reminder of what people in the world were thinking and feeling. Music serves to communicate the concerns and plights people face.

Grunge became popular in the early 90s and was marked by lyrics exhibiting apathy, nihilism, chaos and dissatisfaction. *Nirvana*, often considered the "flagship band" of Generation X and the grunge movement, solidified their position as my favorite band in high school. Their Sartrean lyrics left me with an attitude of rebellion against established authorities and the status quo, and promoted an expression of one's individuality.

As a teenager I wore my Christian t-shirts in part to rebel against the world. "Look at me! I'm different! I'm a Christian!" I was "on fire" for God. I held membership at a church ran by stodgy old men who believed that "if it was good in 1950, then it's good today." I rebelled against a pointless system of rules and regulations by growing my hair long and wearing jeans with holes in the knees to Sunday morning worship. "The Man" wasn't going to keep me down. And while the church elders looked upon me with disdain, "God Save the Queen" by the Sex Pistols played repeatedly in my mind like my own personal theme song of resistance against the Pharisees of my church.

I remained confident in my worldview – until the seed of doubt planted a decade prior began to germinate.

One morning I woke up and went about my business as usual. I showered, trimmed my beard (yes, puberty hit me at an early age and I had a full beard in high school), brushed my teeth, dowsed myself with an overabundance of cologne reminiscent of Noah's flood, and reached in my closet for one of my Christian T-shirts. At that moment, I froze. I don't remember what the shirt said—most likely a "Jesus saves" message in a flashy Gen-X motif—but I remember staring into my closet at the picture of Jesus on the shirt, reading the words on that shirt and asking aloud, "Is any of this true?" I had been a committed Christian, and everyone knew it. Most of my wardrobe proclaimed a Christian message. I even laced up my Chuck Taylors with "Jesus loves you" shoelaces. At that moment skepticism and doubt entered my mind—and both were armed to the teeth and dressed like Rambo.

"How do I know God exists?" I asked myself. I had always simply presumed the existence of God. How could someone *not* believe in God?

Now I thought I was going to become an atheist. *Ew!* I could find no peace. Is there a god? The question continued to fill up my head, and I couldn't shut off my brain.

I did not want to be known as the guy who "fell away." I had listened to many sermons about "backsliders" and people who turned away from the faith. Such people were reprehensible. *Anathema! Anathema!* For a long time I kept my doubts to myself for fear of what people would think of me.

My prayers were reduced to a few simple words, which I repeated every night before bed: "If you exist, please show me you exist. If you are there, and if you can hear this, please answer." Night after night I said these words. Day after day I received no response. I wondered why God appeared to be hiding. As I said, music is a tool of communication and understanding for me, and the lyrics to the song "Smell the Color 9" by Chris Rice (interestingly enough, a Christian singer) sum up my state of mind during this period:

> Sometimes finding you... is just like trying to... smell the color nine...
>
> Smell the color nine? But nine's not a color. And even if it were you can't smell a color. That's my point exactly.

After months of keeping my faith frozen in carbonite, I spoke with my youth minister, who was the preacher at another church. I told him about my doubts and questions. His reaction, at the time, surprised me. Instead of pointing a finger at me and telling me how evil and wrong I was, he said, "Everyone goes through some doubts, and that's okay." The implied message I did not understand at the time was that "it's okay to have doubts... *as long as you come back to the faith.*" Soon after our talk, he let me borrow a few books on Christian apologetics—though I did not know it was called *apologetics* then.

I read those books from cover to cover, over and over again. Even though I demanded something more reasonable than tingling kneecaps, once again my desire for evidence was appeased easily because of my stronger desire to believe. I did not want Christianity to be wrong. The arguments I found in those books were enough to keep me in the faith because that's where I wanted to be in the first place, and I had not yet overcome the egocentrism that prevents many from examining their beliefs objectively.

As I continued my search for answers, I acquired more books on Christian apologetics, and studied them every night. I studied at the feet of René Descartes, Thomas Aquinas, Søren Kierkegaard, and C.S. Lewis. I read that some guy named Nietzsche declared "God is dead," and I laughed along with the writer of the apologetics book at this incredible notion. "Certainly God is not dead," I thought. "God is alive and well. There's so much proof!" I had much more than tingling kneecaps; I had the argument from design! Look at the complexity of the patella, and how it is attached to the tendon of the *quadriceps femoris* muscle, which contracts to extend or straighten the knee. The *vastus intermedialis* muscle is attached to the base of the *patella*. The *vastus lateralis* and *vastus medialis* are attached to lateral and medial borders of the patella respectively. This complexity could not have come from chance. Therefore there is a god.

My exposure to apologetics – coupled with the fact that I had few significant intellectual encounters with people outside of Christian culture – made me more closed-minded in the short term. The introduction to such concepts, however, was my first step toward discovering my life's true passions: critical thinking and the study of philosophy.

After high school I attended Lincoln Christian College in the August of 1993, where I stayed until December 1995. My premature departure was due to poor grades.

After my short stint in college, I returned home and became a youth minister. This marked the beginning of a decade in which I worked in various churches in professional ministry. I also enrolled at South Suburban College, the nearby community college. Getting kicked out of Lincoln was a shot to my ego, so I wanted to prove myself. My thinking became more Nietzschean as I felt I was fighting to carve out a purpose in my life. And my weapon of choice in this fight was the pen. I registered for only one class that semester: *Creative Writing.*

I began writing poetry, anecdotes, and short stories. I also sketched. I conveyed the rage, the confusion, the ennui of my life through my creations. For a time, I turned into the quintessential tormented artist. The following semester I registered for more classes, including an Introduction to Philosophy class. Like I said, I always liked to think, and by now I was somewhat of a scholar in Christian apologetics. I knew I'd like the class. Little did I know *how much* I would like it.

The professor, Dr. Stark, was brutally honest and incredibly intelligent. Every class session he pushed his students to their cognitive limits. He challenged us to think critically about the views of the philosophers we studied, and he challenged us to think critically about our *own* beliefs. A lot of students hated his class. I loved it. He was the only philosophy professor at the school. I took every class he taught. Dr. Stark admonished us continually to seek the truth. He exhorted his students to question everything. His teaching and his passion remain with me still today. He has shaped my thinking more than any other person.

I discovered, through the teaching of Dr. Stark, that I loved learning. That passion for learning grew, and I soon learned to tolerate school for the sake of my education. I must have done something right, though, because I was eventually inducted into the Phi Theta Kappa honor society.

Carl Rogers wrote in his book, *A Way of Being,* about his willingness to take risks in life:

> But perhaps the major reason I am willing to take
> chances is that I have found that in doing so, whether I

succeed or fail, I learn. Learning, especially learning from experience, has been a prime element in making my life worthwhile. Such learning helps me to expand. So I continue to risk.3

So much of my "Christian walk" was based on fear. I spent years too afraid to be honest with others and myself about my doubts; too afraid to be honest enough with myself to keep asking the hard questions. I feared what I might find. My education served to eventually expose those fears.

Carl Rogers understood the difficulties of education, and believed that, sometimes, taking a risk is the best – if not only – option. Dr. Stark, in his lecture on Plato's Cave Metaphor, said that education is oftentimes a violent process. Sometimes one is confronted with an idea that shakes up her paradigms. Sometimes one is forced to consider things from another point of view and cannot help but change her way of thinking, even if it runs contrary to her desires. Sometimes, as Plato's Cave suggests, the move from ignorance to knowledge is a painful procedure. And sometimes, as the Cave Metaphor suggests, others will turn against the one who dares to question long-held beliefs.

If philosophy is literally the "love of wisdom," and if Pat Benatar is right in saying "love is a battlefield," then one should not expect such an education to be easy. I had begun to experience what John Stuart Mill would call "Socrates dissatisfied" and wondered whether I'd rather be a "pig satisfied." But it was too late. I had been dragged out of Plato's cave, and once your eyes grow accustomed to the light there's no going back to the darkness.

---

3 Carl Rogers, A Way of Being (New York, NY: Houghton Mifflin Company, 1980) pp. 77-78.

Risk necessarily implies the chance of loss. The risk associated with education and devotion to Dr. Stark's mandate of "seek the truth" came with the loss of confidence in the paradigms I had embraced for most of my life. The more knowledge I gained the more I realized just how little I really knew. The more education I received, the more ignorance I realized I had. Like Plato's Cave, I saw that what I once believed to be reality were little more than shadows and illusions. The arguments and evidences I memorized in those Christian apologetics books no longer seemed so strong in light of the arguments and evidences I encountered to the contrary. The case for my faith was not as air-tight as I once believed.

This loss of confidence would not blossom into the next full-blown crisis of faith in my life until several years later, after I became a husband and a father.

Crisis of Faith 2
I Should Have Avoided D.O.P.E. in College.
It Nearly Killed Me.

I returned to Lincoln Christian College in the year 2000 for a few reasons, among them being that I grew desperate for a bachelor's degree, and LCC offered what I called the "Get a Bachelor's Degree Before You're 30" program. I also needed to confront the demons of my past. They kicked me out of LCC. In spite of my success at the community college, I returned to Lincoln to prove to the world – and to myself – that I was not a failure.

I got a job as a preacher of a small church in a small town. I'm from Chicago, so to say I experienced culture shock is an understatement; however, my biggest shock came not in rural

Illinois, but on the campus of LCC. Though I worked in ministry during my time at South Suburban, I had been away from a dominantly Christian context for a while; thus, I was not the same person I was when I left LCC five years prior.

Some things about me remained the same. Congruous with my rebellious nature, I continued where I left off in my pursuit to hold the unofficial title of "Student Who Used the Most Swear Words in Written Assignments at Lincoln Christian College." Half the time I just quoted excerpts from *The Ragamuffin Gospel* by Brennan Manning, and that usually took care of my swear word quota. My degree program was flexible, so I was allowed to design my own degree plan. My education focused on apologetics, philosophy, and world religions. There was a mandatory class for any student planning to graduate: Dynamics of Personal Evangelism, or D.O.P.E. for short. This class was by far the single worst event of my educational life.

One of the problems I had with the class was the required textbook: *Becoming a Contagious Christian* by Bill Hybels and Mark Mittelberg. I read it. I hated it. I read it again to see whether I misjudged the book. I hated it even more. The reflection paper I had to write about the book was *interesting* to say the least. I went way beyond my quota for swear words—and I didn't quote Brennan Manning once. If being a Christian meant being a "Contagious Christian," then I didn't want to be one.

I hated the implied secrecy. To be a "contagious" Christian, one must focus on "strategic opportunities in relationships" and making friends for the sake of sharing the Gospel. I know how Christians talk. They talk about their non-religious friends as though they were *projects*, even if they do not view their non-religious friends as projects consciously. If these "contagious Christians" were not Christians, would they be making the effort to build these relationships? Probably not. And the emphasis on evangelistic strategies is a bit unsettling. "Win their trust" so they will be vulnerable. Spies and undercover agents employ similar tactics to those that the authors promote.

One strategy offered in the book is "barbecue first." In other words, invite your evangelism project – I mean, your "friend" – over for dinner, or to a party, and to just "hang out" without making a serious effort to share the gospel. Build trust—then work the gospel message into later conversations.

Each week I sat in Dynamics of Personal Evangelism class, and as I listened to the teacher lecture, I noticed that every time he made a point, every student in the class would nod in agreement; that is, every student but me. I found myself grimacing every time he spoke. I got up and left the classroom the day he started using the "we're the fishermen and the world is full of fish" metaphor.

I found myself disagreeing with the theology taught, the covert tactics encouraged, and the manipulative attitude nurtured.

I left Lincoln in 1995 as a believer and returned in 2000 as a skeptic. Yes, I was a minister, and I came back to Lincoln to earn a degree in theology, and I still believed, but those doubts I had repressed for so long resurfaced when I became immersed once again in the Christian culture. The mask I wore that had fooled the world into thinking that I "had it all together" stifled me to the point where I was choking. I needed someone to talk to. Naturally, I turned to my wife.

Talking to my wife proved to be less than beneficial.

As my skepticism grew, so did my wife's faith in God. I saw fear in her eyes the day I attempted to communicate my concerns to her. She held on to her beliefs because she was afraid of being wrong, afraid that the truth might be something she would not want to accept, afraid that she might not understand the world and herself as well as she thought she did. For my wife, *fear* was her true God.

She wanted me to be silent. She did not want to hear doubt coming out of my mouth. She wanted me to be the good Christian husband she had tried so desperately to turn me into throughout our marriage. That was one of the many times I saw that my wife loved the mask, not the man underneath it. What did I learn from the experience of a marriage that was slowly falling apart? More than I can hope to write here. However, I can explain what this experience did to me: I became afraid.

To quote F.D.R., I feared fear itself. I did not want my fear to force me to hide who I was any longer. I was determined to live up to the definition of *free thinker* as set forth by Bertrand Russell:

> The expression "free thought" is often used as if it meant merely opposition to the prevailing orthodoxy. But this is only a symptom of free thought, frequent, but invariable. "Free thought" means thinking freely—as freely, at least, as is possible for a human being. The person who is free in any respect is free from something; what is the free thinker free from? To be worthy of the name, he must be free of two things; the force of tradition, and the tyranny of his own passions. No one is completely free from either, but in the measure of a man's emancipation he deserves to be called a free thinker. A man is not to be denied this title because he happens, on some point, to agree with the theologians of his country. An Arab who, starting from the first principles of human reason, is able to deduce that the Koran was not created, but existed eternally in heaven, may be counted as a free thinker, provided he is willing to listen to counter arguments and subject his ratiocination to critical scrutiny... What makes a free thinker is not his beliefs, but the way in which he holds them. If he holds them because his elders told him they were true when he was young, or if he holds them

because if he did not he would be unhappy, his thought is not free; but if he holds them because, after careful thought, he finds a balance of evidence in their favor, then his thought is free, however odd his conclusions may seem.4

Thinking freely requires overcoming one's fear, one's prejudices, one's self-centeredness and one's inflated ego; i.e., "the tyranny of our passions." It requires humility and a desire to listen and learn from others. The pursuit of truth requires the courage to question and analyze ideas and to hold "disrespect," as Salman Rushdie noted, "for power, for orthodoxy, for party lines, for ideologies, for vanity, for arrogance, for folly, for pretension, for corruption and for stupidity."

Blind acceptance of a worldview and adherence to Dr. Stark's axiom are incompatible. My wife embraced the former; I held fast to the latter. I suffered in my ministry, in Lincoln, and in D.O.P.E. because I still wanted Christianity to be true. I couldn't let it go. My second crisis of faith reached its climactic peak while I was killing time shooting baskets in the gym and trying to sort through my thoughts when, standing alone in Lincoln's old gymnasium, I cried out, "I'm an agnostic. I can't believe this!" I didn't appreciate the irony in my choice of words at the time. I acknowledged my agnosticism the way a sick person acknowledges she has cancer.

My mind was plagued by the ambiguity of our world; the Kantian antinomies; the apparent limits of our cognitive powers to perceive – much less comprehend – a cosmos that shouts of the glory of a creator and in the same breath whispers that

---

4 Bertrand Russell, "The Value of Free Thought" *Bertrand Russell on God and Religion* (ed. Al Seckel, Buffalo: Prometheus, 1986), pp. 239-40.

nothing exists above or beyond mankind save for the cold, dark, indifferent emptiness of space.

At this point I was in the middle of my internship with a campus ministry in Springfield which, along with being a full-time preacher and full-time college student, kept me busy enough to ignore my marital problems, but served as a constant reminder of my philosophical conflicts. Christianity was not only my belief system, but my occupation and, in many ways, my social network. Removing the mask meant undergoing a complete change of lifestyle for which I was not prepared. As much as the mask stifled me, I was not ready to remove it. So I kept my agnosticism to myself.

I graduated from Lincoln Christian College in 2002 with a bachelor's degree in theology. Earning my degree marked the end of my time in ministry – or so I thought. Most graduates of LCC leave to pursue ministry, whereas I graduated from Lincoln and fled as fast as I could from ministry. I had no idea what to do next. I was not moving *toward* anything, only running *away* from something.

Crisis of Faith 3
I Made a Deal with the Devil.
Think He's Bad? Meet My Ex-Wife.

My wife and I moved to Chicago and bought a house. I had to work four jobs so we could afford it. I worked at a bank, unloaded trucks for a retail store, worked for a cleaning service on weekends, and, in spite of the vow I made to myself never to return, I accepted a ministry position. I took the ministry job because "I needed the money." My wife wanted that house, and in spite of my protests that we could not afford it, I eventually conceded. I took the job because, I rationalized, I had a degree in theology and previous ministry experience; I was a family man with a wife, a new house and a third child on the way: what else was I going to do for money?

I resented our house the way a horse might resent the master's whip. I resented my wife for making me buy the house. I worked to the point of physical and mental exhaustion, too much to care well enough for my family, all the while feeling as though I was not doing it that well. Severe, debilitating depression took hold of me, accompanied by thoughts of hopelessness, helplessness, regret, fear, and suicide. The weaker I grew, the more emotionally detached my wife became. Either I was going to get better or I was going to die, and she simply waited to see which would happen first. Having a severely depressed spouse isn't easy, I'm sure. Sadly, my marriage collapsed in late 2004.

After our separation, I had to deal with financial woes, bills I could not pay, and debts that only grew larger. I was homeless for about a month. During that time, the only place I had to sleep was in my van. I asked God for a sign, in spite of the fact that I had no clue what kind of sign I wanted or should have expected, or what this sign was supposed to tell me. I was six years old the last time I asked God for a sign. Since then I had not been the kind of person who asks for signs from God. Signs are ambiguous. A shooting star is a shooting star, and that's it.

To hell with shooting stars, jumping dolphins or anything else that can be ruled out as simple coincidence. I understand a kick in the throat. I understand cuts and bruises. I know scars, and wounds that somehow never seem to heal. In such wounds I have seen my reflection. I am alive. I am comfortable with the sight of my own blood, and I can survive. There's my damn sign, and that is good enough for me.

I finally quit the ministry and removed the mask for good. My wife married the mask. She divorced the man. I hated her for a long time. I don't hate her anymore (I think), although if she were to suddenly burst into flames and explode I don't think I would be all that broken up about it. I had a hard time believing that life could get better after the divorce. I kept getting knocked down, and each time, just as I got back to my feet, I would get knocked down again. I figured "one step forward, two steps back" was just how life would always be.

After leaving the church in Chicago – an event which signified my final farewell to ministry – I wrote an email to everyone in my email contact list. In an act of transparency I explained in my email that I no longer considered myself a Christian; moreover, I explained, I was unsure of what I should believe. I did not want to believe that which was incorrect, and I had no answers. This, by definition, made me an agnostic.

I received various reactions to my email. One Christian friend of mine remarked on his blog that he was saddened by the fact that I had "renounced my faith." Another Christian friend told me that my being an agnostic was a cop out. Another Christian commented on how I put "head knowledge" above "heart knowledge," whatever that means. She believed philosophy was an evil that caused me to turn my back on God. She quoted Colossians chapter 2, verse 8:

> See to it that no one takes you captive through hollow and deceptive philosophy, which depends on human tradition and the basic principles of this world rather than on Christ.

In the same vein, another Christian friend of mine told me that my reliance on reason instead of God is "making a deal with the devil." He quoted 1 Corinthians chapter 3, verse 19:

> For the wisdom of this world is foolishness in God's sight.

I received positive and encouraging responses as well. I mention the negatives not to cast all Christians in a poor light, but to emphasize that I had to teach myself to not care what people think. I cannot allow my progress as a thinker to be hindered because I'm worried about what others think of me. To give in to such concerns is to don the mask once again. If I care at all about truth, the mask and I must be forever parted. I have to be honest with myself and with those around me.

Bud's Conclusion
If They Only Knew...

Coming to terms with the fact that I am an atheist proved to be one of the most emotionally satisfying moments of my life.

I was content with the *agnostic* label for a long time, but that had become just another mask. I needed to come clean. If my theist friends truly understood what my being an atheist means, they would know it means I am both open-minded *and* a skeptic, and those two qualities are not contradictory. In fact, one can't function properly without the other. If my religious friends knew what my being an atheist means, they would know that it's not an arrogant defiance, or an attempt to act smarter than them. They would see that my atheism is merely a declaration that *I don't know as much as I thought I did.* If they really knew what my being an atheist means, they would understand that all I want and all I care about is *the truth*, and I won't settle for anything less.

All I really know is that I don't know much. The more I learn, the more I discover how little I know. I was a Christian, but when I looked at it honestly and had the strength to be honest with myself, I saw no good reason to continue to believe in it.

3

SALEHA M.

After the Interlude

THINGS CHANGE. BAD MEMORIES AND THE RECOLLECTION OF laughter; everything fades.

The world passes by in a blur.

The beginning

It starts with something small.

The sun is setting, and like always, my dad marches around the house pulling my siblings off computers and down from their rooms for prayer. Here they come, tramping down the stairs with frowns on their faces because they just don't want to, but they have to anyway.

I've grown used to this by now. I obey in silence, zoning out like I always do, letting my thoughts wander to my novel's latest chapter as my father does the *adhaan*.

And then comes my little sister in her five-year-old, princess-like glory, bouncing on her feet, her pink dress that she insisted she'd be allowed to wear every second of every day swaying with her movement.

As we spread out the prayer mats, she waddles up to my dad, who prepares to lead the prayer.

"Papa, can I stand next to you?" she asks. My mother has already tied a purple scarf around her head; it's already coming loose. Nothing can tame her hair.

Dad gives her a cursory glance, the smallest of acknowledgements. He doesn't seem to like her dress.

"You can't," he tells her. I cringe at *can't*. "Boys stand in the front. You're a girl."

How many times have I heard that one before? Angry words come bubbling up to my tongue in passionate fury, but I bite my lips to restrain them. They are dangerous.

Interlude

That wasn't even the first time. The first time I was angry, the first time I wanted to rip the scarf off my head and throw it at my parents' faces. The first time I questioned the existence of an almighty being who was the sole reason I was quarantined in my house. No, I'd experienced all those firsts since the beginning of awareness, since I realized there was something wrong with forcing me to stay inside while my brother roared in laughter in the backyard with his friends, and mine were turned away at the door.

But somehow, hearing my sister be told that she was a girl, that she was not *good enough* to stand in the front with the boys, made my blood boil. My sister's reaction was to shrug and join my side, as if this was perfectly okay. It was not perfectly okay. And the more I thought about it, the more frustrated I got. I'd never allowed myself to dwell on such things, fearing that I'd let my thoughts go too far, that my disapproval for everything we did would destroy me.

And it nearly did.

A taste of freedom

We're in New York, where my cousin lives. Somehow, she and I have found our way outside for some fresh air. Our mothers are not far behind, their voices loud and staccato in the silence of the night. We're going in circles around the neighborhood, and the serenity is so tangible I want to reach out and grab it, douse myself with it.

Yet, maybe I'm doomed to unhappiness. For the umpteenth time, I adjust my hijab, pushing hair out of sight, loosening it from around my neck. Finally, I've had enough, and this time when hair escapes I don't bother to fix anything. Another step, and the pink material slips further down. A few more heavy footfalls and now it's completely off, hanging around my neck. I spread out my arms, and I'm flying. I imagine this is what freedom feels like—not living a life in eternal darkness, hiding behind a silly curtain. I imagine going to school like this, not getting scrutinized by those who don't even know me. I think of the questions they ask. Why do I wear it? What does it prove? To me, "because God said so," isn't enough. My heart swells with the pain that always comes with longing.

I want this freedom to be real.

Coffee break

The school literary art magazine is nearly complete. We're in the final editing process now, and after the endless sweeping through all work, after fixing the tiniest of typos for over an hour, I tug at the part of the scarf that loops around my neck, like a noose.

I step outside. A few of my friends, those who didn't hold out as long as me, are just down the hall. They're playing *ninja*. It looks like a fun game. I've never actually played, so I don't know the rules. I want to join them. But pink fabric frames my face— and it's more than that. It's a curtain that stands between them and me. A wall that stands between their laughter and my tears. Some say, "it doesn't bother me." Some say, "it's *my* choice."

Well, what if it isn't mine?

What if the mere thought of quitting sets my mother's teeth on edge, makes my father question the goodness in me?

And if you truly believe you will be sent to the fiery abyss that is hell if you refuse to cover, if you truly think that men are savage beasts that cannot control themselves and it is up to women to protect their delicate, jewel-like beauty…

Is it really a choice at all?

Interlude

It was the summer of that same year when I finally took it off. I remember feeling lost and scared for a moment there, and going to Muslim friends on Facebook whom I had gone to school with for support. I remember one particular friend who reacted to my doubts as if I had slapped her in the face. "I don't wear one yet," she told me, "but when I do I know I will never take it off." She called me a traitor, someone who had been "brainwashed" by the West. I remember throwing my phone against the wall, and the feeling of someone squeezing my heart in the palms of their hands.

Then I got up and collected the pieces of my phone, and put them back together. I stared at it for a moment before sending a spontaneous message to a close friend who already knew of my liberal feelings towards many Islamic prejudices. I told her how I felt, what had been said to me.

Her response was probably what kept me going in the end. She waited intently as I banged away on the phone's tiny touchpad, letting out my tears through words like I knew how to. And when she responded, her messages were equally as long. She told me I was allowed to do whatever the hell I wanted to. She told me that if anything, be it a measly piece of cloth, ever made me feel less than I was, then she would personally "chuck it in a bin." She told me she was my friend no matter what I did, and so long as I was happy, she was happy.

I cried. Right then and there, on my bedroom floor, clutching my battered phone to my chest, I cried. This couldn't be real. I'd been depressed, and I'd never been able to accept it until that moment. I'd been sad, feeling walls coming in on me. I'd been Atlas, struggling under the weight of the sky, and now it had finally been removed from my shoulders.

My mother, although reluctantly, allowed this small infraction. Suddenly, one day, I was stepping out of the house with nothing covering my head. To many this probably sounds like nothing, but to me the feeling of the wind in my hair was what heaven actually was. I was no longer cut off, isolated from the world—I was part of it. Sure, I was small, most likely meaningless, but at last, I felt like a piece of the puzzle. I was not a pale mannequin who was desperately trying to disguise herself as something she was not.

After all that struggling, I could finally be me.

A new person

Summer camp. Creative writing sessions for three hours a day at George Mason University. My first time out without my scarf, with people who haven't known me before. I enter the room with a little bit more confidence than before, as if it has filled in the missing place of my *hijab*. No one glances at me twice, and I love it.

Interlude

Strangely enough, I hadn't really lost faith in Islam quite then. There was anger, definitely, and other feelings—bitterness, sorrow, passion. But there was still faith. All make-believe was not quite lost. And to be honest, I can't remember exactly when that realization struck. Perhaps it hadn't been a realization at all, just a slow descent to the already known. Because somehow, lying awake one night staring at the ceiling though I couldn't see it, I wasn't quite as surprised as I expected to be, and that maybe, just maybe, death meant closing your eyes and never opening them again. That death meant falling asleep and never waking up, never knowing that you have died. An abrupt end.

But that came later. Because first, I was too happy. Suddenly, I could wear earrings. I bought fifteen different pairs and a new jewelry box. I smiled at myself in the mirror. I didn't feel ugly.

I felt like me.

A light in my eyes

The first day of school at the end of summer. I'm wary, anxious, excited. It's nerve-wracking. I put on my nicest shirt, a pair of jeans. I wake up twenty minutes earlier than usual to enjoy the simple act of doing my hair. I settle for a simple pony-tail. It is enough.

My creative writing teacher is the first to see me. She already knows, has already seen me at summer camp, but she smiles nonetheless. She says she likes my earrings. I grin back.

Everyone is surprised. Friends I have known since freshman year don't recognize me at first, and when they do it is with a flourish of surprised gasps and lots of clapping. Everyone is so, *so,* happy for me. Because there's a new light inside me, and it comes pouring out of my eyes. Because my laughter is more genuine, because there's an air of positivity to the words that leak from my pen.

I talk more. I'm not afraid to defend myself from prying eyes. I stand up for friends being insulted, ex-boyfriends being douchebags. I wear heels, and I don't care if anyone thinks I'm weird. Because when I'm doing something, it is all of my own accord. I try to come up with an allegory that suits this situation. It was as if someone had forced me to wear a Justin Bieber shirt and people had rolled their eyes at me, called me a silly little teenage girl who doesn't know right from wrong. And all the while I wasn't allowed to say that perhaps I didn't like him at all, that in fact I wasn't sure I approved of what he was doing. Instead, when people asked why I was wearing the shirt, I had to make up fake excuses.

And then I was allowed to wear something different. I was allowed to march around hallways with the Jonas Brothers smiling out at everyone who looked at me. This time I didn't care about the stares. The eyes. The snickering. Because I liked them, and I knew why I did, and no one could make me feel terrible for something I knew I cherished for reasons they didn't need to know.

Excuses

Government class. In walks Malaika, the Muslim girl I met last year who has more lenient parents, who is adept at the best eye make-up. She stares at me momentarily, gives me a strained smile.

"Why'd you take it off?" It's something they always ask. I shift my weight uncomfortably from one foot to the other.

"I didn't quite feel ... right in it." It's the best I can come up with. Because this is a girl I can't tell. I can't say I don't believe in Allah anymore. She will stare, and she will no longer talk to me. So I shrug, and I hope it is acceptable.

She smiles now, more easily. "Aw, but you looked so cute in it! You inspired me."

No, I think. *I wish I didn't.* And perhaps I didn't. Perhaps what you were feeling, Malaika, was guilt. Because you somehow thought that it was wrong of you to go bareheaded as an equal to all, rather than a lesser being because you're a girl. Maybe you hated me inside.

But I say nothing.

Interlude

They decided who I was to marry when I was thirteen. He comes from a good family, they said. He'll take care of you, they said. I didn't mind before. I was too young to care about my own happiness. If my mother was happy, I was happy. What more was there?

But then things changed. And I realized if I married him now, I would never be happy. I would grow up miserable because I didn't believe in the same things he did, because his ideal wife was one who didn't let the scarf slip from her dainty little head, and I had torn mine off and crushed it beneath my feet. Because I didn't want to have kids who would be brainwashed into believing what I wanted them to believe. Because he couldn't possibly understand all my little quirks, the way I was set ablaze on the inside at the thought of that new video game. To him I was a child. He didn't understand. And he never would.

What makes him cry?

The other day I asked my brother if he's ever cried watching anime.

"I don't cry," he says, as if this is a token of his unfathomable manliness. "I get watery."

"Didn't you cry when Naruto was reunited with his mother? When she recalled the day she died? What about when Lelouch sacrificed himself for the happiness of Japan?"

"Like I said," my brother brags nonchalantly, "I get *watery*."

"Well, I'm a bawler," I admit, a bit sheepishly. "I cried so much during that Naruto episode I had to pause the video because I couldn't read the subtitles anymore."

My brother scoffs. "I don't cry."

Yesterday. That's when he said that. *I don't cry* my ass. He does cry. He's crying right now, and because he's crying, I'm crying. Because there is this wall between us and our mother, this unbreakable barrier that cannot fall no matter how much we come at it with swords and axes and scythes and whatever other weapons we can use our minds to conjure. And she's looking at us like we've betrayed her, like we are the source of her misery. Why can't we just happily accept it? She keeps asking us. Why can't we just be okay with the people she has chosen for us, acknowledge that we are not mature enough to make our own decisions?

We're not mature enough to make our own decisions, she says. But what, we're mature enough to get married?

It's worse for him. I know it is. And sometimes I wish if I just gave in he'd be able to go free. He's chaining himself down because of *us*. Because he knows that if he makes one wrong move the rest of us may be lose the chance forever for a future without an arranged marriage, without an unwanted religion being shoved down our throats.

I close the door so I can't hear their voices, but everything penetrates that stupid block of wood. I don't want to hear it; I don't want to go to sleep with the sound of my brother, now twenty-one years old, sobbing out the pieces of his heart that remain after these four years of torture.

He can't change anything. Sometime, sometime soon, we'll both be married. For him, she's *fifteen years old*. But they see nothing wrong with this. And mine. Mine? He pretends like I don't exist. After years of reaching out over the Atlantic Ocean in an attempt to talk to him, to create *something* in this tangled mess of miseries, I have received nothing. A piece of "What do you think of me?" finds its way into my Facebook inbox, as if he has not ignored me all these years. How can I say what I think of you, when I have never heard you utter more than five words in the last thousand days?

I don't want to marry him. But I'm too afraid to say, too afraid to take one step too far and secure a fate of despair. But my brother, he-who-does-not-cry, he's my savior. People want their knights in chain mail to be dashing princes from far-off lands. Mine comes from the room next door. He is brave, tall, valiant, loving. But there's only so much he can do. He can fight, but he falls again and again but he keeps getting back up and *damn him because now he's crying* and *what can I do?* One stupid scarf removed from my head and suddenly I don't deserve a college education. Am I selfish to bite my tongue, to let it bleed rather than let go and shower those that have trapped us with confessions? Confessions that perhaps I don't believe in what they do, that there is more to life than praying and hiding inside a house because men—animals, according to some old *book*— may attack me? I don't want to marry him, but maybe I must, because if I do open my mouth, if I do let words fly, I'm not just dooming myself—

I'm dooming us all.

I'm scared.

We're not fighting dragons or hiding in bomb shelters covering our heads, but we're still being cascaded with shrapnel, we are still losing our flesh and limbs to creatures of darkness. We are being buried alive. They say they love us, and maybe they do. Maybe this is what love is in their eyes. Maybe they think if they wish hard enough for our happiness, if they grab our shoulders and force us into kneeling positions, we'll learn to love where we are and kiss the ground they stand on.

They can't understand, we're trapped, he's crying, and I'm so very, very, scared.

Breaking away

I'm still not free. I'm not free at all. My mother stands before me, and she weeps. She weeps because she feels I have betrayed her. She weeps because today, for the first time, I told her I may not want to marry him. What else, she asks? What else am I planning to do? Am I planning to desert her upon turning eighteen? Am I set on turning her life into a living embodiment of hell?

I relent. I cannot do this now. I'm too young, too weak, too dependent. My siblings look up to me. I cannot let my parents take them away in fear of "losing them" as they may lose me.

Maybe I'll have to go through with it. Maybe I will run away.

But for now, sometimes I stare up at a ceiling I cannot see and I think about what lies ahead. I think about writing books, signing hundreds of copies. I also think of shrill cries in the night, of fingers moving over me under the bedcovers, fingers I don't want there. How long will he wait, if I ask him to? Will he wait at all?

I can't do this. I'm terrified of imagining any kind of future. But I push forward. Because I still smile at the mirror. Because I learned how to play *ninja*. Because I don't have to pray at all. Because I tore down the curtain.

Because like all other things, this too shall pass.

4

SERGIO PAULO SIDER

Questioning The Absolute Truth

I AM FIFTY YEARS OLD NOW, AND I HAVE BEEN A "FULL-fledged" atheist for the last two years. The following account is supposed to be my deconversion story, but the name implies that there must have been a conversion first, which is not the case. I never converted and I sincerely doubt that anyone could change their mind and, in a snap of the fingers, start to believe in something they just wished to believe. Instead, what I think actually happens is people hold what they wish to believe as true, and then start the long process of convincing themselves of this "truth."

Every person's story starts before they're even born. Mine started with some Latvians abandoning their Eastern European homeland, as they fled a bad situation in order to pursue new opportunities. Later on, I was even told that it involved an "evangelical reawakening" of some sort, as they believed they were settling in a new Promised Land. Some groups fled to Canada and others to Brazil (as was the case for all of my grandparents). These hardened travelers sold everything that hadn't already been lost in the turmoil of the First World War and its aftermath, and intended to flee the succession of brutal government regimes that had been jockeying for power in the region. They fled illegally in most cases. All this may seem irrelevant, but this chain of events played a very important role in my life, because that was the state of mind in which they raised their children, and ultimately, their children's children.

They were immigrants, with nothing but their bare hands and feet, in a totally different country, with different customs, phenotypes, languages, and weather—and with only the community and their religion binding them together.

Time passed and more than forty years later, I found myself as a kid in my parents' house. Quite a normal family I suppose, except for the fact that my paternal grandparents lived with us in the same house, and they had a silent but very noticeable control over my father.

A Baptist home, my parents and grandparents were severe and authoritarian, so I found very early that any type of rebellion was rewarded with plenty of verbal abuse in the best fashion, or a good beating, sometimes with a painful whack of the belt for heavier offenses. We were members of a local Baptist church which was rather fundamentalist in doctrine, but quite far away from any Christian teaching of humility, helping the poor and so on.

As strange as it may sound, it was a very skeptical family in a very cold and skeptical church. Skeptical of everything *except* for the following *Absolute Truth* and the following corollary (in order of importance):

ABSOLUTE TRUTH:
"God is real"

COROLLARY:
Jesus is real, and he is God.

The Bible is literally the inspired word of God.

God talks to us through the Bible, and we talk to him directly through prayer.

Those who don't believe in Jesus are going to hell; including the idolatrous Catholics (true statue worshipers).

We are the blessed; *they* are the rest, aka the "worldly" hell-bound sinners

At around that time, for me, the above items were taken as the "God given" truth. Christianity is often seen as a homogeneous religion, but the truth is that each of the thousands of sects think they have the ultimate truth. If I had developed critical thinking skills early on, I would have realized that something was terribly wrong when people who supposedly shared basic beliefs denounced each other.

My grandfather was an especially vigorous Bible thumper. He had a virtual list of his preferred verses that he used to justify the harsh authoritarian parenting he doled out. I wonder if he had the secret dream of becoming like Abraham, sitting on a high chair with all the rest of the family below him, just marveling at his wisdom.

Growing up, my family and I were literally forced to attend *all* church activities. We spent our entire Sundays at church, and if there was any extra religious activity during the week, we had to go.

Back then, I suffered from moderate asthma in my childhood. So one lucky Sunday, my mom said I was too ill to go to church. Every time this happened it was like winning the lottery.

Eventually, I learned that everybody lived a double life, as much as they wanted to pretend otherwise. Everyone acted the part of a saint, but when away from church I saw all of my friends living quite 'normal' (i.e., worldly) lives. The same was true for us. We even had a different language, what I now dub as *Christianese*. The phrases, the clichés, the language of church life—there was just one problem, no one spoke that way in real life.

Early on, I started to notice that something wasn't quite right. My parents and grandparents clearly took biblical verses out of context to justify nonsensical dogmas and abusive behavior while many important verses were simply disobeyed, but no one could voice any opinion as to such hypocritical attitudes, because there would be serious consequences.

On more than one occasion, I watched my father verbally abuse my mother, in the car, after the church. Of course my grandparents never uttered a damned word, because they were all for the abusive behavior stuff. After all, keeping the iron fist was the most important trait of a real patriarch. Was this the real Christian life?

All the questions that arose from comparing real life with the Christian life preached (but not necessarily lived) were being stored in my mind for later reflection. I found some Bible stories amazing while others were just plain stupid, like God asking Abraham to kill his son just to test his faith, and the Job story which was a lesson in how God could do whatever he pleases, because we're all just pawns, after all.

You could say I was a rather rebellious youth. I required explanations when something was given as a truth. And I was probably the one among my siblings that suffered the most punishment because of it. But, to be fair, unlike many Christian parents I am aware of, mine were very nice in one sense: they made all the effort to make us play at least one musical instrument, speak more than one language and take any major course or study, whatever it was we wanted to, so as to be prepared for the professional life.

Years passed, and my siblings and I got used to the theatre and the social life of the church. The corollary of the *Absolute Truth* was gradually changing to accommodate real life and the reality I perceived around me. I was noticing how some previous 'truths' didn't have a solid base or had no base at all.

I remember a Bible camp, when the church invited an American missionary who was living in Brazil for years to give a talk. He was quite well known as a sort of 'Bible scholar' and came to talk about the Biblical canon and the Dead Sea scrolls. In the Q and A section at the end, a friend and I asked some questions about the canon, but when we asked, "If someone defines the canon by choosing to dump or keep books from a large list, how can we say the Bible was the true word of God? Or even inspired?"

The pastor intervened and said, "Ok, thanks for listening, but we are past the time now," as if it were ever a problem to extend a Bible study.

Ignorantly, many Christians hold the belief that the Bible is homogeneous, as if God's employees wrote it down all at once. As always, I gave God the benefit of the doubt and saved the questions for later.

As a teenager, one of the main pros of going to church was to meet girls, although in an almost totally platonic way, since sex was reserved strictly for marriage. Before that, anything sexual was a sin.

Unlike some other countries, in Brazil, the time to leave home often occurred after marriage, not by leaving for college like in America. So one of the main reasons to marry was to leave your parents' home and have your own life. I had this wish of building a family totally different from the one I had.

Just before I married, and after the death of Abraham, sorry, my grandfather, the whole family had had their fill of that old church. My brothers and I found a new church, a totally different one. Still Baptist in name, but there was no building; instead, they rented a hotel garage floor, filled it up with plastic chairs, and there was a team of young pastors, and an older one (kind of a leader). They used a more modern language, there was no cold marble, no dress code, and they embodied a Christian way of life that you could live seven days a week. No double life (in theory). It seemed like 'the real deal'. I didn't have to be ashamed of going to a church anymore.

Then, I got married. Almost immediately, my first son was born. Even with a good church, all those years of being mandated to go to church made my visits to the new church increasingly infrequent. But it was quality, not quantity that mattered, I thought.

My wife suffered from asthma too, but a more severe type. When my son was about three years old, she was having constant asthma attacks, even with all the medications. She even had an oxygen canister to help deliver an inhalation. I was always ready, going to sleep only after leaving my clothes out just in case I had to take her to the ER. It was exhausting. It was one thing to pray for candies as a child and not get them, but why do we have to suffer if Jesus told us just to ask and it would be given to us? He was the Doctor of Doctors. Something was obviously wrong.

In one of the visits to ER, my wife just fell down, she couldn't breathe. She was rushed to the ICU. I thought it was over, that she was dead. But the medical staff managed to revive her and put her on the mechanical respirator.

I was totally worn out. A friendly couple, who were members of the previous cold-marble church, were now attending a newer one. It was a 'powerful' church where they could 'see' the real 'power of God' working before their very eyes. They offered to talk to a pastor and have him meet us. After some 'powerful prayers' he guaranteed us that she was *cured*. We didn't even have to have faith, because he was so sure she was cured because he 'felt it'. Other people even talked to my wife after that episode saying that God had healed her and that He had special plans for her (whatever that could mean). We were informed that she could and *should* stop her meds (especially since they were not working well anyway).

I was in still in shock. What was I supposed to do? Tell them to fly a kite or tell the other lukewarm and powerless friends and family that yes, Jesus could still work a miracle, although I had not seen one all of my life.

I was scared. The plan was to see what my wife would do and be ready either for the worst or for the real 'power of Jesus'. She opted for withdrawing her meds (I was now *very* scared), but I thought it would be alright since I would be nearby to act in case of any trouble.

Then, she felt better, as she had never felt before. But I was still scared. I went on a business trip to Japan and Taiwan for a month. To the best of my knowledge at the time she was doing okay; however, I later learned that while I was away she had to go to the ER and had told my mother that she thought it was the end. Seven days after returning, she woke up in a really bad state. I asked my mother to help me, grabbed my wife, and in less than two minutes we were at the ER.

After all the prayers, my mom's loud cries to God, my wife was dead.

Somehow I felt that God intended to relieve her suffering, even leaving a widower and a four year-old child motherless. I was sad and angry, but I still thought God had his mysterious motives. I even started to create ad-hoc justifications for God: that my son being more attached to me than to her was some sort of divine preparation for having to experience his mother's death.

Life went on. Four months after her death, already feeling a lot better and thinking the worst had passed, I started having what I thought was a mild asthma attack. I picked up my asthma canister and used it (as I had done literally thousands of times all my life). It didn't work! I panicked. That was how she died, her meds didn't work. I grabbed and took a potent corticoid, and I had to wait in panic. After long and desperate hours, I got better.

But it happened again. I went to the ER. I thought I was going to die. All my thoughts went to my son. I didn't care about myself, but what would happen to him if I died too? Why would God want that?

More ER visits followed. Cardiologists, pneumologists. I spent an entire year suffering. I left my son with his grandmother and I was literally a thirty year-old grown up living at home with his mother. I felt as if I were a two-year-old child. I tried to sleep all of the time, but the attacks were now occurring during sleep also.

Worse, I had to listen to people saying that I should pray more for God to heal me. Again, I asked myself, what was the purpose of this suffering?

After a few weeks a friend suggested a good psychiatrist. Problem solved: panic disorder. Some pills and in a short time I was ready to regain my life. I thought it a test from God. I even felt I was (or thought I was) closer to God somehow.

Three years later I met my new wife, a Catholic woman. We planned to marry after just a few months after meeting each other. I thought I would have trouble with her family, not with my enlightened, cool and liberal Christian family. I was wrong.

The supposed idolaters were okay with the marriage as long as I actually loved her, but on my side all the old prejudices surfaced. Eventually, we married, but we married at a modern Catholic church with a Catholic priest and a pastor with just a few family members and friends.

The day after the marriage we moved to the US and it marked a new era for us. A good isolation from both sides of the family. No church attendance. Just us and the real world.

My wife was already a PhD in biomedical sciences and was going to the US for her postdoctoral fellowship. I began my layperson interest in science related to medicine. My wife helped me to see things a little bit differently; for example, the nonsense of a human body, with so many defects and with being prone to suffering, somehow being designed by some divine tinkerer. The nonsense of the suffering of an innocent child seemed to suggest a cruel if not capricious God, instead of a loving one. Although she believed in God, she was not trying to make excuses for Him. She just questioned. Plain and simple.

While in the US, my wife almost died due to an acute case of ectopic pregnancy. Another example of a bodily failure that seemed to contradict the idea of a perfectly designed creation. Fortunately, it happened in the US, where 911 worked flawlessly, and in minutes she was at the hospital to be operated on by a skilled doctor. Were it in Brazil she would certainly have been dead before help arrived.

Months later, back in Brazil, we had our baby. It was a wonderful time, and I had made a considerable amount of money working for my own Brazilian company while living in the US. But then something happened that still sends shivers down my spine to this day. We had a nice swimming pool in the backyard, and we put up a fence to prevent accidents. On a warm day in spring, we were playing at the pool, because our two-year old son loved it. The water was cold though. When we left the pool, we forgot to close the pool gate and everybody went to the showers. I was the first to get ready and I went with my son to the TV room to wait for the others to have dinner. He had *never* managed to open the living room doors before. But while I was watching some stupid game on TV, I noticed the usual toddler noise had stopped. I immediately went to the living room to see if everything was okay. It was not. He had managed to open the living room doors. I saw the open gate and I ran. I saw the body of my little two year-old child floating motionless in the shallow section of the pool. The water was motionless too. He had probably been lying there for already a couple of minutes.

In just a few seconds, all my life played before my eyes and I thought, *it's OVER!*

I immediately jumped into the pool and fetched his cold body from the water. In desperation I started crying. My wife arrived at the scene, and we started to perform CPR. But to no avail. My wife said we should take him to the hospital. At the time I was so distraught that I was sure he was already dead, that it never crossed my mind to take him anywhere. Needless to say, I was in total shock.

We ran to the car, and I saw that he was moving his eyes gently. A glimmer of hope. I asked my wife to drive (I could not leave his side). I told her to turn on all the lights, sound the horn like hell, and don't worry about the car... Just pedal to the metal.

Arriving at the hospital, I let him go with the doctors and I felt it was all my fault. My son's pediatrician arrived at the hospital and then took things from there.

Going in and out of consciousness, my son fought for his life. Later that evening he was messing around with the hospital gear and playing with the staff. After all the "Thank God" and "It was a miracle" utterances passed our lips, I was still holding on to the *Absolute Truth*, but I was a little less motivated to try to find excuses for God.

Now it was time for the Fat Cows to die—time for the hungry to eat these fat ones. We faced financial problems and it was difficult to keep my oldest son in an expensive American school here in Brazil, and then to apply to American colleges. Fortunately, he is very intelligent and it was possible to get some wonderful scholarship offers from a couple of colleges. It would be hard to maintain him abroad, but it was still less than what I was already paying for the American school here.

It was time for new prayers, but, as always, nothing seemed to happen at all. I would even accept it if suffering was the rule and joy was the exception, but why did Jesus promise to answer prayers? Why didn't he tell us the truth? My Bible was already reduced to only a few Jesus-related passages. Even those ones had to be reinterpreted.

My son went to college in the US. Things started to get back on track after a painful time of financial trouble. I noticed how things went bad and went well without any relation whatsoever to praying, Bible reading, etc. I started noticing that I was really talking to *myself* at night, before bed. What was I doing wrong?

My mother then got some serious orthopedic problems, and started experiencing a lot of pain. No sign of Jesus, the perfect physician around to help. We had to help ourselves, as always. By this time, I was already an angry skeptic, but I decided to research a little more on the subject and debunk all of the bullshit for myself. In my research, I found the excellent site *skepdic.com*. It started to be my consultation bible for the real life. But every time I searched for one type of quackery, I ended up being shown how prayer, religion, and God were type of quackery too, or at best simply a delusion.

While on the subject of quackery and pseudo-science, I found two amazing videos by an interesting Brit. A biologist called

Richard Dawkins. The first video was "Enemies of Reason." I devoured it. The second was "Root of all Evil?" It was amazing. One thing led to another, and then I was reading *The God Delusion*.

I absolutely loved it. For the first time I tried to suppress that old *Absolute Truth* and everything started to make sense. I reached out and started frequenting some forums about religion, and started to read many books—about fifteen in a period of a few months (I had never read so much or so avidly in my entire life). I will not list here the details of the huge amount of evidence I found and analyzed in order to justify my conclusions. Most evidence is sitting right in front of your face, and you just have to be willing to look. The most important points I took away from my new educated and skeptical outlook were:

❖ How the very concept of God is clearly man-made, and how it's easy to understand how ancient people would have come to invent it. The human mind works to detect patterns and gives false positive results that are not meaningful. People tend to attribute agency and meaning to things or experiences that just happen for no higher reason.

❖ Christianity, in particular, depends heavily on the historicity of the Bible, but proof is lacking for the main part, and the rest fails badly. Even if we dump the Old Testament as most modern Christians would like, the Jesus of the Gospels is clearly a myth. And it's pathetic how Christians think that the New Testament is a solid and untainted piece. Some simple and shallow research on the subject can crack the entire backbone of Christianity.

❖ The concepts of heaven, hell, free will, Jesus' sacrifice, and such, are all preposterous.

❖ More and more scientific evidence shows our 'soul' is just an illusion of the working brain. Tamper with a bunch of neurons and cells or observe the effects of some mental illnesses and you see how one's entire memory and life changes or just washes away.

❖ The diversity of religions around the world. Everyone thinks that theirs is the right one and that others are the deluded ones.

In a nutshell, no matter how I looked at it – whether through prayer, scripture, faith and the concepts of heaven and hell— God and religion failed miserably. Christianity was nonsensical from top to bottom.

What's more, I noticed how everyone's Christianity was forced to change over time to try to adjust for reality when it became too far away from it. Every Christian thinks that this is a normal process when they are growing up, leaving the useless details and focusing on what really matters. But for me, after removing all of those "useless details", there was nothing left, except for the "golden rule" and "love thy neighbor," but, truth be told: there's nothing godly or divine about these (even the golden rule predates Christianity). It's just innate in social and empathetic animals like us.

I turned into a complete atheist in a very short time. Even so, I felt enlightened. It was awesome. I felt the power of discovery. At the same time I felt angry for the previous forty-eight years wasted believing in such nonsense. Even as a watered-down Christian in the latter decades, I felt ashamed of being so brainwashed. I replayed the movie of my entire life in my head, and it was clear I was alone all the time. Just me and my thoughts. Whatever I thought to be the 'hand of God' at the time, it turned to be just plain old wishful thinking and some happenchance.

I felt an intense will to debate Christians and warn my family and friends. We were on the wrong bus. I had to show them the evidence I had found. But then came the shocking truth. *No one* even had the curiosity to know what had happened to me let alone why it had happened. For them it was all settled. I just was a false Christian who knew God was real, but was unhappy to have my prayers not answered exactly as I wanted. There was no need for discussion, because to them, I was against the *Absolute Truth*, so it was plain easy. I was just wrong. Period.

That was a couple of years ago. In the meantime, I have found a set of really good friends online. That's my community now: good, funny, ethical and moral people who just want to spend their remaining lives with dignity.

Looking back, here are a few things I find positive about my supposed deconversion:

❖ Life disappointments. Although people often think that most 'deconversions' are due to disappointments and tragedies during one's life, they actually have the opposite short term effect. You think you get 'closer' to God. Of course, after the 'deconversion', when you recap your entire life, you see that you were alone. Simple as that.

❖ Evidence. Yes, it's important and still is. But I looked to evidence only when I wanted and felt the need. Nobody can push anything down on you if you are not willing to re-examine your position.

❖ I have a personality with a natural tendency to doubt and confront given truths and authoritarianism. And as I was often obligated to attend church by force, I grew a natural aversion for it.

❖ Emotional appeals don't work. I just can't be convinced of anything through emotional appeal. No 'holy spirit' emotional orgasms ever happened to me.

❖ My wife helped me, although sometimes unconsciously, to see the world with a different perspective, even if Christian in essence. I had been taught to make excuses for God. She also helped me see how the evangelical worldview was arrogant and condescending.

❖ A time without communal reinforcement. It is a powerful antidote to brainwashing. A time to compare reality with whatever you were brought to believe by your parents. Consider this: If what you believe is what you were raised to believe, then all you have are the beliefs of others. It's difficult for anybody to truly see the real word if there are always people blocking their view.

Were it not for childhood indoctrination, no one in their right mind would believe in the nonsense of Christianity and religion in general. It's patently obvious that personal gods are manmade. Change the name of the characters of the Bible and the same Christians would laugh loudly, the same as they laugh at other religions and with the same sincerity that they declare them absurd.

There's not a single day when I don't look back and regret losing the best years of my life to false hopes, false certainties, to angst and the ambiguity of faith. Although I might be considered an 'angry atheist', this anger is just indignation, and it is a healthy type of anger. Therapeutic.

Take it from me, it's way better to live without false hopes, false expectations. Life is too short to waste it all living a lie. I now have clear and guilt-free opinions about euthanasia, abortion, homosexuality, parenthood and even suicide. And I am ready to guiltlessly change my mind again in face of new evidence, which I find liberating. It's really *worth* it to be free from archaic religious superstitions and the shackles of faith. So this isn't really the story of my deconversion. I like to think of it as the story of my de-brainwashing, the removal of a blatantly false *Absolute Truth*.

5

ALICIA NORMAN

This Was Your Life

As I sit down to write my de-conversion story, I am finding it a bit harder to do than I had initially anticipated My trepidation may also be due to the fact that there are many facets to my harrowing tale and it wasn't a simple A to Z type of journey.

FOR THE LONGEST TIME I DIDN'T KNOW THAT THE little booklet I had found outside my Dewitt Arkansas home was called a Chick tract. All I knew is that it rained the morning of that fateful discovery and the gray dreary atmosphere seemed to match my mood.

Mother, a diagnosed paranoid schizophrenic, had once again fallen prey to her disorder, an "episode" as was called by the elders of the house, and had been sternly prodded to seek medical help once more. Although I kind of understood that this was not a "fault thing," I still couldn't help but resent the fact that she would be gone—again.

Last time she'd gone away, it was months before my sister and I saw her again—my heart grew heavy at the prospect of losing her and being alone again.

Marilyn and I were now in the care of Blu, our kind-hearted but near-ancient Grandpappy, and his grim-faced second wife Charlie Mae, who believed children shouldn't even be seen, let alone heard.

The rain had stopped by the time we got back from the airport and I sat on the porch trying to wrap my six-year-old brain around the chain of events. It was then that I saw it, in the corner of my eye, a tiny yet friendly looking black and white comic book resting just under the slope of our dilapidated slat wood porch. Although a little wet, I was able to open and read it quite easily.

I was only a child at that time but I was a voracious reader. In retrospect, I can concede that for me, reading had been a bit of a refuge. Nose to pages, I was able to escape some of the near-constant turmoil within my family's small country home.

The book was entitled "This Was Your Life" and it detailed the story of a man who died of a heart attack and was soon found at the throne of God awaiting judgment for his "sins" on earth. A handily convenient angel by his side informed him that he would now have his life put on display for Jesus Christ to scrutinize. Depending on his deeds, the man would learn if he was to be going to heaven or to hell.

At one point in the book, the man's life began to play like a movie on giant screen before him. Based on his life's film, the reader gleans that our protagonist had been a very naughty boy indeed. He lusted after women, stole stuff, told dirty jokes, lied and mused about football scores whilst in church.

So, opening the "Book of Life", he discovers his name isn't in it. He is then told by Jesus that he has to depart into the lake of fire. But all was not lost. The booklet also detailed the life of a good man and how his righteousness allows him to be spared. This lucky soul gets an instantaneous, one-way pass into heaven.

Now, at this juncture in my young life, I had heard of God and Jesus before, courtesy of my mom who would buy kiddie-books that told of a man named Noah and a strongman called Samson.

I'd found these religious kiddie-books with their dumbed-down Bible stories fun to read, but this was the first time I had heard the redemption tale told in this way. It scared me, but I was also delighted that I had stumbled across such wondrous information.

I resolved that, come what may, I would try to be like the good guy in the story, living to be the kind of person that could get into heaven and meet Jesus.

I said the salvation prayer right then and there and felt all at once loved and protected. An unsettling sort of peace would follow me for weeks after. I attributed this to the angelic spirit that was now charged with watching over me now that I had God in my life.

In the years that followed this transition, I tried my best to stay devout and live the kind of life that would make God proud if it were ever to flash upon the big screen. Despite my best effort, I often found myself falling short of my goals.

In my twenties when my understanding of spiritual concepts became a bit more, shall we say, sophisticated, I started trying to locate a religious ideology that fit my temperament.

During this journey I found myself going through several phases and sampling various spiritual wares.

Baptist

Blu and Charlie Mae were both nonpracticing Baptists, so when I had questions about God and faith, when they could spare a minute, they usually answered from a fundamentalist perspective.

By and large, however, my sister Marilyn and I were left to our own devices when it came to life instruction, as Charlie Mae appeared off-put by the presence of children in her life.

If asked at this time, I think I would have called myself a Baptist since I really didn't know of any other denominations. Indeed, even the church in the tiny town of Dewitt had a faded white sign in front with the words Baptist proudly displayed. I never stepped foot inside the place though, although I felt a bit of kinship to it. In my kid's mind, I felt God knew I wanted to go to the old church.

I would continue to personally, if silently, identify with this label until the fateful day my dad gained custody of my sister and me and moved us to California to be with him.

The days I spent in San Bernadino would be glorious, the best years of my childhood, in fact. Sadly, the good times would be short-lived as my dad would seek to flee a charge of theft and move us to Atlanta, GA. where we had relatives willing to harbor us.

Seventh Day Adventist

I was twelve years of age when we came to live in the birthplace of Dr. Martin Luther King and although that aspect piqued my curiosity, I had mixed emotions about the South itself.

The culture shock was immediate. I can recall how the valley had been a laid-back place where labels were seldom used, if at all. I had played with friends of various backgrounds and never truly regarded them as "other."

In the south however, I soon learned there were black folks, white folks, illegals and God-fearing good people. Even though there were no signs saying you couldn't go here or there, people "knew their place" and followed this unspoken caste system without question. This fact became abundantly clear the day I tried to talk to a white girl in the nearly all black school I went to.

Not only did she act surprised by the fact I, a girl of color, spoke to her at all, but my counterparts called me an "Oreo" for the transgression.

A different world indeed.

But it would be dire developments at home that would change the course of my life forever and, once more, propel me toward Jehovah and Jesus.

Dad got hooked on a newly emerging recreational drug called "crack" cocaine. Prior to this experimentation he had been a heavy pot smoker, but aside from making him a more mellow type of fellow, it never interfered with his life or his ability to look after his girls. By the time crack rock was starting to find its way into black communities, and the gay community in particular, he was looking for something new to both excite him and dull the pain that, I can only assume, came from the estrangement that occurred when "Big Daddy" learned my father had a sinful sexual proclivity toward other males.

Big Daddy, my paternal grandfather, was a Baptist minister and ex-military officer who retired with honors from the Armed Services. Of his five sons however, only two remained "straight." Even though I was too young to truly grapple with what "sexuality" was, I somehow instinctively knew that this development was not a "fault thing" but rather, the way it turned out sometimes. Seemed obvious.

Big Daddy ostracized his gay sons out of duty to his Ministry. Because of this, I would lose touch with this side of my family outside of the three brothers, who stuck by one another through thick and thin, sometimes for better and worse.

Interestingly enough, my father's homosexuality was never a concern to me even when family members tried to indicate that it was Dad's sexual orientation that drove my mother to madness. As an adult, I now know that this was not the case, as paranoid schizophrenia is not triggered by sudden traumatic knowledge; rather, it was an onset illness that cannot be forecast. Besides, I also learned that Mom had her own demons to deal with and struggled through a rather rough childhood.

Crack turned my dad from being a flawed father with a profound love for his little girls, to a neglectful addict who must doggedly chase his dragon at all costs—even at the cost of losing his girls. Gone was the fun yet irresponsible rascal my sister and I knew and loved. Our father, William Carnell, was soon replaced by a hollow-cheeked imitation of his former self who became resentful at attempts to get him to fly straight.

At that time, I took my case to a sympathetic teacher who helped me acquire a work release from school and, at a young age, I began working to help keep food on the table and take care of my little sister. In time, however, Dad would come to demand my paychecks from me. I soon found myself having to lie and hide my money in order to keep things afloat.

The final straw came when I arrived home from school one day to find out that my dad had sold a word processor I had won in a literary contest so that he could buy drugs. On top of that, Marilyn had started running away from home on a regular basis as she was constantly fearful of being attacked by one of Dad's drug "buddies." The threat was real enough, as we did not have a bedroom door and Dad loved freebasing with some of his friends at night.[5]

I told my counselor about the issue but she didn't seem to care all that much until I casually mentioned that Dad was gay during our conversation. It is ironic that the drugs didn't compel her to action but that being *homosexual* would give her the motivation she needed to contact child welfare services on our behalf.

My sister and I were then temporarily placed in the care of a church-going woman named Peaches (yes, this was her real name), who was a Seventh Day Adventist. She strictly observed the tenets thereof and asked that, so long as we lived under her roof, we abide by her religious rules. That meant no shellfish and the curious habit of chilling out on Friday at Sundown—no work of any kind as it was the dawning of the Sabbath.

I found Peaches' religion very intriguing and actually didn't mind going to church to learn more about it. She was also very open to my myriad questions regarding the topic as well, which was a refreshing change of pace from those who usually told me to go read a book if I seemed too inquisitive.

But the more I learned the more I was hesitant to call myself a Seventh Day Adventist. Not that I didn't find the folks pleasant or the believers earnest. I suppose what stuck in my craw was the answer I received when I asked Peaches about their practice of going to church on a Saturday.

I was confused by the fact that most churchgoers believed the Sabbath was Sunday and I wondered what that meant for her as a Seventh Day Adventist. What would happen, for example, to the folks who were going to church on the wrong day?

"Oh, they all go to hell," she told me, as a matter of fact.

---

[5] Editor's footnote: to *freebase means to take cocaine that has been purified by heating with ether, and is taken by inhaling the fumes or smoking the residue.

I was stunned; and, upon further rumination, grew infuriated. Wait a minute, I thought. There are many wonderful and devout Christians who care about the word of God just as much as any Seventh Day Adventist. Why would a loving god condemn millions of people to hell for getting a day of worship wrong? Was there no such thing as being sincerely mistaken?

It was then that I knew that the Seventh Day Adventist religion was not for me, but I continued to go to church on Saturday out of respect for Peaches' faith.

Jehova's Witnesses

Around my sixteenth birthday, I tried to commit suicide while under Peaches' care. To this day I am not sure why, but I did. Perhaps I missed Dad or finally caved in to the black, spiraling depression that seemed to come out of nowhere to engulf me on occasions.

I ended up taking some blue pills that were prescribed to Peaches and soon found myself in the hospital getting my tummy pumped with black charcoal.

Not an event I ever repeated.

A week after this event, Peaches contacted the proper authorities and Marilyn and I were sent to live with another foster couple.

Myrna was a former single mother, recently married and a social worker with a heart of gold. I immediately fell in love with her when, after a lengthy discussion, she apologized to me when she realized that she had misjudged me. As a teen, I had never had an adult do anything remotely like that. It spoke of humility, class and fairness that I felt was a truly rare trait in most people.

Harold Slaton, her husband, was a quiet man who didn't quite understand her vocation as a social worker, but he didn't seem to mind her desire to help two strange teenagers out and was very welcoming.

When we moved in to the couple's tiny apartment, neither one of them seemed particularity interested in religion. At first, I wasn't sure what to make of that. I was still under the delusion that good people were usually religious.

The situation was soon remedied by the visit of door-knocking Jehovah's Witnesses, who managed to secure a Bible study after speaking to Myrna one fateful day.

The Jehovah's Witness couple seemed polite enough and although my bored sister refused to sit in, I happily did so with notes in hand, eager to find out what they practiced and why. I had even studied up prior to this visit by reading the few Watchtower tracts that had been left by the missionaries. I recall feeling impressed by their scientific and honest approach to faith, and I leaned toward the idea that I may have found a religious ideology that closely mirrored my own.

When it came to the Bible they were literalistic in their approach, refraining from celebrating American pagan holidays like Easter and Christmas. They even frowned upon wearing crosses or observing birthdays, as they saw this as form of idol worship.

I asked the cute, elderly couple what they thought of divorce.

The woman smiled kindly at me and replied that Scripture made provision for divorcement only in the case of adultery. When I asked if they made any exception for physical abuse, she told me that they would only support legal separation. The spouse in question would have to remain married to the abuser.

"And if she gets a divorce anyway?" I asked, eyebrow raised.

"Well, the church frowns on that," she answered, starting to show the first signs of discomfort.

"The spouse would be ex-communicated," the husband piped up, looking stern. "Not to mention being in threat of hell—"

Whelp—for me, that was my "back to the drawing board" moment. Any religion that would resort to "let me find someone for my spouse to cheat on me with" contortions to get out of a physically harmful relationship was not one I wanted to belong to.

My foster parents were, however, reeled in and after a few more Bible studies, they ended up going to a local Kingdom Hall.[6]

That visit let me know that I had made the right decision when a visiting speaker claimed that the New Testament verse, "Suffer the little children to come unto me," meant little kids were supposed to "suffer" for Christ.

Mormons

I had just turned nineteen when Myrna helped me get a job at the Department of Labor. It was here that I met an effervescent, likable co-worker whom we shall call Devan. Devan, I learned, was a Mormon. The little I knew of the religion had come from the Latter Day Saints television commercials that were very prevalent at the time, so when Devan approached me about finding out more about his faith, I told him that I would speak to Myrna about setting up an in-home Bible study.

To Myrna and Harold's credit, they happily gave me the go ahead, although they were still identifying with (yet never officially a part of) the Jehovah's Witnesses. Although they never voiced this, I got the feeling that they were happy I was actively seeking the answer to spiritual questions and wanted to

---

[6] Editor's note: Kingdom Hall is the traditional place of worship for Jehovah's Witnesses, not unlike a Christian church. The term, as proposed by Joseph Franklin (1935), is preferred over "church", since in the Bible "church" specifically refers to a congregation of people rather than a building.

encourage it. They even sat down to ask the two young "Elders" who came to visit a couple of questions. Interestingly enough, when I look back, I don't recall anything coming directly from the book of Mormon that day, but rather from the Bible. I studied with them for several months and during this time I was making the transition from living with Myrna and Harold to living on my own. I had wanted to leave the nest for some time, so when a mutual friend introduced me to a woman who was looking for a part-time live-in nanny, I saw it as a stepping stone toward that end. As I prepared for my life-changing move, Devan arranged to help me get my belongings to my new place. He also invited me to hang out at a local skating rink with some of the members of the local temple the following weekend.

Standing in the lobby of the rink on a Saturday afternoon, I recall feeling a bit awkward in a tight-fitting top and blue jeans amongst a group of conservatively dressed males. The "leader" of the group seemed sympathetic to my plight however, assuaging my unease by cracking jokes and being an all-out gentleman—which, I will admit, reddened my cheeks a bit.

The name of the said elder escapes me after all these years, but I don't think I would have a hard time recognizing him in a crowd, even to this very day. He was a handsome, imposing figure with ice blue eyes that shone with mith and kindness.

Funny thing too, was that I noticed that most of these "elders" were fresh-faced young men who had been sent to Atlanta in order to perform dutiful missions for their church. I was fast learning that missions were a big deal to Mormons, and while on one, you had to mind your P's and Q's lest you shame not only the church, but also the family who had scrimped and saved to send you.

Still, I always found the term "elder" to be kind of a misnomer since most of the ones I had met were barely legal enough to buy a drink let alone tell folks the way to live godly lives.

The leader of these elders was the oldest—maybe 26 years of age at the most, and did I already mention he was handsome? I recall blushing as he bent down to help me tie my ice skates (I had never been ice skating before and didn't even know how to stabilize my ankles). He saw my distress and silently bent down to help me in my moment of crisis.

As he knelt before me, the younger "elders" marveled at his humility, to which he replied, "Christ would do no less."

Man, I was all kinds of impressed.

Later that evening, I hopped inside the car as Devan, the elder (who was driving), and one other Mormon boy from the rink accompanied me to my new home. We engaged in spirited discussion about our foibles, with some lighthearted banter about how often I had fallen in my attempts to aspire to become an "Olympic" skater. During a lull in the conversation, I quietly asked Devan if Mormons could date non-Mormons. I was told that dating outside the church was strictly frowned upon so most didn't do it.

The handsome "elder" who had tied my skate asked if I was at all interested in Mormonism. With doe eyes, I demurely said 'yes' and he promptly pulled over to a parking area near a lake and told the others in the car to baptize me there and then... *they did.*

I recall feeling exhilarated that night, born again! When the lead elder gave me my own *Book of Mormon* to read a few days later, he instructed me that the Holy Spirit would reveal its truth to me. Well, one could have colored me all kinds of excited and that very evening I put the Book o' Mormon on my bed, knelt down, and prayed.

And got... a tingling sensation... something ethereal, I think.

A few days later, I got a call from my handsome baptizer, and I was thrilled... we talked for a few hours and then, just out of the blue, the conversation curiously crawled towards a more sexual tone.

I hung up feeling a bit bemused, freaked out and saddened by the exchange.

It would be months before I would officially leave the church, however. Numerous other things appeared to be rampant in this local chapter, from drug use, to blatant racism. For instance, two party-goers once showed up in "black face" paint dressed as African American food servers to a church-sponsored Halloween party. I was also told that if I were ever to marry a white Mormon, we would not be able to do so in the temple (the heavenly dream of many Mormon Brides to be), as the church would not officially recognize it.

I ran screaming from the Latter Day Saints and never looked back.

Charismatic/Pentecostal

Like a piece of flotsam caught in a current, I found myself ebbing in and out of religious states. I would spend whole years just doing my thing, working, coming home, dealing with family issues, with nothing much of a social life to speak of.

During this period, I largely kept to myself, dating very little if at all.

This didn't mean the urge to merge had vanished completely, and I would often turn to self-gratification to ease occasional bouts of loneliness and a screaming sex drive. I realized this was not a bad thing in and of itself, but still, I couldn't help feeling guilty whenever I finally caved in to the desire to indulge my impulses.

I usually pulled out the Good Book to find solace and redemption in scripture upon losing such a battle. After a healthy dose of Bible learnin', I'd hit my knees and pray, feeling satisfied I fixed my sinful little misdemeanor.

But of course it didn't, and the cycle of urge to action, to sin, to guilt and prayer again continued off and on until the day I literally fell in love with the son of a preacher man.

Carlton Lowe, called "Solo" by his friends, was a struggling musician who had fallen out of favor with his father, an esteemed reverend with his own church, for the simple crime of wanting to perform R 'n' B music. Carl, it turned out, would be my first serious relationship. He was the man I went all the way with, lost my virginity to and saw a future with beyond dinner and movie.

Six months later, he officially asked me to be his wife, and I moved in with my fiancée along with the other members of his band.

I was working as a temp at this point. Carl and the gang were in the process of recording under the guidance of then manager Auvil Gilchrist, who primarily concentrated his efforts on pitching the album to some of his major label connections, and who had a tendency to be very tight in the area of financial support. As a result, the band only managed to make money when they performed on the road. Unfortunately, gigs were few and far between.

One fateful day, Carl ran into a pastor named Brenda Chase, who would hire him on to play keyboards for a small in-home assembly that served as something of a makeshift church. Pastor Chase would often quote from Matthew 18:30 which read, "For where two or three are gathered together in my name, there am I in the midst of them," to lift the spirits of her small congregation with the idea that one day their church, alongside its message, would grow.

For her, hiring Carl to play solidified the fact that they were indeed a church even if they were only meeting up in a basement every Sunday. She called her ministry *Power of Prayer*, and the group often assembled at the home of Sister Abby, one of her parishioners.

I often accompanied Carl when he would play for the pastor but I could never shake the feeling that she was something of a shyster. I mean, as far as I could tell, she was merely a self-proclaimed minster, and I didn't even know if Chase had a license to preach. The one thing that I found oddly alluring but also off-putting was that she seemed to marry mysticism with traditional Baptist ideals.

A native of Louisiana, her style of religion seemed steeped in the charismatic traditions of Pentecostalism complete with the laying on of hands and speaking in tongues.

I was very skeptical of these practices and Carl shared my concerns. Still, for him, money was money and we both decided it was best to keep our mouths shut and play along. This didn't keep Pastor Chase from attempting to pull us into her *Power of Prayer*. After church we would all pile into our individual cars and seek out a local cafeteria-style restaurant to hang out in. During this time Pastor Chase would take keen interest in me, as if trying to find the "in" that would enable her to coax me into joining the fold.

Carl was also keenly aware of this and, pulling me aside, he would warn me not to get taken in. I told him he needn't worry, as I was far too smart for her tricks. The year prior to Pastor Chase coming into our lives had been somewhat eventful. I had, after many years, reconnected with my father, who was still battling his inner demons with mixed results. He lived with a good friend and on occasion Carl and I would come and visit to see how he was doing. My sister, whom I had also lost contact with after she had run away from our second foster home, showed back up with her newborn son in tow. The father of her child, a drug addict as well, was nowhere to be seen.

Despite the mishmash of issues, I was happy to have my family back. Unfortunately, Pastor Chase got wind of this news and, hindsight being what it is, I can see she used it to her advantage.

I will admit that with so much going on, I was starting to feel a bit powerless and overwhelmed by it all. Carl's career was also hitting a snag and I found my personal and work life suffering.

Pastor Chase stepped in to occasionally offer advice and help and pretty soon my doubts and subconscious warnings about her began to soften to near whispers. In 1991, she helped me get a job as a switchboard operator at the Centers for Disease Control. It would be the first of just a handful of stable jobs that would allow me to be truly self-sufficient in a way I hadn't been before. It was here that I met the feisty and spirited Della Sponge, or Sister Sponge as she came to be called. Pastor Chase and her had been long time friends, with Sponge following her from Georgia to Louisiana.

Now, for reasons too numerous to mention, I desired to move from that band's apartment into my own place. Carl and I were still engaged, but as time wore on this became a somewhat tentative promise. Although we never said this aloud, we seemed to understand that time apart may actually strengthen our relationship.

Interestingly enough, Sister Sponge would soon find herself in need of a roommate.

I soon found myself swept up as I became a regular participant in *Power of Prayer*. In no short order I adopted the mantle of church secretary, and, as promised, the church began to grow quite considerably, to the point where we were looking for a physical building to hold services in. Still, Sister Abby's basement was quite sizable, and more than capable of accommodating the growing throng as Pastor Chase sought a permanent church home.

As time passed however, I failed to recognize how much I had allowed the church to slowly take over my life. When it came to the *Power of Prayer*, we did everything together. We ate together, lived together, prayed together, worked together as well as traveled to numerous places preaching the word of God together.

I even found myself speaking in tongues, something I had once ridiculed. If you asked me how and why, I couldn't have explained any of it. I even experienced being "slain in the spirit" once or twice; and although I have no explanation for it, I think it was invoked by spiritually ominous organ music.

At this juncture Carl and I had broken up and it wasn't a mutual decision. Things had gotten pretty bad on numerous fronts and it was time to move on. Devoid of a fiancée, I abstained from all sexual relations. In fact, I would immediately go into my "prayer closet" if I had so much as a sexual thought, let alone an urge to masturbate. Literally, I'd go into a closet and pray.

At any rate, I somehow managed to stay chaste for three long years, and luckily I hadn't found keeping my celibacy to be all that difficult. Between the church, work and family obligations, I rarely even had time to think about relationships let alone "doing the deed."

I will admit to having found a bit of peace within the folds of *Power of Prayer*. In Pastor Chase and Sister Sponge, I had found a more stable family who could look after me and seek after my best interests. Sister Sponge in particular became my role model and close friend, lovingly taking me under wing and keeping me in line when I strayed. A devout Christian, she was approaching thirty and still a virgin. She was also sensible, capable and well versed in the word of God.

Yet, even with so much stability and support coming my way, I began to have nagging doubts about the direction my life had taken. Particularly, whenever I read the Bible.

The first thing I noted was far too many pastors seemed to misquote Bible verses. I could not say with any certainty that this was on purpose, but some of the discrepancies seemed to be in direct conflict with what was being taught in church, especially when a passage was read in its entirety. Not only this, but as I sat down and read, I noticed something dreadful. My Bible, my beautiful, love-filled, Holy Bible—was one sick book! There were passages about bashing babies' heads against stones, volumes about the capture and rape of women, reams about the wholesale killing of entire tribes and nations.

When I came across such verses, I would blink them away and quickly forget about them. This trick didn't always work since, upon opening the Bible again, there were many more passages of the contemptible sort. None of this brutality and injustice seemed to be in line with my idea of a divine protector who wanted to know and love me.

The New Testament had some jacked-up things in it as well, but it was the Old Testament that gave me the most pause. The first five books, or the Torah, as it is called, grieved me the most. It condoned mass murder, rape, incest and a whole host of other despicable things I just couldn't reconcile with my image of an all-knowing, all-powerful and loving creator.

When I approached Pastor Chase with my concerns, she told me that I needn't worry about it. She informed me that the Old Testament was primarily allegorical and historical. She also explained that God allowed some of these horrible things to happen to show mankind why we needed a savior.

You see, Pastor Chase explained, man was inherently sinful and all the evils that I saw were the work of mankind—not God. Therefore it was our sinful nature that kept us from even having a deep and meaningful relationship with the Almighty. This was why we needed someone to intervene on our behalf.

The New Testament, she went on to say, was the best go-to book for answers on the pathway of modern salvation. According to her, I merely had to read the Bible in context and pray for guidance from the Holy Spirit so that he could open my eyes to what the words of the Bible truly meant.

So I did just that, in good faith. I prayed for a "leading of the Holy Spirit" as it was called, and hoped I would get some real answers. I then opened the book to the New Testament and read about how Jesus said he came not to bring peace into the world, but a sword.

Later, I took my concerns to Pastor Chase and Sister Sponge, but eventually they began to deflect my inquiries with "God works in mysterious ways" or the advice to "Seek God's face."

I did as instructed, but my doubts continued to linger.

The pivotal point came when I was forced to make a decision based purely on reason. I had just been paid and a bill came up that needed my immediate attention. If I had paid my tithes as I had for the last three years, I wouldn't have been able to make the payment.

So, I made the decision to pay the bill and double up on my tithes the following week instead. Curiously enough, the very next day Pastor Chase called to ask me about my decision. When I informed her that I had paid a bill and would double my tithes the following week, she told me that I couldn't "put God on hold" in this way.

Seriously? In the three years I had been an active member of her church, I'd faithfully tithed and had not missed a single payment. When I found myself at the crossroads of a dilemma, I figured a just and loving God would understand individual circumstances. Why would he feel I was putting him on hold by simply being responsible?

This question prompted me to do a little research into tithing practices and what I found was surprising. For instance, I learned that numerous denominations tithed differently. Mormons for example tithed annually; others bi-weekly. In the grand scheme of things, there was nothing wrong with me opting to double my tithes the following week.

At the next prayer meeting, I decided to broach the subject again in order to get a firm grasp on why my decision to double up would have been such an affront to God. I was shaken and humiliated when Pastor Chase rebuked the devil in me in front of the congregation. She then asked everyone to lay hands on me and pray the demonic spirit out of me.

I was furious. I mean, really? This was the treatment I was going to receive for asking a simple question? I was possessed and allowing the devil to use me because I wanted to understand why we were tithing in the manner we were?

Right then and there, I recognized the situation for what it was. Pastor Chase was using that money for her own personal gain. In other words, she wanted the money to keep rolling in. As the secretary of the church, I had seen her purchase $200 dollar dresses on the basis that she was "representing the flock". Heck, during a sermon she once stated that if we loved her, she'd be driving a Cadillac.

But alas, my question was a threat to her money-grubbing lifestyle. If I could get away with doubling up tithes every week, others might follow suit. She wouldn't be able to count on that money coming on a regular basis. So, to keep me and the others in line, she had to shame me for even thinking I could alter the ritual.

In a heartbreaking moment of clarity, I came to recognize the fact that, in exchange for a comfortable sense of belonging, I had allowed myself to be hoodwinked by a shyster.

I was *livid!*

Yet, as angry as I was, it would be months before I would get up the courage to pack up and leave my friends and extended family behind. But, leave I did.

Pastor Chase and Sister Sponge followed me around from room to room, wagging her finger and preaching at me. She tried everything in the book to get me to reconsider, as I packed my things into suitcases.

I didn't have anywhere to go so I ended up moving back in with my dad for a while.

Spiritual Non Religious

For almost a year I had something of a rudderless feeling and was in the throes of self-pity. Amid my despair, I didn't want to work, I didn't want to go out—I just didn't want to *be* any more.

It was my sister who eventually convinced me to get off my ass and do something. She even managed to get me to go to a club in a rich downtown district called Buckhead. This was quite the *fait accompli* as I had never stepped foot in one for the life of me. I almost felt as if I was under threat of fire and brimstone just for stepping foot in the place.

I must have stuck out like a sore thumb. Nobody outside my sister's circle of friends said much to me. In retrospect, I may have put out an unapproachable vibe as I would often carry a near ream of paper with me everywhere I went. As others laughed and drank, I furiously scribbled about my adventures in this strange new world.

One dark and stormy day, an unlikely duo slid in the booth across from my sister and me. There were two men. One was a young man who introduced himself as Dennis Willis. He was a wiry corporate type, his companion was the polar opposite. His name was Terry L. McDonald, a self-assured jovial man in his early forties, with corkscrew gray hair, and sly look to his eye that seemed to house a bit of devilment.

He caught my attention immediately when he replied, "Looks like we have quite the passionate writer in our midst!"

I found myself intrigued and reeled in by Terry's amiable manner and infectious personality.

The night wore on and Dennis, who had promised to give my sis and me a lift home, left the bar only to discover the back tires of his car had been booted by a towing company. After a few terse words, Terry and Dennis called the towing company and found they had to wait until the following morning to pay the fine.

Undaunted, Terry cheerfully announced that he would grab us a cab to make good on his promise to get us home. I balked as I lived quite a ways from Buckhead, but he wouldn't hear of it. True to their word and with no small amount of expenditure on their behalf, we got home safe and sound.

When I offered to pay them back, Terry merely shook his head at me and said, "Darling, the evening has paid for itself!" And with a wink he and Dennis hopped into the cab and headed home.

As time wore on, I found myself excited about the prospect of hanging out with Terry on the weekends, as I was eager to chat him up and probe his intriguing mind. In the course of our exchanges he turned me on to various sci-fi authors such as Asimov, Heinlein, Sagan and numerous others. Before I knew it, I was myself immersed in the colorful worlds of Orson Scott Card's "Red Prophet" series as well as Varley's glorious dark operatic "Blue Champagne," Pournelle and Niven's "Footfall" and even William Gibson's electric cyberpunk works. These writers helped open my mind to fascinating new possibilities for human existence and styles of thought.

Terry also expounded on philosophies like existentialism while pouncing on and tearing apart Ayn Randian style objectivism. He'd deconstruct the merits and benefits, as well as the pitfalls, of human sexuality; the expansive spiritual planes he explored as a child of the sixties. He talked of measured drug use, popping shrooms, pot smoking and LSD trips. All these served as the fertile backdrops for true life adventures that Mark Twain would have surely slapped his knee over.

Terry and I flirted with a romance that ended up being very short lived. He and I both knew that ours was a doom-fated relationship—what with me being half his age and all (his daughter and I were only three years apart). But true to his nature, he took me under his wing and looked after and nurtured me.

The friendship had its ups and downs, of course. Terry, despite his *avante garde* outlook and wherever-the-wind-blows lifestyle was, much like me, broken. He'd come from a shattered childhood that was fraught with abuse and on occasion, I could see the hallmarks of his desire to flesh out something more romantic with me but, despite this, I couldn't forsake our friendship as Terry had come to mean more to me than any other person before. He was a mentor, a guide and yes, I suppose, a father figure.

In the end, no matter where our lives led us, and the dark places into which we oftentimes delved, the one thing Terry constantly stressed was that we are the captains of our own fate and that freethought was a gift worth fighting for.

Even though parting with Terry was bittersweet sorrow, when I reflect on these distant memories, I know I can fully credit Terry with putting me on the path towards freethought and critical thinking—for this I am eternally grateful.

Atheist

Regrettably, I lost my father to HIV AIDS in 2004. Soon after, in 2005, I met and married Michael Roach and later that same year gave birth to a daughter who we named Gabrielle. In 2009 we received a wonderful son name Orion. Throughout all these life-changing events I found time to pursue music, write, draw and delve into animation.

But as we all do, when the quiet rolls in, I wondered about where I stood on spiritual matters. When I met Michael we were both agnostics, in fact, we often mocked the antics of atheists who put up billboards and challenged folks for praying in public.

Yet, one day, it just kinda came to me that, in the grand scheme of things, I simply didn't believe a god existed.

I was an atheist.

Once I realized this, I began to investigate the political movement and philosophies of fellow non-believers. I started watching shows like "The Atheist Experience" and looking up videos online featuring the likes of Christopher Hitchens, Richard Dawkins and Sam Harris.

I began to understand that the media were skewing many atheistic stances and lampooning them to look ridiculous. For example, many lawsuits were brought due to gross legal breaches of the separation of church and state. Contrary to popular belief, this protest wasn't just about some militant atheists getting a bee in their bonnet and trying to spoil theistic fun. No atheist has ever tried to silence individual prayer either, just state sanctioned prayer or religious activities which breach everyone's constitutional rights.

The more I learned the more excited I became, because, as luck would have it, the atheist worldview seemed to closely mirror my own.

There was only one problem. I was still a black woman living in Atlanta, the famous home of religious civil rights leader, Dr. Martin Luther King. That presented a few unique challenges in regard to the largely Christian black community and their reaction to folks like me.

As it stands, only a handful of my friends currently know I am an atheist and, thus far, they have all been pretty chill about it. I am happy knowing that, in 2013, I have shed the religion of African American slave owners. Indeed, I have opened my eyes to a deeper sense of purpose, of movement, steeped in the relevant secular mysteries that keep propelling us forward, and will continue to do so, whether there be gods or not.

I will say that where I am today also seems to make the most sense. I don't feel weighed down or as hampered by my personal demons as I once was. Of course, I am sure I can attribute some of that to growing older and wiser, but I also know that one certainly feels emancipated when they recognize, for example, that masturbation doesn't come with the price tag of eternal damnation in Hell.

Now, I can enjoy intimacy for intimacy's sake... and when I love I do so with vigor and passion, understanding that this is my one and only life, and by gum, I need to do live it to its fullest. There are no do-overs.

It seems Oprah Winfrey's claim that "God is the Awe" is mistaken. God is not "the Awe." God is, simply speaking, naught. As atheists, the awe we experience is ushered in by the very thought that in the vast emptiness of space, we exist on this rock, against all odds, by mere happenstance. For those who understand the value of this revelation, we stand in reverence of the brief, flickering flame we call life.

6

ARSALAN

Through the Fog: A Journey to Extemism and Back

I WAS BORN TO A MIDDLE CLASS FAMILY IN PAKISTAN TO practicing Sunni Muslim parents. My parents, like many people in Pakistan, were moderate people with an intense love for Islam but no hatred for anyone else. From my pre-teen years I used to observe fasting throughout the month of Ramzan and would pray five times a day. My parents were very proud of my composed nature and the fact that I had been observing religious practices from an age that few others do.

The story of my deconversion begins when I was living in Peshawar. Unlike the Punjab province, the religious outlook of many of the residents of Peshawar and much of the Khyber-Pakhtunkhwa province leans towards the extreme. I was a square peg in a round hole, as the sole Punjabi in an all-Pathan school who hardly understood their language; I had to work hard to earn respect but I gradually managed to settle in.

During my early days, I got on well with my Islamic Studies teacher who was a certified "Mufti" or cleric. He had been impressed with my habit of praying regularly and my tenacity in dealing with the challenges of earning my place among my peers. He taught Islamic Studies to the entire class but would offer everyone a break half an hour earlier so that he could preach to me and two of my closest friends.

I was deeply impressed by him and listened to whatever he told me with religious dedication, as if it were the word of God himself. He told me that I needed to stop shaving as it was a grievous sin. I complied with his advice and let my beard grow out, much to the protests of my mother who thought that having a beard made me look much older than my age.

Impressed by my dedication and piety, the cleric made me his "Naib-Imam" (deputy prayer leader). I was very proud of myself at the time and I revelled in the praise and admiration that the cleric showered upon me. Yet slowly he started making other demands on me which he ensured were met. I was asked to wear my trousers above the ankle because lower than ankle reflects too much pride; I was quick to adopt the said practice and once again faced much opposition from my mother whom I brought to tears with my blunt reasoning. I was quick to reprimand her over her actions to try and hinder my efforts to achieve enlightenment and I saw her attempts to stop me from wearing my trousers above ankle length as a particularly dastardly act as the cleric had told me that it signifies great pride in one's self and anyone who does not wear their trousers above ankle length will be doomed to oblivion on the day of judgement. The cleric told me vivid stories of how God would look away in disgust from anyone who did not conform to this dress code and that my failure to do so would just condemn me to damnation and the rest of my good deeds would have been in vain.

It was quite heart-wrenching for me at the time, to have made my mother cry to satisfy someone who I had known for less than a year, but I consoled myself by thinking that I was doing this for the favour of God and not any mortal; that at the end of the day it would be worth it. Moreover, I reconciled myself further by thinking that it was my mother who was at fault because she had weaker faith and was more worried about what the world might say when they saw her son with a beard and skull cap, his trousers folded to above his ankles at every gathering, than she was about pacifying God by meeting his demands. Now when I think about it, I am forced to commend her foresight as she had a very fair idea of where this entire episode was headed.

When significant trust had been established between myself and the cleric, he got to the real order of business and started telling me to avoid Shia Muslims and not to accept any food or drink that they might offer me.

Let me give you a bit of background about one of the most divisive aspects of Islam—the ongoing sectarian battle between *Sunni Islam* and *Shia Islam*. The issue has its roots in a political struggle for the *caliphate* (Islamic state led by a *caliph*) that erupted after the death of Muhammad; Shia Muslims believe that Ali, the prophet's nephew, had first right to the caliphate and the seat was usurped by Abubakar, the prophet's best friend and his father-in-law. They further believe that the next two caliphs that came before Ali finally became caliph were also illegitimate successors to Muhammad. Sunni Muslims on the other hand believe that the order of the caliphate is not open to question and followed whatever logical chronology that was decided best by the prophet's companions.

Arguments over these points still get heated and violence has broken out on more than a few occasions. What once started as a political dispute has since then grown into a religious divide that has often seen both sides declare the other to be non-Muslim. Shia Muslims glorify Ali and his grandson Hussain, who was killed at Karbala, to the point of worship, and commemorate the incident with a 40-day mourning period and processions in which they engage in self-harm. Some Sunni sub-sects consider both these activities to be against the spirit of Islam which leads them into conflict with the Shias. The rivalry between the two sects has, in the modern world, evolved into the Saudi-Iran conflict with both countries serving as the fountainhead of religious power for the followers of either sects. Even today, Arab Sunni conservative sects like Wahabi and Salafi are quite vocal and confrontational in their opposition to these practices and other purist, pro-Arab sects like the Deobandi in South Asia follow suit. That is why they are often engaged in some degree of hostility with Shia Muslims. It must be highlighted at this point, though, that some Sunni sects, especially those belonging to the more mystical Sufi orders, detach themselves from this conflict and generally avoid being involved in these debates though the Sufis are themselves resultantly declared to be heretics by the purist Sunnis.

Back to the issue at hand, when I asked the cleric why that was so, he told me that Shia Muslims spit in their food and water to win you over to their beliefs. No amount of blind allegiance to the cleric could allow me to accept this preposterous claim and I retorted that if that were so, wouldn't it be easier for Sunni Muslims to just stand on a street corner and spit at oncoming non-Muslims to convert them, rather than spending so much time and effort in preaching to them? He dismissed my question by saying that *there was no space for doubt or critical thought in matters of faith* and *they must be accepted for what they are.*

For the first time in my life, I felt that I had been severely let down by religion. Where there was previously idealism and hope, now skepticism prevailed. I went home that day, thinking about what I had been told, how stupid an assertion it had been and how my attempts to set it right, or at least better understand the spirit behind it, had been dismissed with such an insufficient answer. The cleric who I believed to be the fountainhead of all information and knowledge had failed me and his reputation had been left soiled in my eyes. But I was still far from questioning faith, at least at this point in time.

For some time, the cleric avoided this topic as he realized that I was not quite partial to it yet. After about a month or so, though, he asked me to stop spending time with my Shia friends because he said that he could visibly see them corrupting my faith through their influence. I had been brought up in a very moderate family that bordered on having secularist beliefs: my parents never taught me to treat a non-Muslim or a Shia any different to how I would treat a Sunni and my upbringing told me that the cleric was wrong. So I told him that I did not think this was the case.

This was the first time I had said no to any religious belief or demand that had been shoved down my throat; it was a liberating feeling. I had just used critical thinking to reject what a religious authority had said. Whereas it would seem common sense to do so in the Western world, it is considered a very audacious move in the East to be so outspoken, and in some cases has escalated so far as to see the person questioning a cleric or prayer leader to be declared an apostate and killed. These minor transgressions can lead to major consequences.

My affair with critical thinking had just begun and I started relapsing back to my former self, my trousers slowly regained the normal length and now rested gently over my shoes instead of being suspended three inches above them. Then my beard went because, at this point, I realized that what I believed in need not manifest in some physical form and not everyone who displayed these physical indicators of piety really believed in the spirit of them.

Soon, however, I began to question God himself. I began to ask if God really *is* that benevolent, why is there so much suffering in the world? Why do people kill in his name and he does nothing? Why would God ask me to praise him all the time? Is God really like a five year-old who needs my constant attention and cajoling or he will throw a tantrum? Is the maker of this world and beyond really so immature so as to allow for hundreds of religions and ask people to play Russian roulette with them because they all claim to lead to heaven and at the same time say that all others lead to hell?

God began to sound more like a pampered brat than an "All-knowing, All-seeing" power. I was now an agnostic and read about other faiths to see if they were any different but I found a profound monotony between them all. I was not sure what to do in order to satisfy my spiritual self.

Life had lost all account of normalcy at this point; I was in a vacuum and everything around me seemed so distant. I still prayed regularly when I was with my family. However, now it was not because I sought the approval of some deity but because I did not wish to upset my family who were quite proud that I had been praying from such a young age and saw it as a reward for some good deed they must have done long ago. I did not have the heart to see them lose their optimism and pride so I decided to continue praying for them whilst I loathed myself for being two-faced.

I was trapped.

On the one hand was my spiritual liberation, or lack thereof, and on the other were the hopes and aspirations of my family. I was afraid of even considering that I had become an atheist. I shuddered at the thought of what would happen to me if my family or friends found out what I believed (or didn't); I would surely be disowned, and yet at the same time I feared even more about what would happen if someone else found out, someone who had no relation to me. I had heard stories of people being lynched by large crowds for desecrating the Quran, claiming to be prophets or uttering unflattering remarks about Allah. I had no intention of upsetting anyone or hurting their religious sentiments but would they really allow me to offer any clarification in an attempt to allay their misconceptions about the nature of my beliefs? I doubted it and so I let all this emotional mess brew inside me as I kept all my questions locked up, in fear of asking the wrong crowd.

I looked to the internet for help, to online forums for atheists where I was met with taunts of being a "Paki," "Towel-Head," "Sand-Nigger" and "Terrorist." It was a tough time for me and I realized that hate prevailed globally—it was not some localized phenomenon. My people would not tolerate my beliefs and those who would tolerate my beliefs would not tolerate the colour of my skin. I was smack in the middle of a clash of civilizations and I would not wish even my most bitter enemy to face such a situation, much rather an inquisitive 18 year old, detached from what he had been taught to accept as the truth, as I had been at the time.

The only positive that I could see at this point was that I had moved out from Peshawar and I was no longer in regular contact with the cleric who I had started to avoid earlier on. It had been that our proximity and past interaction which meant that I had to share his company at least twice a week. Now, with him out of the picture, I could think much more clearly and I was accountable to no one for how I chose to dress and conduct myself. Better still, my parents were all too happy to see their son reverting back to his normal self.

I had moved to Lahore, the capital of the Punjab province and one of the hubs of the arts in Pakistan. It's a very liberal and progressive city for the most part, especially in comparison to Peshawar. Indeed, the cities are poles apart in their tolerance for others. Lahore is all-welcoming and a typical metropolis, bustling with life and people of all kinds who share their love for two things, good food and fine art (the staples of Lahori culture).

It was here that I became acquainted with Anis. He was the first vocal Pakistani atheist I had seen and before meeting him I was convinced that that there were no atheists in Pakistan. For the first time in my life, here was someone who could provide me some support in my transition from life as a Muslim to that of a non-Muslim. I now knew why I could not find peace within the existing system as I, too, had been an atheist at heart but had just been too afraid to accept it. Seeing Anis gave me the courage to embrace my lack of faith. As it turned out, even my best friend Khawar was an atheist but he too had been too afraid to admit it. Indeed, he had earlier met my question about whether he had been an agnostic with significant disgust but later gathered the courage to acknowledge that he was atheist as well. It was quite an awkward experience now that I recall it. I had shared a joke with him from the ex-Muslim forums where someone had proposed a secret code to check if the other person was an ex-Muslim and someone had jokingly posted the following questions and answers as a possible secret password:

1: Do you flat press? (Are you an Atheist?)

2: Cheeseburger. (Affirmative)

In the spur of the moment, I asked Khawar the same question who responded with the right answer. It was an awkward moment but in over 8 years of knowing each other, this was the first time we had admitted our atheism to one another and it was quite a liberating feeling, so much so that we no longer saw the joke as being a comment made in jest but rather became indebted to whoever wrote it for allowing us the vehicle to come to terms with a notion that we might not have been able to admit to if it had not been sugar-coated as a comment made in jest.

Now, I talk to people to try and recognize if they are atheist and if I find anyone who shows the signs, I offer them support and a sympathetic ear. I've often been told that I have a nose for finding atheists and sometimes I even know of people's atheism before they are prepared to accept it. I am asked what signs I look for an in atheist and I believe they are quite simple to observe once you know what to look for. These signs include but are not limited to:

1) A less than sympathetic response to religious material, as people are often expected to show extremes of emotions in order to reaffirm their piety and strength of dedication.

2) A tendency to argue the one-sided sectarian narrative.

3) Most ex-muslims are against the controversial law that declares Ahmedis (a particular religious sect) as non-Muslims.

4) A style of conversation where God is often brought into critical question; regular discourse in Pakistan usually avoids mentioning God unless for praise.

These are some of the common signs to observe; it is often a combination of these in addition to many personalized signatures that allows me to make an assumption. I initially introduce myself as a "Non-Denominational Muslim," also a rarity and somewhat an oddity in Pakistan, and then spend some time gauging the other person's response before deciding whether they will be tolerant to the big question. It's playing with fire every time you do it but you can generally guess because Muslims, even those who never prayed in their life and engage in acts forbidden by Islam on a daily schedule, will be quite vocal about their love for Islam and their devotion to God. It is hypocrisy, but rampant nonetheless.

Offering another atheist some support is a huge service to offer anyone in a country where atheism is criminalized by law and apostasy from Islam is punishable by death. In that sense, I am like an atheist preacher who is helping people realize that there is nothing wrong with being an atheist and you can be an atheist without being a terrible person, contrary to the popular perception here in Pakistan.

Some of my closest Muslim friends know that I am an atheist and many of them are okay with it. Of course, others try to convert me back and say that I left because I gave into my impulses, which is a laugh because many of them preach about piety and how I am dooming myself by leaving Islam during the day but during the night they drink booze and attend rave parties high on ecstasy, all forbidden by Islam. I, on the other hand, do no such thing. I abide by social norms and respect society's limits; I just reject their deity and consider it my right to believe in whatever I believe or in nothing at all, as I see fit.

I still maintain the illusion of being a perfectly pious, practising Muslim for my family. I pray regularly and still fast during Ramadan because I fear that my family will disown me if I confess to being an atheist. I just hope that one day I am able to tell them the truth and I hope that they will just smile back and tell me that it's fine and they are at peace with my choice. But that seems like a long shot at this point.

At the time of writing this, Anis is studying to become a doctor and I am pursuing a degree in International Relations. Khawar has left for the UK where he is completing his engineering from amongst the top universities in London and is open to the ex-Muslim community there. He urges me regularly to consider moving to the UK as it promises much greater religious freedom and welcomes individuals who are ready to be contributing members of society. Yet even though I have visited the UK on multiple occasions and found the people to be quite sociable, my online interaction with atheists of the Western world has left me scarred. I realize that I will never look anything like a European and if I am to be discriminated against, I might as well be discriminated against at home. The culture of atheists in the East and particularly in Muslim countries is vastly different to that of our counterparts in the West, we have to put our life in jeopardy for our beliefs and I guess that is why we tend to be more sympathetic towards each other. We thrive in secret communities and live double lives but are always there to offer a word of encouragement, advice or caution to our fellows. We attained our atheism after considerable thought and deliberation, we fought to the truth through decades of propaganda and came out better people.

I just hope that if anyone reads this, whether they be in the East or West, they will have a more sympathetic approach towards ex-Muslims and try to understand them better.

7

VYCKIE GARRISON

Fertile Ground

The Idea

I AM REALLY JEALOUS OF PEOPLE COMING IN TO THE skeptical movement today, with all of their support networks, and social media, which allows a sense of community and belonging, whether it be the Center for Inquiry groups which have popped up, or Skeptically Drinking in, say, Washington DC. (Though I wonder how that works. Perhaps "I *doubt* there is enough rum in this coke!"). I was never able or inclined to know what the "other side" were up to. My story is one of becoming more and more entrenched within a Christian network and worldview until I was blind to the existence of such others. My world was the *Quiverfull* world.

What is Quiverfull? Well, it's not a denomination, it's not a set of doctrines. I like to describe it as more of a mindset than anything. It is a very powerful head trip which affects every aspect of your life: home schooling, home birthing, home churching. In fact, I was "HOMEier than thou," as I used to say. The whole process of becoming part of this movement was incremental, one step leading to the next and then that to the next, and so on—it didn't happen all at once. Quiverfull, essentially, is about having as many children as you can in order to parent soldiers for Christ, as I will now explain.

It began when I started home schooling. I ended up going to a Christian home school convention, which I liked to call "fertile ground." The proliferation of this family lifestyle is basically marketing. If you go to home school conventions like these, you might have a workshop where they tell you how to teach advanced math and there might be a couple of parents trying to learn that. But more likely and more popular will be the sorts of workshops titled "How a woman can use reverence to build and save her marriage." They'll bring in speakers from *Home School Legal Defense Association* and *Vision* Forum and they essentially teach a patriarchal, Dominionist ideal. And Quiverfull.

The idea is unapologetic. We are going to take back this world for Christ, and the way we are going to do that is to simply out-populate unbelievers. As Psalm 127 states: "Happy is the man that has filled his quiver with them: he shall not be ashamed when he speaks with the enemies in the gate." (NKJV)

We were told that the gates of "the city" was the place where all the civil matters were decided; that's where the rulers, the leaders, the deciders of politics, met. They met and did their deeds at the gates. The whole point of having this quiverfull of children was to train them up as leaders and to put them in these prominent positions of power: of government, education, media, religion, business, arts and entertainment. You have these seven mountains of influence, and they were the targets for our children. The goal is to train up these children to go in and infuse those arenas with biblical Christian principles.

In my case, I already had my eldest daughter, and my now ex-husband was really good with kids. My husband, Warren, was blind. Well, I guess he still is (I don't want to make it sound like he was cured, or is dead)! We started figuring out how we were going to do this relationship thing. At the time, I was still going to college—I had a 4.0 grade point average—I loved learning and college life was great. I enjoyed working, too. Warren was on disability allowance and he didn't really have a way of making an income, so it made sense to us that he was going to stay home and look after the house, look after the kids, and at any rate, he loved to do laundry. Who was I to disagree? I was going to go out and get my degree and get a big job and support the family. For us, this was the most suitable way of having a relationship and of having a family.

But then we started hearing this sort of indoctrinating message. We went from the Salvation Army to this fundamental Baptist church and I remember the pastor talking about biblical rules for husbands and wives, biblical family values—God's plan for families. The basic story is that God made man to be the head and the woman to be the helpmeet. The man is to be the provider and the protector and the woman is to be the supporter for whatever calling God has for *him* and his life. Hearing this message over time, we started to mull over what God thought about our approach to the relationship, to our jobs and to our family. It was a gradual thing but eventually I got conviction that I was abandoning my kids, off doing what *I* wanted to do, and was neglecting my role. That was not really what I was supposed to be doing, what God had called me to.

In other words, I needed to *come home*.

This meant quitting college, quitting my job. I came home. It was my time to be a helpmeet, which our personalities didn't really suit. Warren was not much of a leader. He didn't particularly like making the decisions; and me, well I was fine making them! But we learned that that was not life, this was not the way it was meant to be. We were simply not conforming: he needed to be the leader and I needed to be his support.

We soon took on the idea that we had to leave our family planning up to God which meant that we started having all of these babies. Because Warren didn't really have a way of making an income, we needed to find a way to support this burgeoning family so I started a Christian family newspaper. Of course, by "family", I mean very political and very radically pro-life. It was pro-life not just in the way we supported the "right to life" but in the way we also questioned how we could talk with any authority or moral integrity about abortion if we are accepting the same mindset that children should be planned rather than allowing them to come at the behest of God. We were saying that if you really trusted in God, that he is the Author and Creator of life, that he is in control through his eternal decisions as to whether humans come into existence, then you need to leave that in his hands. Trust in divine family planning. The newspaper became a mouthpiece for this worldview, selling it to others.

Northeast Nebraska is very conservative, so the newspaper went over really well and we were able to support our family fairly comfortably off of that income.

The Relationship

In one simple word: patriarchy. When you have this total imbalance of power, this form of relationship submission, the person who is the head can easily suck you in with promises steeped in biblical authority. Ephesians 5:25 was a favorite: "Husbands, love your wives, just as Christ also loved the church and gave Himself for her" (NKJV). I call this the *peanut butter and the patriarchy trap*. This is what draws the women into this whole Quiverfull 'women's movement'.

What I have learnt since leaving this particular world behind, since starting the *No Longer Qivering* website, is that it seems the case that it is often the women who are pushing these biblical teachings on the men. Why? It's the whole "husbands love your wives" thing where you think you are going to get to be the wife of this servant leader, like Jesus. You believe that you are going to get someone who loves you like Christ loves his church. When you have this ideal embedded in your mind of what kind of husband you are going to get, and you are willing to pay the price, and the price you are going to have to pay is submission and obedience... Well, it's twisted. Unfortunately, as you may guess, I didn't realize this until much later and I got out. Too late, some might say.

When I finally recognised the insidious nature of the headship and submission scheme, here's how I described it:

The very first thing that I had to learn as a Christian wife was submission. I needed to honor and obey my husband. And I had to be such a devout, godly woman that my husband couldn't find any fault in me—and in that way, I could "win him without a word." Of course, the Bible study ladies who were teaching me about this submission, in one meeting, reminded me that it was God's job to get my husband saved, but they also assured me that I could do my part by following their advice and being a loving, respectful wife. What I took away from that meeting was this: all I had to do was be the perfect wife and the perfect Christian; and God would honor that and save my marriage.

Now, I'm sure you're reading this and thinking that obviously it's impossible to be perfect—but that wasn't so apparent to me at the time; it seemed doable. I had little doubt that I could carry out all that those women told me I must do—I was young and I had a lot of confidence in my abilities—and when I did it, when I became this submissive helpmeet, God would have no choice but to come through for me. He would make a really great husband out of Warren.

This, as I have said, is twisted. Morally twisted and logically twisted.

When you counsel couples who are in co-dependent relationships, it is clear that you cannot change each other; all that you can do is focus on yourself. The equation here, though, is complicated when you throw God into the mix. Of course, I felt like *I* didn't have to control my husband because God is the one who would be controlling him in honoring my obedience. The web of manipulation, or illusory manipulation, was quite intricate. And this has been the same for every patriarchal relationship which I have witnessed since breaking free. The more the man is submitted and catered to, and given this special place of authority and responsibility within the home, the more and more he begins to resemble the God of the Old Testament—that crazy and capricious *man-God*. And the wife? She looks more and more like Jesus, the sacrificial lamb. "Though he slay me, yet will I trust in him" (Job13:15 KJV). What you have is the husband becoming ever more narcissistic, ever more feeling that he is superior, whilst the wife is becoming progressively more of a martyr, self-abdicating. The website which I set up to help people out of this mindset, out of this world, is called *No Longer Qivering*, and it drives people mad because they don't get why there is no 'u' in the word "quivering". It's simple: there *is* no *you* in Quiverfull. As such, that is the subtitle of the website. One often talked about JOY: Jesus first, Others second, and Yourself last. This was the mindset which guided me; or to put it in biblical context, "Greater love hath no man than this, that a man lay down his life for his friends" (John 15:13 KJV). In the patriarchy paradigm, within Quiverfull, this is your expression of love. The wife completely subsumes herself for the good of her family and for her husband. For God. It's all for God.

Again, the themes here are manipulation and, equally sadly, dysfunction.

And if it isn't working, then whose fault is it? Surely we are not doing it right, not trying hard enough, not praying enough, not being submissive enough, we haven't found just the right scripture… So you buy another book from Vision Forum. But the take away idea from it is always the fact that it is never *his* fault. I see this all the time, these days, in dealing with the aftermath of such relationships; that it ruins the men and it ruins the women. You would think that a set up which caters to the man would suit them just fine, but on reflection it infantilises the man. Christianity is apparently always dealing with love and respect—the women need love, the men respect—but as soon as you adopt that patriarchal model of relating where you are completely submitting to another person, there is no respect in that. In reality, people need to take enough responsibility to foster respect for themselves. To earn it.

However, this did not occur to us, we were so heavily involved in this mindset that everything was twisted. I considered myself a fairly intelligent person; I wasn't stupid. But I was told from the beginning, from the Bible and Christianity, about myself as a human being, that there was something wrong with human nature. I was born with this *sin nature*; I had an urge which was trying to take me away from God, that was trying to rebel against him, leading me down worldly ways and down Satan's path. I knew this about myself, and used to say, "My heart is deceitful above all things and desperately wicked." I was taught that the person whom my heart most wanted to deceive was *me*. So whenever something started to make sense to me, I had to think, well that can't be God, and because I was a woman, I was taught that I was inherently more susceptible to deception by Satan. For example, "And Adam was not deceived, but the woman being deceived was in the transgression" (1 Timothy 2:14 KJV). I had such a doubt over those years that if something seemed like a sensible and commonsense idea (especially if it was something that *I* actually wanted to do), then it could not be right—I was being deceived. I would have to figure out the opposite, because obviously whatever seemed right to *me* would lead to self-destruction.

My Blessings

My husband and I got further and further disconnected from reality, building this little fantasy world up inside our heads. But reality didn't go away; pregnancies were killing me, and I don't say this frivolously. I had had some health issues after my third to the point that we were advised not to have any more children. We thought three were plenty. Warren had gone and got a vasectomy.

But this was all *before* we set off fully on our Quiverfull journey... We read Nancy Campbell's book *God's Vision for Families* and Mary Pride's *The Way Home: Beyond Feminism, Back to Reality*. In these books, they talked about giving your reproductive life over to God. The more we spoke to people who had done this, people from the Quiverfull movement, the more we felt convinced that we needed to put our reproductive lives back in God's hands. Warren went ahead and had a reversal and we had four more children (we always called them "blessings").

What made demanding things even more difficult was the fact that three of my children had inherited my bone condition which I have been struggling all my life with. Because of this, we were always taking them up to appointments in Minneapolis and between the three of them they've had about twenty-five surgeries (and one time, all three of them had operations simultaneously!). That was consuming a massive amount of our time and a lot of our life, and we were just about bringing in enough income to keep things ticking over.

Quite often you hear that these large Quiverfull families are a drain on the welfare system, but this is not the case. Quiverfull families generally will not accept public assistance because it will be a bad witness. They are generally very Republican, anti-'socialism', so we were having to do all of this without food stamps and Medicare; we only had healthcare. Luckily, there were *Shriners Hospitals for Children* who provide orthopaedic care, so the children's healthcare was thankfully free, otherwise I don't know what we would have done.

Where we really failed, sadly enough, was with the home schooling, because you can't do it all. The Quiverfull lifestyle is unsustainable when it creates such a demanding life, and I now feel like we failed them.

With my last pregnancy, I had a partial uterine rupture during the delivery and had to have an emergency C-section. We had this Catholic doctor whom we chose because of his pro-life view. He took a long time to stitch me back together and he left my uterus. He even told me not to have any more children. But if God had wanted me not to have any more children, he would have taken away my uterus, *but it was still there*. Being so into that Quiverfull mindset, I fell pregnant two more times. However, I miscarried early with both pregnancies. In a sense it was a relief because I didn't know how I would have coped with them. The last successful one nearly killed me, and it nearly killed the baby. I was thinking, how are we going to deal with this situation? What was my husband going to do? He was blind, we had seven kids...

It got to the point that I just broke down. Mentally, physically, emotionally: it was all too difficult, this lifestyle that we were leading. It was impossible, and yet it didn't start out as an overwhelming life, it was all very gradual.

I started seeing that this was not good for my kids. They were not thriving. With life being so regimented, they were in many ways *oppressed*. We had taken the notion of sheltering children to the extreme. The children had no friends; they couldn't even go to Sunday school because there were public school kids in the Sunday school; they certainly couldn't play with the neighbouring kids. As a result, the only people they could associate with were our adult friends or the children of the families we were home churching with.

It even got to the point where we thought that the independent fundamental Baptist church we were attending was too compromising—way too liberal! This is what prompted us to start the home churching. We ended up isolating ourselves and our children and they started suffering. And I began questioning why this wasn't working. After all, I had been doing *everything*, way beyond the call of duty, *to the point of death*. I was at that point where I was risking my life for this ideal that I felt God had called me to. I accepted that it was unrealistic to want everything to be perfect all of the time. That was not my expectation. But it could at least stop being such a bitch all of the time!

And then I met my uncle.

My Uncle Ron

I found my father, whom I had never known, on the internet at the age of thirty-seven. My parents had separated when I was young, but biblical commandments demand that one honors their parents. After all, the fifth commandment calls for us to honor our fathers and mothers. If I was going to honor my father, then I needed to share the Gospel with him! Upon calling him up, it turned out he was already a Christian. A fairly fundamentalist type of Christian who had been married to his wife for some thirty years. He had heard about our family and was really pleased for us; he saw us, with a beautiful family, as walking with the Lord. We were publishing a pro-life, Christian family newspaper and we were quite well known in the state of Nebraska. For example, in 2003 we were honored as the Nebraska family of the year, awarded by the *Nebraska Family Council* which is associated with the *Family Research Council* and *Focus on the Family*. The reason we were awarded such an 'honor' is that we had helped to get DOMA (the Defense of Marriage Act, the law which allowed states to reject same-sex marriages) in Nebraska. That was where we were and who we were at the time. That was us.

Some three years later I got to meet the rest of my father's family (three brothers, a sister and a mom who all lived in Northern Arkansas). Before I went there, my dad warned me about my Uncle Ron. "He's not a believer, and he's kinda tricky, and he will try to confuse you!" I had been warned, but I was so insulted! I was the most committed Christian I knew. I had studied apologetics, I knew my Bible, I had all of this figured out. My faith was so strong and God was so real to me that there was no way I was going to have the least doubt; if anything, *he* was the one who needed to look out! Such low confidence in me!

As it turned out, I really liked my uncle, Ron.

Upon meeting him, there was this instant clicking. He just felt, instantly, like an awesome person. That's just how it happens sometimes. We talked for quite a while when I was there, and when I got back from the vacation I had an email from him. "I'm really impressed with your family; I can tell you are really intentional about your way of life; that you are trying to be counter-cultural in the way you are living and trying to go against the flow. I think that's something that's very noble. I was wondering if you wanted to get to know me better, to exchange an email or two?"

Sure! Great! I wrote back in one of my first responses, "But, you know, the bottom line with me will always be Jesus. Not some abstract Jesus, but God as revealed in history through Jesus Christ!" Et cetera...

Over almost a year we exchanged about a thousand emails. This opportunity was presented to me to talk about the big ideas of life, of Christianity, theology and doctrine. In Quiverfull, as a woman, you don't get this chance. After home church, we would have our fellowship meal, after which the men would go out into the living room and discuss doctrine, theology and church matters. And the women went into the kitchen to talk about home schooling and child training (which was interesting, of course, and I was into it, but at the same time I was always trying to figure out what *they* were saying *out there*). We women didn't talk about those kinds of things, and we especially didn't talk *to a man* about them!

However, because Ron was my uncle, I was allowed to talk to him, never mind that he was effectively a random stranger who just so happened to share some DNA. We were able to correspond and it gave me a chance to start rethinking. I knew something wasn't right; that there was something that I wasn't *getting*. As a Christian, it wasn't like I shut my brain off—I never stopped thinking. The difference was that I confined my thinking to the Christian, the biblical, the orthodox. Within that little box, I could do all the thinking that I wanted and use my powers of logic; but those powers were constrained to that biblical box.

Here I was explaining to my uncle (who was very interested) why I was having all of these children, why I was homeschooling and so on. From his point of view, this was not what people did these days. But how did I explain this to him, how would it sound *to him*, since he didn't accept all the premises that I did… without sounding completely nuts? What a challenge! The more that I did it, the more that I allowed myself to look into what I believed and what I was basing my life on from that perspective. What if this stuff and these premises weren't true? How could I justify my beliefs?

I realised that I couldn't. They *were* crazy. They *were* unrealistic.

There came a point in our correspondence where I realised that I just didn't believe enough about Christianity. I stopped believing that the Bible was the Word of God and just saw it as… as… this old *book*. And it really didn't have anything to do with our lives these days. I didn't believe in Jesus any more. When I realised that, I figured that I didn't believe enough about these ideas to be able to call myself *Christian*. And yet I had this extremely Christian-based life: our income, our parenting, our social lives. Everything. It had got to the point where we didn't even know anyone who wasn't Christian, who wasn't a fundamentalist, Quiverfull Christian.

Reeling from this, I scrabbled around for some time wondering what I could hold on to or salvage from our lives. If I could say there was still *this much* that I still believed… But with fundamentalism, once that foundation has gone, once the Bible is not the word of God, it all falls apart like a house of cards. If those bricks upon which it is built are taken away, then all you have left is this castle in the air.

After that point, when it all evaporated, everything changed. And I guess I have my uncle to thank for that.

The Aftermath

Out of Quiverfull, divorce, enroll kids into public schools. Like dominos.

It was a terrifying experience not believing anymore. I lost my faith, but everything I had built, everything in my life, was centered around holding that belief. The Christian newspaper, my social situation, my children.

I remember hearing in church that atheists have no morals, that they are only rebelling against God because then they would be able to sin without feeling guilty. The late Christian apologist, Francis Schaeffer said that "atheists have both feet firmly planted in midair." As a Believer when I first heard it, I thought that was *so* clever. And then I was that atheist. I had built my whole life on that firm foundation of Christ the Rock, and all of a sudden I didn't have that basis of my everyday existence. The concrete stability of chapter and verse for everything was missing. Now what? What should I do with my life? I was fully expecting to get depressed, for my life to fall apart, since everything I was doing was for Christ, and Christ had evaporated. What would I do to keep it all up? Bring on the crash and burn.

But what happened instead was finding out that life goes on. I had got my divorce and we had decided to put the children into school. Day by day, you would have to make choices. No I didn't have chapter and verse. Instead I had to rely on common sense and research tools. It was not like I was stupid the whole time, only now I could think outside the box; I had to weigh pros and cons to come to decisions just like everybody else. As I did that, time went by and I realized that I wasn't depressed.

This was summed up by an experience in the mall one day with my kids. They didn't have all of this rigid structure any more. They had this opportunity now to have their own opinions without being constrained and they really started finding and reinventing themselves. It was no longer a case of saying, "What does the Bible say I am supposed to be? What is God's plan for my life?" Instead, they got to start thinking, "What do *I* like? What are *my* interests? What do *I* think about this topic, or that?" They were able to express themselves finally. It became a really fun time for us all. So when we were at the mall, we were goofing around with their friends. And while this was going on, I felt really *odd* and I couldn't really figure out what was going on. Was I having a low blood sugar moment? I just didn't feel normal. Not bad, though, just odd. The whole time we were walking around, window shopping, having conversations, laughing, in the back of my mind I was thinking, "What is this I am feeling?"

It took a while, but eventually I realized that what I was experiencing was energy.

For the first time in decades, I didn't feel like if I lay down and shut my eyes, I would pass out for a week. At that point, when I started feeling human again, I started looking back and realized that, now that I wasn't depressed, all those years I *had been* depressed! I had confessed during those years that I had had the joy of the Lord in my heart and I was always talking about how wonderful that was but it hadn't been until I had experienced this actual energy and actual enthusiasm for life, this optimism, that I could say that I really had been depressed. Simply put, I had been unable to acknowledge it because it wouldn't have fit with my Christian testimony.

As somewhat of a celebrity among pro-life moms and the Quiverfull movement in Nebraska, I realized that I could not continue to publish a pro-life Christian newspaper. I myself was no longer a Christian. Perhaps I could make the paper more liberal, change the focus, but this wouldn't have worked in the community. The paper worked so well because it was a very conservative community. So I turned the paper over to one of my editors and got out.

From there, I started a website, *No Longer Qivering*. I had never intended to start it, just wanting to blog about my experience. Naively, I agreed, thinking that I had an obligation to let the people who knew who we were understand what had happened. It was a very sensational headline: "Losing Her Religion: Local Woman Is No Longer Quivering In Fear Of God."

"So that's what happened to her!" and "Wow, she's really gone to the other extreme!" were the general reactions.

Interestingly, the pastor's association in our town called a special meeting to talk about how they were going to deal with this situation. Because we were so fundamentalist, and over time we had become more and more insular, isolated and, well, fundamentalist, we had pretty much left every church in town. We became more extreme than them and rejected them one by one. We had really cut ourselves off from the Christian community personally, and so there was not really a lot of ostracizing going on. We had a nice house, we were settled and I didn't really have enough money to take my kids and go to somewhere like Seattle where they have a wonderful freethought community. We were stuck there, and so the community would just have to deal with me and my family.

There was a moment when some of the Christians we knew from the home school community really started to vilify me. They knew my faith was very real so they either had to accept that somebody could be *that* committed and then go the other way, or they just had to make up a story. So that's what they did. Of course, my real story was a threat to them and their beliefs.

I started the blog and shared my story and other families like mine came to the blog. However, at first this was mainly to gawk. At the end of the day, I was very vocal in the Quiverfull magazines and media. I wrote articles and testimonies. Our reversal story from vasectomy was featured in Nancy Campbell's book *A Change of Heart*, a collection of reversal stories from vasectomies and tubal ligations from a Christian point of view. When people started hearing about us on forums such as the *Above Rubies* forum, they started saying, "Poor Vyckie, I wonder what happened." One of the editors of a magazine which had carried some of my articles ran an editorial entitled, "My Friend Died." What this particular reaction represented was the idea that I'd had some kind of spiritual death, which is the most grievous death of all. I was dead to them.

But there were others who came to read the blog and it resonated with them because the Quiverfull lifestyle is exceedingly demanding, being such an investment and personal commitment. You put so much of yourself into it and so when you start seeing that the results in your family, your marriage, your relationship with your children are not the rosy picture that you had imagined, or seen on *19 Kids and Counting*, it becomes a struggle. The honest ones in the Quiverfull community were bold enough to admit this to themselves, and they found the blog.

At first the visitors to the blog who commented were often defensive, claiming my family was *that* extreme because we didn't have a television in our home, or some such similar psychological ploy. But the more that they dropped by and the more that they read, well, it wasn't very long before they started getting out of Quiverfull too, and sharing their stories to the point that the website became a collection and a collective. These were raw stories from the women who had struggled through this lifestyle and these challenges, from health to relationship. One common thread was poverty because it really isn't possible to support a very large family on a single income. Trusting God meant they couldn't accept government aid, and the woman was supposed not to work, and so it was invariably very tough, financially.

Not only is there financial deprivation but also educational deprivation: the home school neglect resulted from the fact that you couldn't keep up with everything. That meant that something had to go, and this was usually the education of the children and the woman's health.

The stories that we started writing soon made me realize that we were creating a counter-movement of sorts. When the young adults who were being raised in these homes discovered No Longer Qivering, and they began reading, it was a shock to their systems. They had not known anything else; their lives had been controlled in every aspect, having only these narrow perspectives. As a result, they felt ripped off, which itself led to anger. They were forbidden a childhood, an adolescence and very often they became second parents or a second mom.

There is such an emphasis on the father-daughter relationship in Quiverfull, being a huge core value, that often the older daughters become emotionally second wives for their dads. The wives become so strung out with childcare and running the house that the dads often unload everything on to their eldest daughters. This creates a huge emotional attachment which becomes an emotional strain on that relationship to the point that it becomes pretty twisted. You get children taking care of children. Many of the daughters have such a strong connection to their younger siblings, sometimes more so than their mother does. With my last pregnancy and the uterine rupture and emergency C-section mentioned earlier it meant that I had to spend a lot of time rehabilitating in hospital. It was a month before I really properly woke up. As a result, my eldest daughter had this newborn baby of mine. And it was *her* baby. She was the one whom he woke up to, whom he was conscious of. She would bring him to me to nurse and I wouldn't even wake up for that, hardly, barely being able to get out of bed as it was. I missed the first month of my baby's life, and my daughter was his mommy.

When the older siblings in these sorts of families start questioning, start thinking that "this isn't right," the parents and the younger kids who are still in the home will shun these older kids. There is so much control in Quiverfull households that the families can't allow this rebellion. So if a child comes in and starts to vocalize concerns or raise questions, that child is cut off. Now remember the idea that these older children might have really close relationships with some of the younger siblings whom they have almost raised themselves and you can see the devastating effect that such ostracization can have. This very traumatic experience is very much like putting a contagiously diseased person in quarantine for the good of others so that the deadly disease cannot spread.

However, now these young people are able to write, using the power of being able to tell their stories and get feedback. It's almost like a kind of group therapy where the writers can process their thoughts and feelings and work through their problems. These people weren't crazy. *I* wasn't crazy. But what happened to us *was* crazy. There is no wonder there are psychological issues involved with such a lifestyle since I consistently felt like such a failure before God, felt guilty and inadequate, hating my life and myself. All because I couldn't fully give myself to this ideal.

I always encourage these contributors to start their own blog and start writing for themselves. Some of these writers have gone on to their own successes, like the writer of *Love, Joy, Feminism* on the Atheist Channel over at Patheos. It's almost like a phenomenon. All these people feel like they have been ripped off and so they get angry. They are invariably young, with a definite energy and enthusiasm coupled with a sense of idealism.

And many of them have younger siblings whom they want to in some way protect, so many of them are working to get more regulation put in place with regard to the home school laws. In this way they hope to curtail the freedom with which parents can totally and utterly control their kids' lives. There is definitely a sense of activism about many of the writers who pass though No Longer Qivering. I seemed to have stumbled across creating a movement which, fantastically, has become so much bigger than me and my story. It's about spiritual abuse survival.

Spiritual Abuse

Spiritual abuse has such an insidious nature to it, being like regular abuse, but confusing the matter by having God thrown into the equation. People have struggles; we are all trying to navigate through the difficult waters of life and we don't necessarily have all the maps and the tools to do that. We can't always figure things out. Yet this is made all the worse when you involve faith since everything gets redefined. When women find themselves in abusive, co-dependent, dysfunctional marriages, the questions change and the language changes. Rather than saying, "He's really hurting me, what should I do?" it becomes, "Is God testing my faith? Should I be considering my own welfare? He's got bigger and grander things to think about over all eternity than my suffering here. If I decide to walk away now, how is God going to be able to work through me to alter my husband's life?" The dominance, control and manipulation is spiritualized and given chapter and verse to defend it. It's all made to sound like God's will. The woman is always trying to do what is right for her husband, her children and, most importantly, for God.

The situation becomes so much more complex with God in the picture. Very good and noble intentions end up being used against the person, against you, so that it is crippling and you become trapped. But it gets worse. You are taught about acceptance and self-denial and you start to get to the point where if you can see good in the situation, if you can see where God is using you for a bigger purpose, that he has some eternal scheme in mind that you are a part of; then when you see a situation where you could stand up and get out you feel like you are thwarting the plans of the Holy Spirit. Not only do you start to accept your own predicament, but you also start co-operating in your own oppression. You feel like you need to submit yourself to the situation, to embrace it and even thank God for it! He is being glorified in my sufferings. At the end of the day, Sarah, in the Bible, suffered in her relationship, and she got praised for it!

To make matters worse, the Quiverfull movement is one short step away from polygamy, as defended biblically. Such feminist regression!

Because Quiverfull is an all-encompassing worldview, it consumes every aspect of a woman's life; it IS her life. It is difficult enough for an abused woman to leave her husband, but add in half a dozen or more kids, no marketable job skills because she never went to college and has been out of the workforce for decades, loss of her entire support system since her extreme ideals have led to the alienation of all but a few "like-minded" Believers who will shun her the minute she questions the principles and... Yikes!

Stir in the whole God-thing, and you have an overwhelming challenge. But if anyone can make it, Quiverfull women can; they are the some of the toughest, most resourceful and determined women ever. Through No Longer Qivering, I have met dozens of women who have left, or are in the process of leaving, the

Quiverfull lifestyle. Not all become atheists, but none escape without serious modification of their faith.

By the time the reality of my abdication of choice caught up with me, I had seven children—five of them girls—and none of them flourishing due to the ignorance, isolation, negligence, dysfunction and outright abuse of my fundamentalist belief system. As hard as I had tried to deny my own self-determination, I could not escape my personal responsibility when faced with the obvious toll the imposition of absolute, non-negotiable gender roles was taking on my kids.

It's common to hear women who self-identify as "pro-life" say something like this, "Yes, it is my body, but it's not up to me to decide whether an eternal being will come into existence—that is God's prerogative alone—it's not my place to play God."

And by "play God" they mean: evaluate, judge, determine… in other words, Choose.

Passivity is a choice. Choosing not to choose is simple, but the relinquishment of power does not mitigate the harsh and inescapable consequences of indecision. Now that I am taking ownership of my life, I am finding that although most decisions are complicated and some are even painful, having many options—rather than being limited by religious tradition and hierarchical authority—ensures that I have real choices which I will never again surrender for the semblance of simplicity.

8

COUNTER APOLOGIST

Love Thy Neighbour

BEFORE I GET INTO MY DECONVERSION, I WANT TO EXPLAIN how intertwined religion was with my life.

Being born into a Catholic family, I was baptized as an infant and attended Catholic school until the third grade. I attended mass and took my first confession and communion.

At the age of eight, my family converted to evangelical Christianity. Specifically, we were Baptists. I then attended Baptist schools from grades three through eight. My family had moved to a new state at this point, but we were still in a very conservative Baptist church. At age eleven, at a youth retreat, I couldn't recall the exact details of my "conversion prayer" which I had made at age eight, so I re-affirmed my salvation and "accepted Jesus into my heart."

Later, for high school, I attended an Evangelical Christian school that was not directly affiliated with a church; however, I still attended the same conservative Baptist church until I was seventeen.

Every day at school from fourth grade until my senior year of high school I had Bible classes that covered scripture, doctrine, and church history in detail. Every facet of my education until college was taught through the lens of the Christian worldview.

Looking back, my childhood was kept firmly in a reinforcement bubble, even outside of formal schooling. Throughout my childhood, I always had one extra weekly event to attend related to church. As a young child, I did the AWANA[7] program where you get candy for memorizing Bible verses, and then I attended youth group with yearly summer youth retreats. I had Young Earth Creationist science classes, Sunday school, church service, Bible class, Bible tests, and then weekly chapel at school.

The point of all this is to hopefully make it clear that I understood the doctrines of Christianity pretty well. I've had about as much formal training and theological understanding as you could expect of someone who hasn't gone to seminary. I've read the Bible; I know the mainline interpretations of the major passages. In fact, I'd put myself up against most other Christians on a test of theological knowledge and I think I'd come out ahead. Today it's hard to think back and realize that in all that time I never once questioned the existence of God.

However, this isn't that surprising on reflection: it is what happens when you're taught that God and Jesus exist at the same time that you are learning that water is wet and that 2+2=4. It's a bit worse when you have the same people teaching you both sets of "facts," not to mention that atheists were demonized any time the subject came up. I remember being told "humanism" was a form of devil worship.

At this point you may be recoiling in horror, but I don't want anyone to read this as some sort of condemnation of my parents.

---

[7] AWANA stands for "Approved Workmen Are Not Ashamed" taken from 2 Timothy 2:15. This is a non-profit ministry in the US that has curriculum for churches for children ages 3 to 17. The program has children meeting once a week in the evening for Bible lessons, games, and treats.

They actually sacrificed quite a bit to send me to Christian schools. Those schools were almost always a better option than the public schools where we lived, and even when they weren't, I was begging them to let me go "with my friends" to Christian school. My parents sacrificed a bit to do what they thought was best for me and my sister. I have no right to complain about my childhood; my parents did very well by me and my sister.

After spending my whole life in this reinforcement bubble, I went to a non-Christian school for college because engineering programs at Christian colleges generally aren't all that good. This is where you would think that a sheltered Christian child loses their faith, but it wasn't. To use Christian terms, I certainly "backslid" in college (I wasn't living a life consistent with Christian teaching); however, I still believed.

This means I started having sex, largely because hormones are more powerful than Jesus. Moreover, I had stopped attending church because there was a schism in the church I was in, and because my parents went through a divorce at the time. That was scandalous in the eyes of the church; on the other hand, both of my parents were disgusted by the schism. I lived with my mother but was going off to school, and the eighteen credits a semester for a Computer Engineering degree left very little free time to worry much about spiritual matters.

What's odd is that I actually had a renewal of my faith towards the end of my college experience. So when I got out of college, I took my girlfriend (who's now my wife) and I converted her to being an Evangelical Christian. We went looking for a church, and as a result of our renewed commitment to God, we actually stopped having sex until we got married. I only add that bit of information to stress how seriously we took our beliefs.

We had joined an Evangelical Presbyterian Church (our denomination is known as the EPC-USA). This is a conservative denomination that broke off from the mainline US Presbyterian branch in 1980 once the mainline branch started to liberalize.

For those that don't know there are quite a few differences between Christian denominations. I grew up a Baptist, but was now in a Presbyterian church which was essentially a Calvinist version of Christianity. While we initially liked the church, their doctrine was a bit different from my Baptist upbringing, which caused some hesitation on our part. Fortunately this specific church was "liberal enough" on the specific doctrines of Calvinism to admit that they didn't know if Predestination vs. Personal Election[8] was correct, but that they leaned towards Predestination. They admitted it came down to how to interpret various verses in the Bible, and joked in Sunday school classes that this was "one of the first questions to ask the Lord when we get to heaven!"

Since the church was not stringent on holding to the Predestination view in order to be a member, we stuck with the church. I was particularly impressed with the EPC's motto: "In Essentials, Unity. In Non-Essentials, Liberty. In All Things, Charity; Truth In Love."

At this point in my faith journey, how and when baptisms happened wasn't the big issue for my version of Christianity. I didn't think God cared much. What God cared about was whether or not you believed that you were a sinner. He cared if you believed Jesus died for your sins; and he cared that you

---

[8] Predestination vs. Personal Election is a major doctrinal point, and is one of the main differences between Baptists and Calvinist denominations. Predestination squares the problem between free will and omniscience by denying free will. It means that before creation God chose who would and would not be saved and "elected" into heaven vs. the reprobate of people condemned to hell. Personal Election is effectively the opposite in that it affirms some kind of compatibilist idea between divine omniscience and free will, holding that humans personally chose to accept salvation as a free gift from god.

accepted that the only way to heaven was by accepting Jesus' sacrifice. There was no real difference in the "core" parts of prescriptive behavior between my Baptist upbringing and the EPC—"the greatest commandments" still held: "love the Lord thy God with all thy heart, and with all thy soul, and with all thy mind. And the second is like it: 'Love your neighbor as yourself." (Matthew 22:37-39).

We went there for roughly eight years, and I was a volunteer for the sound team almost for the entirety of our membership. My sound duties necessitated that I be one of (if not the) first people at the church *every Sunday,* and I was at the Tuesday practices almost weekly—for almost eight years. I was a trustee for about four to five years and I volunteered for various ministries and events. I tithed 10% weekly and I attended a Church small-group[9] regularly for about three years, towards the end.

That's when I deconverted.

I want to stress that there was no major event that really changed things, no traumatic experience. Things were, by and large, going very well for me. The problem was that, ever since college, I had started to liberalize both politically and personally.

My circle of friends expanded as a result of my wife and college. You see, back before college, I didn't know anybody who wasn't my specific brand of Christian, let alone wasn't a Christian at all. I had made one friend in particular while working at a video game store while I was in college. This person turned out to already have been friends with my wife from before I knew her, and, as a result, we became good friends.

Eventually this person came out as gay and I effectively *freaked.* My wife was instrumental in pointing out that I was

---

[9] A church small-group is where a subset of five to six people meet weekly outside of church for prayer, in depth bible (or Christian book) study.

being an asshole, and that I was not supposed to be freaking out about this. She pointed out that I had no problems with this person before I knew he was gay and that this was not a good reason to stop associating with him. As a result, we stayed friends.

At this point there is something you need to know about my growing up. Someone being gay was pretty much the worst thing ever. They were effectively the most "demonstrably wrong" thing a person could be. So my wife actually did quite a bit of work making me not as bigoted towards gays, and so did my friends. They put up with a lot of shit with the way I acted initially. I learned to stop using the word "gay" as an insult. I stopped using the word "faggot" because that made people I cared about uncomfortable. As a result, I eventually stopped being a bigot and grew as a person.

Not too long after my wife and I got married, our friend found a partner. One thing I haven't mentioned is that my wife and I are pretty big geeks. As a result, we hung out more with our "geek friends" more than our "church friends" since we had more in common with them than most of the people at our church. This meant that my friend and his partner were hanging out with us more often than not on any given weekend.

We became very close friends with them, which was causing a bit of cognitive dissonance for me. Cognitive dissonance is the mental stress where one holds two contradictory beliefs at the same time which causes the mind to try to harmonize those views in weird and wonderful ways, or one set of views or evidence in favor of the core belief. This isn't something that's limited to just religion, but it impacts us all in a variety of ways. Many of us go through minor instances of it daily; however, it becomes a potent effect once you become aware that you actually hold contradictory positions on topics that are important to you. Religion was extremely important to me, but I had a group of friends who not only weren't saved, but their lifestyle made it near impossible to bring up the Gospel! My church at the time said that the way to deal with this was us being a "light for Jesus." We were supposed to have our lives exemplify the values of Christianity, and that would eventually convert our gay friends to Christianity.

But then there was another problem. I was in this fantastic marriage which caused some reflection in me. I realized how much I truly am in love with my wife. I realized that I knew what true love was. Through my relationship with my friends, let's call them Jason and Tom, after knowing them for eight years, it was clear they had the same kind of loving relationship that my wife and I had. They went through the same kind of couple issues my wife and I had. In fact, as far as couples go, we were so similar it was uncanny. Basically, I knew what love was, and it was clear as day that they had it. Jason and Tom were in love, and that is a good thing!

The problem was that, eventually, I could not call their relationship wrong. There was no way you could tell me that *love* was wrong. Having a loving relationship is probably the most wonderful thing that you could ever experience, and to call that wrong just didn't compute for me.

This view on their relationship was in direct contradiction with the Bible. What's more, it was about this time that I was going online and debating politics and eventually came across some general criticism of religion. And while normally that would be something I'd blow off, I couldn't do that once I started seeing problems with the Bible. After that initial crack, I started finding lots of problems with my holy book.

The biggest problem I found with the Bible was *hell*. It became more real to me now that I actually had friends whom I cared about that this doctrine applied to; my friends, who were clearly in love, and were wrong for their love according to the Bible, were going to hell—a.k.a. eternal conscious torture.

And that shook me quite a bit.

As a result, all this criticism of religion stuff that I was reading started to stick with me for the first time. What didn't help my faith was that this all came to a head for me while I had taken a temporary work assignment that had me living in another country for six months. During that time I was working so many hours that even though I had my wife with me, we ended up not going to church during that time just because the work schedule made it so we were travelling most Sundays.

I was able to do a lot of reading, however, though I kept it to myself. I started investigating arguments against theism and I finally broke through and asked myself a question that I realized I had never asked in the twenty plus years I had been a Christian: "Why do I believe in a God?"

I had no answer to this. Now one of the things I realized when I asked myself this question was that I was taught this Jesus stuff since I had been an infant. In fact, (as mentioned earlier) I was taught this by the same people who taught me more concrete things: ice was frozen water, 2+2=4, and then the claims like Jesus Christ was the son of God who died for my sins.

Ultimately, every argument I found for Christianity fell back on "You have to have faith" or if it was a problem with Christianity it was "Well we can't expect to know God's reasons because he's so far beyond us." And, really, that's not a satisfying answer.

So I read the arguments, the counter-arguments, the counter-counter arguments, and eventually when I came back home and started talking to my pastors and church friends about these doubts I was having, they really couldn't get past the first set of

counter-arguments and things came back down to the whole faith thing.

The argument that did it for me was the Argument from Hell. This is because if you believe in Christian theology, then the only thing that has existed eternally is God. "Eventually" this God had to decide to create the universe, and God knew that if he gave man free will, which apparently he really had to do, then God would have to create a hell.

So God is faced with a choice at this point: either he creates the universe and creates a hell to go with it, or God can simply not create. What's worse is that according to Matthew 7:13-14 we're explicitly told that the majority of mankind will be condemned to hell. So for the vast majority of creation it's far better off to not have been created if you're going to eventually be condemned to eternal conscious torture.

So why create? God is the perfect being and before the creation of the universe he exists in a triune Godhead of mutual fulfilling love in the most perfect state possible. He literally is perfection according to Christian theology. So he had to create for creation's benefit, not for his own benefit or any need or want on his end.

But most of creation is better off not being created! Even if it was a small subset of creation that was better off not being created, the only moral choice is not to create anything!

And that's pretty much the argument that made me lose my faith.

One day, I eventually broke down and started crying. I realized I didn't believe the crap that was taught to me as true my entire life. This was a problem because I had converted my wife, the most important person in my life, to being an Evangelical Christian.

It all hit me at once. My entire family was Christian. I realized that I would not be seeing my dead relatives ever again; I might get disowned; what was going to happen to my marriage? All these ramifications and questions… Why was I lied to my whole life? Why did I convert people to this terrible religion?

All that hurt, but it was also liberating at the same time. Unfortunately, the "liberating" part only lasted a little bit before the social fear took over. I told my wife and she became very upset. She still believed, she wasn't nearly as conservative as I was and so didn't see the problems I did since she didn't have the indoctrination that I had had.

So when I showed her things in the Bible to back up my case that according to what she believed, hell had to exist, homosexuality was wrong, etc., she was shaken but she still believed in a God and she still remained a Christian.

Not wanting to be fighting with my wife, let alone the rest of my family should they ever find out, I threw myself into apologetics to re-convince myself that Christianity was true. Fortunately (concerning my wife), in our discussions, we made it clear that our relationship with each other was more important than our religion. I didn't want her to give up her beliefs because of me and she didn't want me to believe just because she did.

That said, I wanted so desperately to make myself go back and believe that shit again so my life could go back to normal. I spoke to pastors, I spoke to friends, I did everything you could think of—I read William Lane Craig, CS Lewis, Tim Keller, even more liberal theology stuff by people like Kenton Sparks. I read debate after debate online, reading every possible argument I could get my hands on. I tried to go back, I really did, but it didn't work.

There was no argument that could make me believe that stuff again. This put a stress on my life, a palpable dissonance between what I believed and what I was trying to believe so I could have peace at home. Eventually we stopped attending our conservative church. My discussions with people there had roused some feathers, and my wife agreed with me on doctrinal issues like how hell couldn't exist, and that love between homosexuals wasn't wrong. I was able to extract myself from my duties as the sound technician and as a trustee, but we were still "members" that didn't show up much. My wife and I had stopped talking about religion for a while after that, and we had a few months of relative quiet on the topic. However, I was still devouring everything I could apologetics-wise and still couldn't *believe*.

Eventually, I told my father, who was now even more fundamentalist than when I was growing up and the discussions had not gone well. My father is a trained and very skilled pharmacist, yet told me that he was a Young Earth Creationist. He told me that people could actually live to be 900 years old in biblical times because there was so much more oxygen in the air back before and right after the flood. I was absolutely shaken by the rationalizations I got from him defending views he very well should have known were demonstrably false: that there was a global flood, that the universe is only six to ten thousand years old. My father is a very intelligent man; he is a pharmacist and has quite literally saved lives. As a child he taught me to be skeptical of advertisements for products when they name herbs or "special ingredients" being in some pill or product you can get without a prescription. However, when it came to religion he allowed his beliefs in the inerrancy of the bible to trump all other scientific training I know he had. During the conversation with my father I was treated to a litany of Young Earth Creationist defenses against clear scientific evidence for the old age of the earth and the cosmos.

That really shook me, to see someone I love and respect be taken in so completely by a set of beliefs that it trumped all evidence and experience we have. I broke the unspoken treaty of silence on religion that my wife and I were maintaining and I brought up the discussion I had had with my dad. What followed in our discussion that night was groundbreaking for me. My wife told me that after thinking about things lately she didn't believe anymore—that she wasn't a Christian. This was a watershed moment both literally and figuratively.

I cried again, just like when I had first realized I didn't believe, but this time it was tears of joy. My wife cried too, realizing what I was still doing, and at how we were in agreement on religion again. The conversation lasted most of the night, confirming that my wife wasn't giving up the faith just because of our relationship. At this point, I was free from having to try and make myself believe again. My deconversion was a rollercoaster that had lasted about 3 years at that point, and it was finally over.

I truly am lucky for it to have worked out so well. We aren't in full agreement; my wife is more of a nominal deist but doesn't really like being specifically labeled. She just knows that she is very specifically not a Christian. That was good enough for me. We spent a long time working out what we did and didn't agree on, and specifically what to do if we had kids.

That last part was key because not too long after this happened my wife became pregnant. It was another stroke of fortune on our part, partially because we had wanted children for years but were unable to conceive for medical reasons. The other part was that it happened after we came back into agreement as a couple, and I can't describe how happy I am that my daughter will not go through the same indoctrination that I did as a child.

Because of the arrival of a baby, we eventually did have to tell the extended family that we weren't Christians. After all, there would be no baptism or christening, and we absolutely did not want any religious gifts or talks with our daughter until she is old enough to fully comprehend its implications.

This has caused some problems, but it wasn't a disowning like I thought it might be. We're lucky enough that we've not really lost any family over it; however, we've still conveniently neglected to tell one section of the family who is highly fundamentalist.

The worst of it was when my father and my stepmother thought my wife was still a Christian but I wasn't, right after our daughter had been born. It was around Christmas and they informed us that my wife and daughter would get presents, but that I would not. They were more than a bit upset by the earful my wife gave them about how she also was not a Christian, and how insulting that was.

The end result of this was that we do not exchange gifts and we are not allowed to visit with them on Christian holidays. They claim it would be disrespectful for us to be there with them, because we're not celebrating for the right reasons.

While this is extremely upsetting, we've still been able to maintain an otherwise decent relationship with them.

Other family relationships haven't been quite as dramatic, but they've been impacted. I've already had to decline to accept gifts for our daughter that were religious books for children, and reinforce our wishes about how and when religious discussions with her will happen. There have been all sorts of passive/aggressive moments about us not being religious, but so far it hasn't been unbearable.

Our relationship with people from our old church has effectively been severed. Most of them were not into the same kinds of things we were hobby wise, so once we weren't meeting up to talk about religious topics, things died off. We both went through a few Facebook blow-ups once it was public that we weren't religious, but we had little compunction in unfriending people. I had to meet with someone to turn over the set of keys to the church I had, and it was done with forced smiles and near to no discussion. There are a few people we're still on good terms with: I have had a few good discussions with my former pastor and small group leader on atheism, but by and large we simply don't see them anymore.

I'm lucky in that it hasn't been a problem with my best friend, who is far more religious than I ever was. One day I let him know what had happened, and while a little upset, we agreed to simply not discuss it. Ironically, others in my circle of friends from college have independently deconverted in recent years, and I feel somewhat sorry for my best friend as all of us are now unbelievers to the point where we don't discuss the topic only when he is around. We are still close, and I'm honestly glad that we've been able to keep this from affecting our friendship.

Fortunately, my family lives in a fairly secular part of the country where religion isn't as much of an intrusion on daily life as it is in other places in the US. There hasn't been much else that's affected us as a family as a result of leaving Christianity, though it's one thing to be accepted as an atheist but it's quite another to identify as someone who actively advocates against religion. It is fairly diverse in my area, and this peace is enforced by the social norm that it is simply not polite to talk about religion. More importantly I admit that I'm a bit fearful of how things will go as my daughter grows up, and family pressure intensifies to "share the gospel" with her. The last thing I want is for her to go through what I did as a child.

Still, I look at my deconversion as one of the best things that has ever happened to me. It has led me to find a love of philosophy that I didn't have before, which has in turn driven me to help others questioning their faith to "see the light" of atheism.

9

WILLIAM LUCAS

Something Better

IT'S HARD TO DECIDE WHERE TO START. FROM AN EARLY age, I've always had a Douglas Adams bent: a need to figure out life, the universe and everything. I've worried that bone since the dawn of self-awareness. Where did we come from? Why are we here? What should we do about the situation? And is there anything better on the other channel?

Round about the time that I first wondered about Santa Claus—Sinterklaas in Dutch—I received a valuable life lesson. My paternal grandmother showed me a picture-book Bible to illustrate the significance of Xmas (Kerstmis), but the Calvary etching quite repelled me. It made me realize that society is a mob. "Conform, or else" was what I intuited. Don't dare to be different. Don't veer from the straight and narrow lest we nail you to a cross.

It's just as well that, in my family, the practice of any form of religion was not enforced.

That point is significant. It must be traumatic to be forced to abandon a belief system that a person has been born into, rather than one that she or he has adopted of their own free will. It's like a fish and water—it's almost impossible for it to sense that element, much less be objective about it. To drag itself out from that environment would take a superhuman effort requiring not merely a change of mind but virtually an amputation. Thankfully, that isn't something that I've ever had to do.

I would tag along to church sometimes with a friend (you might get offered a cup of tea with a biscuit.) I wanted to socialize with others, but needed help in that department, so this was a means toward that end (I was a shy lad, but a resourceful one). On the whole, I like people, but I find them hard work. I can tolerate company only in small doses.

It's only recently that I've cottoned on that I may have a mild form of Asperger's syndrome. Though it sounds like an affliction—the word rhyming as it does with Alzheimer's—it's beneficial on the whole. I'm what they term high-functioning in that I'm creative and a lateral thinker (and you could blame it for my zany sense of humor). Nevertheless, it often makes life problematical for me. Oh well, we've all got our crosses to bear.

Anyway, what went on within those church walls never came close to enlightening me. I mean, really, when you apply the test of reason to any religion, what do you find? A Martian on a visit to Earth is not likely to want to return home bearing a trial sample. No, I was never drawn to organized religion. In that respect, I emulate Olaf Stapledon[10], the science-fiction author, who, according to Wikipedia, was an agnostic hostile to religious institutions but not to religious yearnings. I have a constitutional need for a practical philosophy, which both calms me and yet shoves me in the direction of absolute truth.

The need for a mental tool to keep my head screwed on peaked as I entered adolescence and developed a tendency to go

---

[10] William Olaf Stapledon (1886 – 1950) —known as Olaf Stapledon—was a British philosopher and author of several influential works of science fiction.

off in tailspins of free-floating anxiety at the drop of a hat. Monsters stirred inside my teenage soul. I felt unsettled and uneasy, as if poised at the event-horizon of an ominous black hole. It needed filling, but with what?

Then, one day on the news, I heard about something that might do the trick. Indeed, it seemed tailor-made for me. Even the Beatles—who had recently broken up—gave it their seal of approval. Subsequently, I went along to a couple of public lectures on Transcendental Meditation (I'll use its initials TM from now on). Their charts and graphs had a more positive effect than Oma's Bible to convince me, and I decided to take the plunge if I could afford it. It turned out that there was no across-the-board cost. Instead, you 'donated' a week's income. For me, of course, that represented a bargain. I was only fifteen, and so for five dollars—what I might reasonably earn as pocket money—I received my secret mantra (Neil Young, I believe, was charged $35).

For a while, TM™ did the job. One simply closed one's eyes (both of them) for ten or twenty minutes. You could do it anywhere—at home or at school. I must have been thought of as a right nerd: that guy who you always see sleeping in a common room armchair.

But my diligence lasted only a couple of months (although my weirdness persisted). Thereafter, my practice of the TM technique grew sporadic. I don't know exactly why. Perhaps I wasn't quite ready for it, not sufficiently mature. My excuse was that the practice felt lacking. Though the meditation practice itself felt okay, and I was happy to retain it as my drug of choice, I was after something with a little more *Voom*.

It is said that when the student is ready the teacher appears. In my case the guru arrived in the guise of a book. Libraries, I've found, are dangerous places. Science fiction and fantasy were safe enough, but I was done some long-lasting damage by a tome written to churn out "well-adjusted" adolescents. Part of the advice was about how to 'date' correctly (it was an American publication). It told you to resort to cold showers whenever physical urges threatened to overwhelm you. It didn't quite claim that masturbation caused hair to sprout from your palm, but for all the good that the book did me, it may as well have.

I tossed it aside and leaped from the pan into the fire. In the Philosophy section, I discovered a couple of books about something called the Radha Soami teachings. They also called it Sant Mat, which meant 'the teachings of the saints'. Other terms bandied about included Santon Ki Shiksha, Surat Shabd Yoga, and The Science of the Soul. Goodness me! If they threw in a little Kung Fu, I'd be made!

Both Katherine Wason's *The Living Master*, and Julian P. Johnson's *The Path of the Masters* alluded to a philosophical TOE—or Theory of Everything (which is a set of ideas that endeavors to explain the cosmos). Its concepts attracted me greatly. I was impressed with how neatly it ironed out and laid straight life's curly questions. Nothing that I'd come across up until then came close to achieving that, and so I felt that it behooved me to dig deeper.

Sant Mat was claimed to consist of a Q document as it were, or original set of teachings. All major world religions were meant to have been identical, essentially, before they gradually changed. They became corrupted by people with a vested interest, or fossilized by empty traditions. As with the Baha'i Faith, which sees other religions as primitive versions of itself, Sant Mat also regarded all religions magnanimously. To me, Surat Shabd Yoga appeared all-encompassing.

The big difference between it and the other contenders was that it was current and vibrant. You needed a living master, not one who had snuffed it. You wouldn't seek help from a doctor from the bygone past for a current illness, now would you? You don't get any information from a radio that's not switched on. Why pray to a picture of someone who is no longer in range? Surat Shabd Yoga[11] presented itself as a philosophy, science and yoga. You meditated as form of self-experimentation. All that was asked was that you gave the practice an honest shot. You tried it out to see what happened.

To me, the philosophy's real beauty lay in the fact that that there was nothing that you needed to take on faith. In fact, it insisted that you didn't believe in anything. You just accepted the set of teachings as a working proposition, until you proved it for yourself one way or the other. And to top it off, you were instructed not to proselytize. Now, that was radical. The Radha Soami sect was not interested in growing its membership. No knocking door to door or going on overseas missions. And, would you believe, it was free as well. I would not have to hustle for any five-dollar deal.

Financial considerations aside, I appreciated how reincarnation and karma explained how the cosmos worked. It seemed fair and just that you got more than one chance to get your life right. Those cyclic, action-and-reaction principles made sense to me. I could see the universe operating in that fashion. No priesthood existed to dictate or intervene between a person and God. Your practice was entirely up to you. Not satisfied with being able to reach heaven only after you die? Seek it out while you're still alive.

To cut a long story short, I decided to enroll, but not immediately. I couldn't act upon my decision just yet, as I was about to embark on a two-year cycling tour. The plans had been finalized and the visas arranged. I would follow this new lead afterwards, perhaps cycling overland from Western Europe to

---

[11] The etymology of the name of the discipline says it all: "Union of the Soul with the Essence of the Absolute Supreme Being."

the sect's headquarters in India. But for the time being that idea was relegated to the back burner. I was twenty-one. I had a life.

It must seem strange that I was never actually recruited or converted by someone with a gift of the gab. That happened— or rather the attempt was made—in London, after I arrived there. Within days, I was buttonholed on the street. A girl invited me upstairs into an office. If I took a multiple-choice test, she promised me, I'd be given a cup of tea and a couple of biscuits (that same old hook).

The results of the test showed, she claimed later, that I was unhappy with my life, and that I yearned for something bigger and better. I agreed with the earnest young woman, but instead of enlisting in I-did-not-know-what, I replied that I preferred to go about in that state. That's what life is like when you're a seeker—you tough it out. You utilize that dissatisfaction to fuel your way forward. Years later, I figured out that it must have been the Moonies that I'd narrowly escaped (which is not to disparage them).

Instead, I continued my adventure. I obtained a tent and a second-hand ten-speed. I was in a hurry to hit the wide-open road, but because of a TV series, not Kerouac's book. A couple of years earlier, David Carradine in his role as Kwai Chang Caine in Kung Fu had inspired me. I, too, desired to roam the world in search of not a long-lost half-brother, but wisdom. Someone, somewhere—and he or she need not live on a mountain top— ought to have the answers. Why not learn such nuggets from them? To me, that seemed an eminently sensible plan.

A month or two later, when I had completed only the Netherlands (where I visited Oma in her rest home) and a corner of West Germany, I was overcome by the blues. I could no longer keep the thought of India on hold. By now, I was too impatient to cycle, so I purchased an air ticket. This is what I had to do, or die in the attempt. I was fully prepared to devote the rest of my life to achieving my goal. I'd seclude myself in a monastery, take a vow of silence and give up my worldly possessions, whatever it took.

Looking back, I was pretty naïve, arriving as I did at an ashram in the middle of the Punjab, and in the middle of the Indian summer, sitting in a donkey cart. It must have appeared quite biblical. Wondering what to do next, I sat sweating under a tree until a group of Indians took me in hand. They led me to the door of 'The Living Master'. Graciously the man granted me an interview the next day. In the meantime, I was given a meal and showed to my room. At that stage, a cold shower was just what I needed.

The next morning, Charan Singh Grewal suggested that it would have been better to have gone through usual channels. I ought to have contacted the New Zealand representative. In due course, he explained, after I had become initiated and had practiced for a few years, I could have applied to spend a month here at the Dera where every spring and autumn as many as a thousand westerners are made welcome.

This being the off-season, I was given a couple of days to get my act together. The office would help me obtain a rail ticket. After studying the teachings in my own country, I might then decide if I wanted to follow them. There was no need at all to renounce the world; just live a normal, moral life, and think about earning a living. I swallowed hard and accepted the man in the turban's advice. I felt a little let down, but at the same time relieved.

Back in my room, I did a stock take. There was no denying the man's integrity. He could so easily have taken advantage of me. This proved the cult's integrity, did it not? Surely it indicated that the group was benign. I became determined to play my part well, too. A day or two later, in Bombay, I bought a couple of dozen books about the teachings direct from the publisher.

Forthwith, I gave up animal products (you had to be vegetarian for at least a year before asking to join up). I had eaten my last egg (in Afghanistan).

Eventually, I made it back to New Zealand (a word of advice: never consider arriving in India without funds and on a one-way ticket). I knuckled down at home to do the groundwork. I discovered a husband-and-wife couple also on the Path, and made contact. Otherwise, I was still alone. Thinking back, it's curious that I had linked up with a brother-and-sisterhood of roughly a million members worldwide without meeting more than a handful. It wasn't the people who had 'captured' me; I was captivated by the vision.

That point, too, is telling—that no other person was ever a factor. Since I had talked myself into it, I retained the power to talk myself out of it too. When the time came for me to set that construct aside, then it would not be an insurmountable hurdle. My conviction had all come from within, from the books that I pored through. As no person in the flesh was instrumental in persuading me to think or behave in a particular way, I remained open to my own advice (though decades were needed).

In the meantime, I girded my loins and set out on the business of finding out whether one could reach God's level through earnest endeavor. Through meditative yoga this was meant to be possible. It would certainly be a neat trick, but I didn't get my hopes up too high. And I drew up a loophole—sort of a prenuptial agreement. I promised myself that I would persevere until and unless something better came along. That was only fair and sensible, I reasoned.

Without going into too much detail, I undertook to meditate two and a half hours daily (which is to say ten per cent of the day). This was needed to 'burn off' the accumulated karmas from previous lifetimes. When that had been accomplished, one's consciousness would then become buoyant enough to arise. It would follow an internal sound current and radiant light (like an out-of-body near-death experience) and transcend the astral and causal planes.

On a more pragmatic level, I returned to university to complete my degree and then to train as a teacher. That's how I'd make a living, avoid alcohol and drugs and lead a "moral life." I felt I'd finally found the higher-powered version of TM that I was after.

Two and a half hours of meditation was just manageable if I broke it up into two periods: early morning and last thing at night (if nothing else, it weaned me away from television). During the rest of the day, I would not have seemed different from anyone else—no more different than before. I certainly felt normal and sane. I wasn't fanatical, and I fancied that I retained an open mind. I remained in charge of myself. I hadn't put myself in anyone's power (excepting the habit of continually repeating five holy names to yourself whenever you weren't mentally occupied).

The meditative practice kept me on the straight and narrow. Though it never resulted in any mind-blowing moments of enlightenment, it was good for me in a mental and physical sense. Those TM graphs and charts from back-in-the-day hadn't lied about the positive spin-offs and side effects. The vegetarian diet—no meat, fish, or eggs—did me no harm. I trained for and ran several marathons. The rut that I was in felt groovy, everything was right with the world, and there was no pressing need to make changes.

I'm startled now to see how many years slipped by—over a quarter of a century (and another ten since I 'made the break'). What happened to me during that time? Was I in a state of suspended animation or an existential limbo? Should I regard that period as time wasted? Ought I to begrudge the passage of years?

Somehow, I do not. Though it's true that I cannot point out, or write about, as many 'happenings' over that interval as in my youth, I don't feel that I remained static or failed to make progress. True, I was a little bit smug and complacent. I lounged inside my cocoon feeling superior to ordinary folks (sorry guys). I nibbled mainly on information that corroborated my worldview; I didn't actively challenge it. But I believe that I matured, and that I accumulated a spiritual nest egg. In which case, what was it that eventually shoved me out of the nest? What was it that prompted me to fly?

I'm going to blame my wife for that—and I'm only half joking. The dissolution—or my disillusionment—dates from the time that I met her. Back when millennia were a-changing, Mami knew only a little English. However, she used what she had very freely. She didn't worry about making mistakes—a rare attribute for a Japanese native, so the lack of language did not pose a problem. We enjoyed each other's company, and we took part in many activities. That included the weekly satsang, or group meeting, that I attended at the home of the American couple I mentioned earlier. The four of us would listen to Q&A tapes.

Mami occupied herself by scribbling down any phrases that she managed to catch. The Indian accent couldn't have helped, so I admired her dedication. Later, she would ask me what the words meant and how they linked. This forced me to explain the philosophy in simple terms. In this way, I revisited concepts I hadn't questioned in years. It made me take an objective look at myself. Ah, so this is how vegetarianism, reincarnation and karma appear to an outsider.

As Mami's English progressed, her thinking did too (well, that's how it seemed). By now she was selecting her own books, and I'd read them too for us to discuss. She'd arrived from Japan with a paperback by Shirley MacLeane. It was heavily highlighted with words she didn't know, but within six months of study she could read it with ease. As her interest in matters philosophical grew, she began to peruse the self-help and new-age genres independently.

One day she returned from the library with her own dangerous book: Neale Donald Walsh's *Conversations with God*. I studiously ignored it for a week or two, but when I did pick it up, I discovered a resonance within. The contents spurred me to complete my process of self-examination. In short, Walsh's words (and those of the big fellow that he claimed to have spoken to) jolted me from the rut that I'd been stuck in. I took to them like a thirsty duck to water.

That is how I came to remove The Science of the Soul from my curriculum. It no longer did the trick for me. It had gaps that I'd closed my eyes to. It was riddled with quirks and foibles. Some of its aspects were silly, and others downright bizarre. It came across too much Old Testament. It did not sit comfortably, all that eye-for-an-eye stuff about karma and being born in sin. The I-and-Thou duality that it pushed felt false; I preferred Walsh's level playing field. How had it once made sense to me that humans were at one and the same time the "highest form of creation" and the "scum of the earth"?

Naturally, the disengagement process—from Sant Mat, not from my wife—did not occur overnight. But over the next several months, I slowly reconstructed my worldview. I'd discard this, and select that to build up an eclectic amalgam. I certainly didn't swallow all of the CWG material hook line and sinker. Having recognized my previous entrapment, I was not about to plunge into another belief system. No more pans; no more fires.

I did keep meditating for a while. I owned that activity, and it did me no harm. Indeed, it had helped to instill a sense of balance, and for that I was grateful. But to be honest, where consciousness was concerned, it hadn't helped me to make any great leaps. The experiment had not yielded any fantabulous findings.

The day arrived that I asked to be taken off the official mailing list. No more newsletters, please. I packed away my collection of books and tapes in cardboard boxes. They would never again see the light of day. The final thing to fall by the wayside was my vegetarianism. Wasn't I my own judge now of what was 'wrong' and 'right'? To mark the occasion, and to test my hard-won freedom, I went out to sample, not eggs from Afghanistan, but chicken from the local KFC.

Hey, where did those extra few pounds come from?

These days, spirituality remains as much of a focus for me as before. I've progressed further on my own, I feel, than I managed with the help of an external 'master.' I've sculpted out a fantastic set of abdominal muscles—nah, just kidding. But I am proud that I've finally cobbled together and set out my own metaphysics. It works for me, as a TOE (Theory of Everything), much better than anything I've previously run across—bearing in mind that I've used that phrase before. I feel that I've finally stumbled across the real thing. If I didn't feel that, then I'd be wasting my time. But along the way I've picked up the humility to realize that I could be wrong. Been there, done that.

I'll continue to explore and to study, though maybe with less intensity and zeal. I reckon that I've mellowed—which could well be an age thing. But in spite of my casual approach, I'm serious about the path that I follow—no—the path I 'forge.' I won't ever rest on my laurels. And I'll provide a poignant illustration of that.

A year or two ago, I sat at my father's deathbed. He slipped into the big sleep as I stroked his brow. I counted down his last breaths and then felt his body temperature drop. Don't get me wrong—it was a beautiful experience, and I'm glad that I witnessed it, but goodness, such an event is a powerful motivator. Not since the epitaph I'd once read on a gravestone was I so deeply affected:

> Remember man as you pass by, as you are now so once was I, as I am now so you will be, prepare yourself to follow me.

Our generation is the next to go. That's the stark reality. How can anyone not feel the need to address that fact? The philosophical urge to find answers to the big questions in life is an integral part of me, so it's a wonder to me how most people seem to be doing their utmost to remain blind to one of the few things in life that are certain. As George Harrison said in one of his last interviews, "I get confused when I look around at the world, and I see everybody is running around and yet nobody is trying to figure out what's the cause of death, and what happens when you die. I mean, that to me is the only thing, really, that's of any importance. The rest is all secondary."

The one thing that I'm truly adamant about—the one constant—is that people should figure out the meaning of life from within the context of their own lives. Remain wary of well-meaning friends, gurus, organized religions and pre-packed philosophies. We're born with lenses of our own, and it's best that we utilize those.

I suggest that we learn to examine ideas in a non-judgmental way, initially. Let's see how everyone else sees the world, and then cherry-pick to form our personal philosophy. Everyone has a story to tell. Everybody has something to offer.

My own brand of 'thinkering' is not that hard to locate. Search for it online under *Will? I Am! My Theory of Everythink* as a blog or maybe an e-book. My thoughts revolve around the premise that time does not exist. Seen from that angle, I've tried to puzzle out how life might operate. Has anyone else tackled that subject? I'm always interested in reading what people have to say.

My worldview works for me, and parts of it may work for other people. I'm perfectly happy to share what I've got, as I feel a certain obligation toward my fellow man. However, I refuse to get into arguments or debates. All I can do is to couch my ideas in terms that aren't likely to offend, because I've no wish to go through the crucifixion experience first-hand. Be gentle, because every new idea is born drowning. Go easily and with a spirit of tolerance. Take or leave what people say, just don't emulate me and spend a third of your life over it!

I'll close with a cliché. They say that no one is more anti-smoking than an ex-smoker. However, I bear no one any ill will. I'm kindly disposed towards every person who follows her or his own path, just as long as they don't compel others to join them. My former cult associates are sincerely engaged in what seems reasonable to them—good on them, I say. They have my respect. I don't begrudge the decades that I 'lost' in their company, for if there's no time, then what exists for me to have lost?

Onwards, upwards.

10

TRISTAN VICK

The Case of a Demon Haunted Mind

LITTLE DID I REALIZE, I BEGAN ATTENDING CHURCH SERVICE before I was ever born. I was born into a Christian family and raised in a Christian home. Shortly thereafter I was baptized—probably to seal the deal. After I was born and baptized, I was promptly inculcated into the faith of my mother. That's how I came to be a Christian. In fact, that's how most people acquire their religion(s); by birth and by accident.

A Spirit Thing

Church hopping was a large part of my early childhood. After my parent's divorce, my mother took us from church to church. At that time, for whatever reason, my mother decided I ought to be re-baptized.

The day of my second baptism (I was baptized as an infant too), I was waiting nervously in the wings. This particular church had a fancy baptism pool which was at the end of a small catwalk. The front of the pool had a plate glass viewing panel,

like a sort of aquarium, so the entire church congregation could witness the children being dunked. It was a spectacle for sure.

Somebody ushered me out and then the minister was babbling some sort of prayer, kept mentioning somebody named Jesus, and then placed his warm hand on my forehead. I was waiting for him to count to three or something so that I would know to hold my breath. He suddenly pushed me under.

It was so unexpected that I gulped in a huge reservoir of water. I came up hacking and gagging—looking all pitiful like a wet cat. Somebody took me by the arm and yanked me out, then I was ushered out the back and handed a towel. Nobody even told me what the entire baptism thing was important for. Unbeknownst to me, my mother was trying to secure the eternal salvation of my mortal soul (since being dunked into the water three times somehow turns your mortal soul into an immortal one—never mind how that works—I was told to take it on faith).

All I knew was that I had almost been drowned.

Time Slip

Jump ahead ten years and I would be helping to lead an interfaith ministry between my humble Montanan Assemblies of God church and several other Evangelical churches out of Seattle. I was on fire for Christ—and loving it.

Slowly, but surely, my faith began to define me. I was on a mission from God to spread the "good news." How did I go from that small boy afraid of wetting himself in Sunday school to a bold and daring young Christian leader? The funny thing is, I can't really say.

When I turned fourteen my mother entered a serious bout of depression. She stopped socializing, she severed all ties with the

outside world, and stopped going to church entirely. But, for some reason and after years of inculcation, stopping cold turkey just seemed wrong to me somehow. So I decided to go back to church on my own accord.

Soon afterward, I would become the veteran in my church's youth group. The other youth leaders had all graduated from high school and went off to bigger and better things. Most of them trucked off to college. Only a handful of us "regulars" were left, and I somehow found myself involuntarily voted into the position of the unofficial youth group leader.

Not long after that, my pastor took notice and called me to his office one day to tell me what a "natural born leader" I was. After our meeting, he invited me to share the position of youth pastor with one of my other good friends. Without hesitation, I accepted. Now instead of simply attending the discussions and Bible studies, I was leading them! I was spreading the Gospel word; teaching people about the saving power of Christ—I was doing the work of the Lord! I felt God working in me daily and I prayed he would guide me according to his will.

I was a true Christian—there was no denying it (and if you deny my past faith then how come I spoke the language so well?). By this time, I was attending Church nearly five times a week. Three times during the week and twice on weekends. You might say, I had become possessed—by the Holy Spirit, that is. So, like many American teenagers my age, I decided to become a born again Christian of my own volition.

My entire world revolved around my Christianity. In fact, I felt that it defined me as a person. Moreover, it defined how I lived my life. My faith was my culture, my religious identity was analogous to my personal identity, and everything was rainbows and sunshine. I felt blessed. My life was good.

You might be asking yourself, "How in the world did this fine young Christian man become a hardened skeptic and a godless atheist?" Well, this is the story of how my faith failed me and why I became a nonbeliever.

A Phallic Singing Cucumber Prophet

My entire teenage life revolved around my desire to be a vessel of Christ, but my lofty devotional goals kept getting interrupted by worldly temptations. Everywhere I looked there was temptation. Always something threatening to take my mind off of Christ and cause me to veer dangerously away from a path of righteousness and toward a path of sin and corruption.

I viewed sex as the supreme vice and, indeed, the very idea of sex is preached against by most Evangelical Christians. Premarital sex was bad. Masturbation was bad. Gay sex was bad. Oral sex was bad. Porn was bad. Even cyber-sex was deemed a sin. Sex represented that perpetual temptation which works to lure the devout away from their relationship with Christ.

That summer I accompanied my church's youth group on a retreat to Seattle. Along with my church pastor and friends, we packed into a van and made the long trek from Montana to Washington. We were going to attend Jesus Northwest (JNW). For those that don't know, Jesus Northwest (now defunct) was exactly like Creation Northwest. It was a rock concert themed revival showcasing popular Christian singers and bands and it invited numerous popular Christian speakers to host workshops and speak on a range of pressing Christian concerns.

It was 1994 and we were primed to rekindle our flame for Jesus Christ. At JNW we were sheltered from the outside world. Surrounded by fellow Christians our own age, we let the ecstatic energy lift us up to the highest high, to the point where we felt closer to God than ever before.

During the long road trip, I had read Josh McDowell's apologetics work *A Ready Defense*, collecting his best essays defending the Christian faith. I distinctly remember my excitement at hearing that Josh McDowell would be the special guest speaker at Jesus Northwest. I had highlighted the *bajebus* out of his book and I was really looking forward to hearing his talk.

While we waited in the stands to see McDowell appear on stage, the large video screen lit up and the adorable Veggie Tales character Larry the Cucumber came onto the screen and did a "Silly Songs with Larry" segment. Singing and dancing vegetables are certainly the opposite of controversy. What's more, Larry the Cucumber was genuinely funny. It was priceless.

After the video McDowell ran out, then proceeded to lecture the attending audience on the "sin" of masturbation for a half hour. So after watching a giant talking cucumber sing and dance we were told not to wank off. I wasn't quite sure if McDowell was fully aware of the content preceding his talk, but it was amusing, to say the least.

The problem was, as a pubescent teen (discovering my body for the first time) all I could do, it seemed, was think about sex and masturbate to relieve the unruly licentious thoughts forcing me to lust after everything. What was simple biology, at the time, seemed like a radical disease to me. Our very thoughts about sex were deemed sinful and we were chastised for having ever entertained such thoughts. But I admired Josh McDowell for wanting us to walk the road of righteousness and be honorable young men.

On our return trip home, I vowed to myself that I would never masturbate again. It only threatened to take my mind off of Jesus. Little did I know that this vow would ruin any potential I had to get a date, find a girlfriend, or, for that matter, just have a normal relationship with a girl. Distorted by a sexophobic

155

creed, women were all relegated to temptresses, in my mind. But I still couldn't escape sensual urges and sexually explicit thoughts I was constantly having about women. Every single day, without warning, the thoughts just appeared in my mind's eye. And the more I fantasized about sex, the more I masturbated, and the more I did that, the more guilt I felt. Until, I came to the horrible realization that the Devil was using lust and the temptation of flesh to deter me from my path toward righteousness.

I was unaware at the time that this small seed of guilt would begin to grow into a massively paralyzing fear of intimate relationships. After a while, I couldn't take it any longer, and so I decided to become a veritable monk, and ignore sex altogether. But that only made things worse. The more I tried not to think about it, the more I couldn't resist thinking about it.

Nightmare World

Every night, I was "sinning" to the thought of pretty cheerleaders and other girls at my school. The fact that I couldn't even approach a girl meant I would fantasize about them that much more—forbidden fruit indeed. It became an addiction—I couldn't stop masturbating even though I desperately wanted to. What was wrong with me? Suddenly, I was feeling a darkness surround me, I was disgusted with myself, and I felt weak and pathetic. Meanwhile, all of my friends had girlfriends.

I kept telling myself that the Lord would provide; that if I stayed true to his cause I would be blessed with a godly woman who would complete me. The only problem was I didn't expect God to go out of his way to hook up a young follower of his.

Especially some masturbating, sex-crazed, delinquent sinner such as myself.

Now, more than ever, I believed that I needed Jesus in my life.

At about that same time, I started having vivid nightmares. Usually it involved a succubus who would seduce me, then, as we were having sex, she would turn into a demonic monster and attempt to choke me to death. The dreams were so real that I didn't know that I was dreaming. I would wake up gasping for air, my heart pounding.

Eventually girls from my school were appearing in my dreams—and they too would turn into demonic succubae and stab me, tear my flesh off, and devour me alive. One night I woke my family up screaming in my sleep!

Silly thing for a teenage boy to be afraid of women—let alone have nightmares about them. Even at the time, I thought that this couldn't be healthy. Soon, everywhere I looked, I felt a dark presence out to get me. It haunted me, just beyond the corner of my right eye, I could sense it stalking me—whatever it was. Every night before bed I would clutch my Bible to my chest and pray out loud to Jesus, asking him to send his guardian angels to watch over and protect me from the demonic attacks.

I felt I was being attacked because Satan wanted to derail my walk with God—and obviously I was succeeding—or he wouldn't be trying so hard. I knew the Devil was out to get me, so I armed myself with the sword of Holy Scripture. Only, the nightmare was just beginning.

Spiritual Warfare

Darkness descended upon me. It hung over me like an impenetrable shroud. In the hollows of nothingness, an uncontrollable feeling of despair topped with horror pored over me. Trembling, I feared for my life.

With a panther's hiss, the demonic voice quickly turned into a growl as it spoke to me. I remember looking fearfully around for a trace of light, but nothing. Everywhere I looked was darkness. I felt motion in the air, but the black veil which had descended upon me was thick, and I couldn't see a thing. I could only hear the demonic voice call out to me.

The hideous voice shot fear-laden chills down my spine. My ears were ringing with the shrill sound of its voice. Then back to the demonic taunting, the cruel words, the deep rattle in its sticky throat.

Suddenly, I felt a weight slam down upon my chest. The demon began choking the life out of me. Then it picked me up off the ground, and I felt as though I was levitating in the air, as if something had reached into my chest and tried to rip out my very soul.

"You think you're special? You think you're God's little soldier, don't you?" it snarled.

I refused to engage it. Instead, I began praying out loud to Jesus—the Savior—the Lord on high. Calling his Holy name, I prayed to Jesus that he might save me from the clutches of this evil darkness. Every time I said the name Jesus, an interesting thing occurred. The demon growled and hissed angrily as if the very utterance of Jesus' name was an affront to the damned creature.

"Don't say *that* name!" it howled out in agony.

"Jesus, I accept you," I cried. "Please heal me, please take this burden of sin from me. Please, Jesus... protect me from this evil," I pleaded and prayed, and cowered.

Suddenly, two streaks of light flashed by before me. They sounded like fighter jets buzzing overhead. Fast. Powerful. A loud earth-shattering *THOOM* suddenly shook the very ground beneath my feet. Then the demon began shrieking for its very life. This insufferable screaming was followed by an even louder KRA-KOOM! And then the terrible voice was silenced.

Standing before me were two enormous and magnificent figures—with wings. They had elaborate golden laced armor which shone hot white with heavenly light. They looked at me and a wave of fear, even greater than that which I had felt with the demon, rushed over me. Raising my hand to block out the brilliant light, I closed my eyes to deter the hot pangs I felt from its radiance. Then a masculine yet soothing voice came forth, and said, "Do not be afraid, my child."

Opening my eyes again, I saw one of the guardian angels pointing past my shoulder. I spun around to see what he was pointing at. Hovering in the sky, like Superman, was Jesus Christ. Stretching across his shoulders and rising into the sky were what appeared to be two giant wings. No, not wings. I squinted hard to force my eyes to focus. They weren't wings, they were two enormous battalions of warrior angels all decked in the same radiant armor as my two protectors.

This was the Christ of Revelation leading his army, preparing for the return, where he would overthrow the old Devil, Satan, and take his proper place at the head of the Kingdom of God— to be established here on earth.

Unexpectedly, the glowing visage of Christ transported down to where I stood, and abruptly materialized beside me. We had a long conversation, although I cannot remember what was said. Only that I felt quieted as a flood of love washed over me and cleansed me of the darkness.

That's when I woke up. Tears streaming down my face. "What sort of dream was this?" I asked myself. No, not a dream, but a vision!

In Retrospect

After my potently spiritual experience, I began having visions on a regular basis. I spoke with angels and I was certain that I was seeing demonic forces prowling the streets. Shadows I caught in the corner of my eye and the disquieting feeling of nervous unrest would pore over me. Eventually, my visions started coming even while I was awake, like waking dreams; this otherworldly sight-beyond-sight confirmed what I already knew. There was, indeed, a spiritual war happening right under my very nose. It was exactly as my Evangelical church had taught: Satan and his minions were working overtime to take as many of the faithful down with him.

At my church, my pastor began talking about the youth that would lead the next generation of Christians in preparation for Jesus's return. He spoke of the visions they would have and the chosen prophets who would arise among the Christian ranks. Even as he assured us this would come to pass, I was too timid to share with anyone my experiences. The visions, as real as they were to me, seemed so outlandish and surreal that I feared everyone would think I was pulling their leg.

A few years later, when I had graduated high school and was halfway into my university education, my mother took my brother and I to see a rabbi, or to be specific, a Messianic rabbi—or *Jews for Jesus* as they are commonly referred to. He put his hands on my brother and me and prayed for the Lord to shield us from the evil that always seemed to be nipping at our heels.

Now before you write me off as a crazy person, just know that many religious people, of various religious backgrounds, experience "visions" and "nightmares" of the sort I am referring to. When you are under the control of religious thinking, the lucid phantasmagoria which you are experiencing seems real, and your brain interprets it as such.

Such visions often have real physiological and psychological symptoms and effects. The person experiencing them cannot always tell the difference between the vision and reality. Like Saul of Tarsus (before he became known as Paul the Apostle) on the road to Damascus, you fall down onto the ground convulsing, cowering in the dirt at the visions of light, which dance blindingly in your mind. You fear the voices and heed their warnings. These strange voices are not your own, because you couldn't imagine anything so terrifying and life-shaking as this.

Of course, now I know better, because I know the scientific (real world) explanations for what I experienced. I know about both the physiological and psychological responses and the stimuli which triggered them. I know about migraines and seizures and the way they can trick your senses into perceiving reality incorrectly. I know about false memories and the psychological burden of religious indoctrination and years of programming. I know about the side effects of anxiety and stress. I know about the amped-up hormonal drug-induced dreams which become hyper-real. In fact, it is these very same hormones that make a young man's wet dream such a pleasurable experience, but which can also cause him to have the most vivid and terrible nightmares imaginable.

But back then, none of this was known to me. What I experienced was as real to me as anything. And the only way I could come to terms with what I was experiencing was via my religion—precisely because I lacked the real scientific explanations.

Burnt Out on Faith

At about this time, I realized I was burnt out on school and burnt out on faith. I had practically finished a four year degree in two years (including two sessions of summer school) coupled with endless hours of study. My weekends were filled to the brim with religious activities as well, and I was still having the visions. I just couldn't take all of the stress any longer. So I decided to take a break from it all, and I applied to my university's study abroad program. I did a student exchange and moved to Japan.

I arrived in Kumamoto, Japan, on September of 2003. It was my first time to Japan, and it would be my adopted home for one full year while I studied Japanese language at Kumamoto Gakuen University.

While in Japan, my religious visions stopped. The horrible bouts of anxiety-driven fear relinquished. And in the land of the rising sun, amid the glistening rice paddies, in a world of bonsai trees and cute cartoon characters designed to soothe the soul, I felt a calm peace come over me for the first time in my life. I believed God had healed me. He had answered my prayers! (In retrospect I simply changed my high-stress lifestyle for a more leisurely and recreational one in which I had time to wind down and wasn't always pushing myself to my limit.)

As I studied in Japan, I took in both the language and the customs. I learned to respect other people's beliefs, which wasn't easy. As an American, I thought that surely I was righter than everyone else. As a Westerner, I thought certainly I was righter than everyone else. As a Christian, I felt that I had the one true faith and everyone else was wrong. Being an American Christian Westerner, I was a hopelessly deluded and completely self-absorbed individual. The way I came to this conclusion was via a series of culture shocks which would wake me up.

Culture shock is basically the experience of a foreign, or alien, culture to your own. One in which the norms are so entirely different that you are shocked by the strangeness and dissimilarity of them. Culture shock is often the catalyst which forces one to re-examine her inherited worldview by contrasting it with an adopted (alternative) worldview. Only after we've stepped outside of our inherited worldview, and experienced a differing worldview, can we truly begin to see the "bigger picture" as they say. This can be a daunting task, because you may come to discover that everything you thought you knew, everything that you held to be true, was merely a fanciful illusion generated in the echo chambers of your closed belief system.

You see, as I was learning to grow accustomed to my new life in Japan, I realized something. We can't change our minds about our beliefs until these beliefs are challenged. Whether they are culturally derived beliefs, religious beliefs, or philosophical beliefs, until we put them under the microscope for fair scrutiny—until we get up close and examine our beliefs properly—we are simply naïve.

Culture shock has a way of showing you that what you thought was the norm is not necessarily true. Once you leave the comfort zone of your own cultural worldview, it's all holds barred against the world, and then it's a fight to keep your identity or else re-forge it entirely. Those who aren't up for the challenge usually opt to get out, and they go back home. I've seen many simply give up and head home. Hey, no problem. Japan isn't meant for everyone. Those who persevere, however, become better people for it. They push through the wall of stereotypes and false preconceptions to get at a real level of understanding. And in that process, those who survive their initial culture shock become more open-minded individuals. At least, this has been the case in my experience and of those countless others who I have seen make the same life-changing realization.

I have laid down how I perceive culture shock impacts one's cultural worldview for a very specific reason. It explains the catalyst of that which forced me to step back and re-examine my own worldview—including my religious beliefs. You see, my whole life I had been raised in a Church which taught that if I married a non-believer (that is someone who wasn't a Christian), I'd likely be tainted by their ungodliness. I'd be tempted to follow their sinful ways and would fall from grace and end up in hell. So it is no wonder that I avoided dating Japanese girls at first. But I kept getting asked out. By the end of the second month in Japan, I caved in and went on a few dates. What could a coffee or two hurt? The girls were sweet, and the dates were fun, but nothing came of them. But then I met a wonderfully intelligent and cultured Japanese woman named Sayaka. After meeting Sayaka, and falling deeply in love with her, suddenly an eternity in hell seemed like a risk worth taking.

Sayaka showed me there is more to people than unfounded stereotypes. She opened my eyes to other ways of thinking and taught me compassion and empathy for other people—no matter their race, gender, sexual orientation or background.

Suddenly, my faith didn't seem to make sense anymore. My faith was telling me I couldn't love the woman of my dreams because she was a corrupting force tempting me away from God. My form of Christianity taught that I couldn't be with her—that if I chose to love this woman that I was choosing her over God. Indeed, it dawned on me that in order to love her unconditionally I would have to become an infidel. I felt devastated. Love had turned my whole world upside down.

So as it turned out, my fundamental outlook wasn't, indeed, compatible with a more multicultural and open-minded view of interracial relationships. I believed God was all-loving, but only of his chosen flock. But here I was, finally lucky enough to find someone who I loved and who loved me back. I didn't want to be a lonely bigot preaching about the power of God's love but know nothing about real love. When it came to devotion to my faith, or devotion to my future wife, I chose my one true love over the religious ideology. Other than a fool, who in their right mind would give up a chance at true love if they found it? Not I.

More than learning to let go of certain aspects of my faith, I also learned a great deal from Sayaka about unconditional love. The more that I observed her, the more that I began to realize that the love and compassion talked about in my Christian faith was grotesquely inferior by comparison. Not only this, I had to seriously start questioning my faith and what it taught. Naturally, I realized that I had to make a choice, a difficult one too. Either I could continue to believe in Christianity, or I could go back to square one and re-educate myself; find a new belief system, and as heretical as it was in my mind at the time, maybe even a better one.

Black Diamond Deconversion

Ultimately, three events happened during my crisis of faith: 1) my beliefs, and my worldview, were all challenged head on; 2) overcoming my initial culture shock taught me the critical skills required to step back, take a better look, and re-evaluate my personal beliefs; and 3) love changed me—for the better—when it showed me that my Christian ideals could, in fact, be inferior to non-Christian ideals.

Talk about a revelation!

If I could be wrong about Christianity, I wondered, then what else might I be wrong about? It was the perfect blend of intellectual and emotional turmoil which lead to my crisis of faith and eventually pushed me into my current skepticism.

Coming to Japan and meeting Sayaka was the catalyst that caused me to go back and re-evaluate my whole life. Everything from who I was as a person, to what I believed, to who I wanted to become. But even with all the change going on in my life, I still wasn't fully ready (or willing) to relinquish my Christianity.

Studying abroad allotted me a surplus of study time. I used a lot of this additional time to brush up on my reading. I tackled the works of C.S. Lewis and read every single religious book he had ever written. I delved deep into his Christian writings as well as his personal correspondence while he was shifting between philosophical worldviews, just like I was.

As a Christian, I had a fairly good idea of what Christianity meant, to me as well as to other Christians. Having been active in interfaith ministries growing up, and having taken comparative religion classes at college, I was well aware of the varying doctrinal and theological viewpoints of the minute differences between denominations. But I was also aware of what linked us all as practitioners of the same faith. It was that common thread, or narrative, which tied all of Christianity together. Something which Lewis referred to as "Mere Christianity."

Sure enough, C.S. Lewis was Christianity's great apologist, and he had an answer for every criticism and doubt. In my time of uncertainty, his words soothed. What's more, his arguments made sense to me. His reasoning was clear, his points were eloquent, and his analogies simple yet profound. But even so, Lewis didn't have all of the answers. So I began to read. A lot. I read everything from Thomas Aquinas to Anslem and Aristotle to Lao Tsu. I read ancient Chinese and Japanese Zen parables as well as the Koran. The more religious works I read, the more it seemed to me that this common experience of *experiencing* God was what united the human race. Actually, it seemed like the best evidence for God I could think of.

Like the seventeenth century Christian theologian Thomas Traherne, who wrote in his collected work *Centuries of Meditation*, I too felt, "There are invisible ways of conveyance by which some great thing doth touch our souls, and by which we tend to it."

And when he asks, "Do you not feel yourself drawn by the expectation and desire of some Great Thing?" Deep down in my heart I knew that the answer was, "Yes."

God, for me, was real. As real as anything.

But soon enough, I strayed from the works of religious writers and moved into the field of philosophy. I began to study the writings of John Locke, Thomas Paine, Joseph Conrad, Thomas Jefferson, H.L. Mencken, David Hume, G.W. Foote, Freidrich Nietzsche and William James. All of their razor-sharp intellects and impossibly hard ideas chiseled away at my faith from every possible angle. But still, I clung to an obstinate faith.

Imagine my embarrassment, then, having to admit to you hear that the book that changed my mind, that forced me to do a 180 degree about face on my beliefs, was a little polemical written by the world's most infamous biologist. Yes, it was this oh-so-shrill god(s)-hating biologist Richard Dawkins and his quaint, little, theologically unsophisticated, book called *The God Delusion* (TGD) that drove me to my turning point. But before you say 'what a joke' it is, or state how a well-read fellow like me should have known better, let me explain how that damnable book helped free my mind.

That Damnable Book Freed My Mind

Not even part way into *The God Delusion* I got to the page where Dawkins criticized my personal hero, and champion of

Christianity, C.S. Lewis. Dawkins' biting comments sent me into a rage. I became so distraught that I threw the damn book against the wall so hard that you would have thought I meant to break its poor little back. If Dawkins was around at the time I probably would have lobbed his stupid book at his big fat atheist-bloated head.

How dare he take a cheap shot at my literary idol! How dare he attack my faith! Why did Dawkins have to attack my cherished beliefs when I didn't feel the need to attack his? There was just one problem. The reason I was so outraged wasn't because of Dawkins' "attack" on my beliefs, but that I had no real answers for the simple, very mundane, even simplistic criticisms Dawkins was lobbing against my religion.

Maybe it was because it was the first real criticism of my faith I had ever read that *The God Delusion* got under my skin. Perhaps it was because many of the arguments and questions Dawkins raised seemed so deceptively simple that a child should be able to answer them, and yet, I was baffled by the fact that I had no good answers at all. I had read the best theologians of Christianity, and I had a large wealth of apologetic materials by modern writers such as Josh McDowell, Lee Strobel, and Norman L. Geisler. I had even read Sir Arthur James Balfour's book, *Theism and Humanism*, which ultimately convinced C.S. Lewis about the truth of Christianity. All my bases were covered, so why did Dawkins and his rubbish book bother me so much?

A couple of things spring to mind. The first is like I stated earlier, I didn't have any ready answers for many of Dawkins' highly practical concerns. Like the logical positivists, such as the American philosopher Willard Quine, Dawkins is a staunch naturalist who rejects metaphysics. But he entertains the possibility in TGD (taking the position that Kant did) by allowing for metaphysics insofar as it is tied to reality at large. If this is true, then science will surely be able to detect all the subtle metaphysics going on. Dawkins then pushes the question: If science can potentially yield the answers for all our practical concerns, then why hasn't it answered our metaphysical and religious concerns? This denotes either a failure of science, or more likely, something is wrong with our religious beliefs and metaphysical assumptions.

Secondly, and more importantly, Dawkins is smart. *Real* smart. He is an eminent, world renowned, scientist who has devoted his entire life to teaching people about science and how science works. Heck, his writing is taught in universities across the globe as a prime example of how to illustrate a point using finely crafted allegories, metaphor, and prose. His non-fiction work is among the best in the English language—it's even included in many creative writing courses as a 'how to' of writing non-fiction. Dawkins knows how to use the power of words to get you to think in new and different ways. To his credit, he does it with an eloquence and a poetry rare in this day in age, and this happens to make all of his reading a joy—even when you adamantly disagree with what he's saying.

Those who criticize Dawkins' book and pooh-pooh his intellect as being theologically unsophisticated have missed the entire point of *The God Delusion* and have underestimated the genius of Dawkins. TGD is not meant to be sophisticated. It's like calling the film *Alien* a good romance flick or Rambo a bad art-house film because it isn't sufficiently sophisticated. You're mixing up your genres. Dawkins' book amounts to "Atheistic Apologetics" but unlike the majority of Christian apologetics it is far better written.

But if you think Dawkins is merely an evil atheist who is lashing out at religion—although he is that too—you might miss how radical *The God Delusion* is as a question starter. Dawkins expertly turns the tables and forces us to ask the difficult questions. For example, if religion provides a clear-cut moral code, then why aren't religious believers any more moral than nonbelievers? If you believe the Bible or the Koran are the best moral guides for living a good life, then why are secular and atheistic countries happier and have less crime? Dawkins brings up these questions and many more like them. The goal isn't to tear down theology, or insult anyone's faith; rather, his goal is simply to try and get us to think.

I was so infuriated after reading *The God Delusion* that I went online to listen to Dawkins and the rest of these pompous, so-called intellectual, atheists speak. I wanted to hear it from the horses' mouths, so to speak. All four of them (Dawkins, Dennett, Harris and Hitchens). I wanted to see them debate Christian intellectuals and be thoroughly humiliated. In retrospect, however, this was a big mistake.

Their intellectual rigor, eloquence, and sophistication were much more than I expected from skeptics and atheists. Every time I listened to them talk, I was amazed at how much I learned. It was more like listening to my college professors' lectures than to my pastors' sermons, probably because all of them, with the exception of Sam Harris, were professors. When I listened to my religious teachers, however, all I got were anecdotal stories, which self-reflexively tied back into some doctrinal teaching based on some theological assumption or other. My pastors made sweeping claims, hasty generalizations, and unsupported quips about the opinions of others. But when I listened to these atheist speakers, they were careful to use fewer fallacies and often had facts to back up their claims. At the same time, they peppered their talks with references to studies, polls, surveys, and scientific research, which gave their claims greater weight than the mere opinions told by many of the religious speakers I had heard.

The thing that stood out the most to me about the New Atheists, however, was that they all professed to support reason over faith. That was new to me.

As a Christian, I was taught to put faith in the wisdom of God, not in the wisdom of men. In my circle of Evangelical friends, Proverbs 3:5-6 was one of the most popular phrases cited. "Trust in the Lord with all your heart and lean not on your own understanding." We were told that more knowledge would only bring us more grief (Ecclesiastes 1:18). During Bible studies in college, when someone was troubled by something their atheist professors said, we were reminded of Romans 1:22 which states "Although they claimed to be wise, they became fools." My whole life I had been taught to esteem faith above all else, and be highly skeptical of my own feeble ability to reason. But for these godless atheists, personal conviction played second fiddle to systems of belief which demonstrated their claims. Religion, on the other hand, asks us to take a Kierkegaardian leap of faith first and ask questions later—and only when necessary—and sometimes not even then.

As I continued to read more and more secular and atheistic works, I realized my faith was faltering. Not all at once, but gradually. My faith was like a snail trying to cross a six lane interstate during rush hour. It always had the horrible realization that it was on the way out. I too came to the same realization about my faith. It was just a matter of time before it would suddenly be gone—all it would take was a blink of the eye.

Beyond an Absence of Faith

After a year in Japan, and having met the love of my life, I returned to the U.S. and graduated college. I poured myself into my studies. I tucked religion away and focused on my intellectual growth. A year later I was on the first flight back to Japan to teach on the JET Programme.[12] Once again I was re-united with my love Sayaka, and she immediately accepted my newfound skepticism. In fact, to my surprise she not only embraced it but she informed me that she was relieved. She had never said anything until this time, but she despised all my religious talk. It was simply white noise to her. This was a huge relief to me as well. Not only did I get to keep the love of my life, but our relationship was stronger without the wedge of religious interference.

One day, while I was walking along the river in a small village in Hiroshima Prefecture, I looked down at the beautiful *koi* (carp) all swimming around in the river. Some were golden, some were black, white, and red spotted, while others were a dark metallic brown. Off in the distance, rice paddies glistened amid the misty mountains, and crisp morning air invigorated me as I walked along the old farm road which hugged the river. The valley smelled fresh with the left-over scent of early morning rain, and the sun rays warmed my face as I looked out toward the horizon. *With no fence but for the sky*, I thought to myself. Bob Dylan knew exactly what he was talking about when he wrote those lyrics. Then suddenly it dawned on me, so this is what happens to nonbelievers who go beyond an absence of faith.

---

[12] Japan Exchange Teaching (or JET) Programme is an inter-cultural teaching exchange program run by three Japanese ministries, 1) *The Ministry of Internal Affairs and Communications*; 2) *The Ministry of Foreign Affairs*; and 3) *The Ministry of Education, Culture, Sports, Science and Technology* (MEXT). The program is administered by CLAIR (the Council of Local Authorities for International Relations). The goal of the program is to integrate English learning at the grass-roots level in Japanese society. Since Japan has limited contact with foreigners, only 2% of Japan's population consisting of foreigners (mostly Asian) who live in Japan, the JET Programme is a healthy way to bring cultural awareness to Japan. JETs are viewed as cultural ambassadors as much as they are teachers and educators. You can learn more about the JET Programme by visiting: *http://www.jetprogramme.org/*

They find peace of mind in the tranquility and splendor of what they are a part of, and comfort in the realization that their minds are set free.

When I was religious I would have thanked God for such a beautiful, awe-inspiring day. But not this time, I thought, a big grin stretching across my face. I had finally come to terms with the fact that the natural world was all there is. In that moment, it felt as though my eyes were truly opened for the first time, and I looked out at the world with a deeper understanding lending to a deeper-felt appreciation. All the beauty and grandeur made more sense to me now, knowing that it could have happened only this way, naturally, than to assume some magic deity did it because he liked fat goldfish and sunshine.

Contrary to popular opinion, I am afraid if God created everything that it all would cease to have meaning. Things mean more when they are precious and rare, like a gem that you can't ever really put a price on. Or your first love. Or your forever love. These things are special because they only come once. No two will ever be the same. They are the rarest of the rare. Life is a lot like that. Our lives are one-off events. Why waste them away with time-consuming religious rituals worshipping figments of our imagination?

Our very existence is precious because it is rare. Those who believe in an afterlife cannot say this since life would cease to have any significant meaning if it is just bound to be eternal. More of the same does not make something more precious and rare. It makes it superfluous and unnecessary. Things do not gain meaning when they are infinite supply. They have to disappear, like the cherry blossom fading away in a summer breeze. In order to give these small life moments any meaning, like the cherry blossom, we have to acknowledge their passing. If they were with us forever, or if we lived forever, life just wouldn't be meaningful. Life seems more beautiful to me without God.

As I crossed over the bridge of the small river, I paused and looked down at the koi swimming beneath the floating pink petals, shed by the cherry blossom trees, washing under me, heading downstream. After they passed, my thoughts turned to how I could find purpose and meaning now that I had embraced my faithless atheism. Without religion or God, where would I get my purpose for living a meaningful life? Well, luckily our destinies aren't written yet. I firmly believe that we write our own futures.

Nowadays, I find purpose for living life by living for my beautiful wife and wonderful daughter. I find purpose in keeping them happy and safe. I find purpose in learning to be more open-minded and accepting of others. I find purpose in gaining in knowledge, wisdom, and patience. I think you'll find that this is all the purpose anyone really needs to live a truly fulfilling and meaningful life.

Striving to live a good life, loving others, and perhaps contributing something which future generations might be inspired by, or that might help to make the world a better place, is what makes life worth living. One doesn't need God or religion to be good or live with empathy and kindness toward others. What's more, it goes without saying that I am much happier now than ever before.

Perhaps just as importantly, I am liberated from a suffocating faith and I am free to love my Japanese wife without religious rules or regulations dictating whom and how I ought to love. I cannot tell you how to live your own life, but I will say this much, the secular life provides an equally rich and fulfilling experience. May you all live well and be wise.

11

MINDI ROSSER

Cultic Devil Daughter

Disclaimer: Enter my world at your peril: what you
discover may be psychologically disturbing.

IMAGINE BEING UPROOTED MALICIOUSLY FROM MODERN CULTURE
and transplanted into the medieval ages. Women are viewed as
sex objects, for the titillating fantasies of the male dominator;
brainwashed into bearing children as their redeeming quality,
females exemplify lust, the physical depravity of humankind.
Cloaking themselves in layers of fabric to disguise curves of
sensuality, cult seamstresses labor to design hideous attire for
their daughters' protection. Scathing sermons are the norm for
the impressionable youths. Ranting about the dangers of the
opposite sex, gods (referred to as *leaders*) proclaim damnation
upon those fringe dwellers exhibiting sexuality through hand-
holding.

Jolt yourself back to the present. Could you believe that such
a modern subculture thrives with tens of thousands of followers?

My entire journey of recovery from that segment of life is a
book-length adventure in itself. Here I am today, a young

woman freed from the bondage of the past. Have I been through an earthly hell? Most would answer affirmatively if they knew all the details. What happened to my former friends? There are two from the past whom I can still call my friends. Do I still experience traumatic moments related to my past belief system? More than I would like to admit. Have I fully recovered? That is an unfair question. The Cult never vacates the alcoves of the victim's mind. My past life feels like a tale of fiction. I pinch myself to remind myself that I lived that nightmare. I survive to share my story, the *Cultic Devil Daughter* of the First Baptist Church.

Asking the Questions

My life reads like a tale of escape from a modern-day Jonestown. Born the preacher's daughter in a burgeoning fundamentalist society, I battled critical thinking as the unforgivable sin. I challenged the patriarchal cult leader face-to-face. My story is not unusual to those who have also left religious extremism. Mine was not a simple deconversion, if there is such a thing.

I was born into a society of religious perfectionism. I followed the rules. I listened in church. I always behaved myself. I was the ideal Baptist believer. My family was an integral part of the First Baptist Church of Hammond, Indiana, an unabashed independent fundamental Baptist church.[13]

I cannot remember the first moment I questioned my belief system, but it happened during childhood. Faith. Just have faith, and God will take care of everything. Was it so simple? I

---

[13] Note: not all of the churches associated with this movement would be considered cultic, but my mega-church matched the characteristics of religious cult as described in Margaret Thaler Singer's book, *Cults in our Midst*.

wrestled with unbelief, but I suppressed it beneath Bible reading, unrelenting sermons, and evangelization. A near-perfect role model for my religious peers, I won senior superlative for "Most Spiritual" in my Christian High School. Throughout my teenage years, I plastered on the fake smile too common in cultic groups. To outsiders and insiders, I looked happy. I should have been. I was following every ridiculous rule. Something was missing though. But just what was it?

Lack of knowledge prevailed, circular reasoning dominated, but I began questioning nonetheless. My leaders did not tolerate kids who questioned God. An innocent question threatened to set ablaze their carefully constructed straw house of convoluted messages. So, I kept my thoughts to myself. I figured that there must be some aspect of this faith that I was missing. I searched through all the leaders' books for the one piece that strung our group together. I took extra-curricular biblical and doctrinal courses. I tried to meet their standard of teenage perfection. In the process, I lost my personal identity. Objective reality was non-existent because every thought was forced through a biblical filter.

Depression, eating disorders, body dysmorphia, psychological trauma, and night terrors—I accumulated all this baggage because of the indoctrination, but according to the leadership, these collective ills were all *my* fault. I must not love God enough. I must not have memorized enough Scripture. The sinful nature inside me was the reason I doubted, they said.

Good girls just followed what their men told them to do. Women were not supposed to have brains outside their husbands' limited minds. Submission was a prerequisite to womanhood. If I ever wanted to become a woman of God, I must match *their* checklist. I strove to become that worthy woman at any cost, almost losing my sanity.

My religious group purposefully suppressed its members beneath fear and guilt, so that I felt I could not leave the group, even if I had wanted to. They entrapped me in the "system." It was too costly, both financially and socially, to leave. It was easier to pretend to "fake it until you make it," as one of the prominent teachers in our group dictated. Suppress. Suppress. Suppress. Until there was nothing left. I became a shell of a human.

My quest began. I decided to shun my doubts and prove my faith. The only way to test my beliefs? Examine the evidence. The evidence would prove my faith, or so I thought. First step was to read outside the sect's approved books. I chose to read Christian celebrity author, Ted Dekker. His speculative novels portrayed a very different Christian God. I craved the God of his books: one who accepted and loved me unconditionally. Not the angry God I was reared to serve. This newfound philosophy of a loving God propelled me toward drastic measures.

Leaving My Man

Every woman I knew dreamed of falling in love with the perfect preacher boy. It was the only way to achieve recognition within fundamentalism. Without being married to a man in our movement, a woman's highest position was a spinster secretary or fuddy-duddy teacher. My future status within the cult depended upon my marriage.

His name was Peter Moffitt (changed his name to protect his confidentiality). He was charming, popular, and the captain of the soccer team. We dated for three and a half years. We kept all the dating rules, which excluded all physical touching. We planned our lives and future together while attending Hyles-Anderson College, the church's college. There was no question that we were a model couple for our peers. We were perfect. I should have been happy. My future was secure. I had a preacher man with all the right connections. We talked for hours about belief, faith, Christianity, marriage, sex (though that was a big no-no), and children. I asked him a fatal question that sent me roiling for weeks afterwards. "What if everything that we believe turned out to be false? What would you do?" He paused before answering, "I've worked too hard to get to this place (in our church). I would stick with it no matter what. Loyalty is more important to me." I tried to mask my shock. At that moment, I realized something. He was only parroting our leaders. *Unquestioning loyalty.*

I could not agree with him. I could not tie my life to a man who was uninterested in truth and unwilling to address the tough questions.

To break up with him as a junior in college would dash my chance of a sparkly fundamentalist future. (Girls in our group were encouraged to have a man lined up to marry upon graduation from college, or we risked a life of spinsterhood.) He was my best option, but I wanted something more than this provincial life.

One night, I felt that God was speaking to me while I wrestled with this predicament.

"Mindi, are you willing to give up this man to follow Me? No matter what the cost?"

At first, I resisted this seeming call from God for several weeks. I did not want to give up my future with Peter for that small voice of the Holy Spirit. Finally, I made my decision about Peter (looking back, I realize it was not God speaking but my own psyche searching for a way out of that mess).

I broke off my relationship with Peter. At that point, it was the hardest thing I ever did. According to my father, Peter nearly committed suicide after our break-up.

I sought pastoral counsel after the relationship ended, but the pastor only berated me for getting "too close" to Peter. He said that he knew we would either break up or "fall into immorality." I could either accept my pastor's guidance to rebuild my relationship with Peter or accept that I was a rebellious woman. So I left.

As a result of my confrontation and ensuing flight, my psyche was altered beyond that of the American girl-next-door. Being a voracious observer and obsessive thinker, I abandoned all my friends and family, who were stuck in cult suppression. I followed my gut instinct in pursuit of freedom and self-discovery.

Losing My Education

I was distraught because I had no dictating belief system any longer. I discovered that Peter was my major lifeline to the group, and now my life was my own. I needed a break from Hyles-Anderson College to examine my beliefs. At the start of the second semester of my junior year in January 2007, I withdrew from college. In this sectarian college, I had studied courses ranging from *Understanding Your Husband* to *Baptist Distinctive*.[14] Quite an education to prepare a sheltered woman for a culture outside the group! But it was just another tactic to deter deserters like me. My college was proudly unaccredited, so my credits could only transfer to like-minded Christian colleges. All those years I had invested in my education—gone in the blink of an eye.

---

[14] See: http://en.wikipedia.org/wiki/Baptist_Distinctives

I spent the next four months working at a nearby pet store and living with my parents, who were still entrenched in the First Baptist Church. Though my parents encouraged my decision to break up with Peter, their pressure on me to cling to their religious beliefs was unbearable. I could not think for myself without my parents spouting sermons from our pastor. I had no relevant job experience to pursue a viable career outside the cult, and I felt trapped. If I confessed my mistake to my pastor and returned, I could salvage my image. Otherwise, I had to begin thinking for myself, like a child learning the ABCs of critical thinking.

Growing up in a socially isolated religious sect, my network was solely populated with cult members. This meant that I had no secular friends or family members to talk to about my doubts. My friends love-bombed me to pull me back into the group. I had no idea how to interact with people outside my social circle. Outsiders did not understand my church lingo or my bizarre perceptions of reality.

I also lost any potential financial security. As a sheltered woman, I had no clue what else I *could* do besides becoming a preacher's wife. My official college major was *Marriage and Motherhood*. I was ill-prepared to enter the workforce, but I had to do something while in my catatonic state.

I had no hobbies or interests of my own. Up until this point, every activity of my life had been structured to meet the needs of my future husband or further the group's propaganda. I was like a seven-year-old child suddenly released into an adult world. Minor aspects of daily living overwhelmed my limited understanding of the "real world." I needed someone to tell me what to do, how to make decisions, and how to think. But, I resisted the urge to return to the cult. I would learn. It would take years, but it was the only way to freedom.

Exploring My Religion

Taking this step back from immersion in the cult, I realized that I had other options in religion. Thus began my exploration of denominations. Starting in my local area, I attended various churches from the rock-and-roll mega-church in South Chicago to a pacifistic church on the North Shore. God was different here. He was not about to strike me down for leaving the supposed one true faith. Still, I saw the shallow billboards of these church's beliefs. Since I only noticed the *differences* when compared to my former cult-church, I did not grasp their eerie similarities.

In April of 2007, I took my religious exploits cross-country. I thought I felt the call of God to New York City, specifically to the uber-pentecostal Brooklyn Tabernacle church, a far cry from my staunch Baptist upbringing. After watching their music DVDs, I wanted what they had: an overwhelming passion for God. I packed up all my belongings into my battered Toyota Camry and moved to NYC without knowing a single person there. The only connection I had was a phone conversation with a mission center called New York School of Urban Ministry (NYSUM). I landed an unpaid internship at NYSUM, which included food and housing. At least this opportunity physically distanced me from my past and allowed me space to heal. I joined the Brooklyn Tabernacle choir after only a couple of weeks.

During this time, I completed my college degree through correspondence studies at a sister school to Hyles-Anderson College. I continued working at NYSUM for five months until I could no longer bear city living. I packed up my bags and headed back to Northwest Indiana, the only place I knew to go. Because I still lacked social support, I went back to the cult-church, enrolled in the Hyles-Anderson College Masters' program, and rejoined the ministry in which my ex-boyfriend served.

It was tragic. I had made so much progress up to that point, and then I relapsed. But, my stay was short-lived. After my journey over the past several months, I realized I could never again be "one of them." I had seen too much of the world outside their cloister. A world filled with normal people just living good lives without these unsubstantiated beliefs in an ancient holy book. I left FBC and Hyles-Anderson for the final time, but my parents and family stayed behind. Looking back, I think I was simply frightened because I had no friends outside the religious society and community.

I turned to the Chicago Tabernacle for support, an offshoot of the NYC Brooklyn Tabernacle. I poured myself into this church to suppress my doubts about God and religion. I began fashioning my persona from the ashes of the woman I had decimated. If I had this "God Hole," even God was not filling up that space. The questions still plagued me.

And what were they, these questions. Well, like many readers here, no doubt, the God question plagued me most... whether or not there really was a God. Other religious philosophical questions plagued me, but they became moot once I realized there was no God. The problem I most had with "belief" was the "blind trust" we were supposed to have in a God that I was no longer sure I believed in.

Floundering in Options

I convinced my parents to leave FBC and try out Chicago Tabernacle. I was one step closer to freedom than they were, so they followed my example out of the cult. Why? They saw a profound and positive change in me after I left FBC.

My luck changed when I met an agnostic friend online, and we began having lengthy phone conversations about the god questions. I met him through an online forum, with the hopes of developing a romantic relationship... which did not happen. At the time, I did not know he was agnostic. I was definitely not thinking within the confines of my upbringing, as it was a horrendous sin to be chatting with "an unbeliever." I kept emailing him because of his intellect. He was far more psychologically advanced and intellectually studied than me. I was intrigued by his arguments. Something resonated with me in our discussions, and I could not help it but keep the discussions going.

Over the course of our contact, he taught me how to begin critically analyzing my presuppositions. His concepts were foreign to me, but I could not help but find his arguments convincing. I was still living with my now uber-pentecostal parents, so I had to hide with the phone in the corner of the house to voice my doubts out of earshot. Once my parents realized what type of conversations I was exploring, they advised me to cut off my communication with this friend immediately. I did, but his words never left me.

Skepticism was one aspect I never explored during my transition out. Skeptics were bad people, who relied on evidence instead of faith in God. Skeptics burned in hell for eternity because they dared to question. Skeptics were worse than mere unbelievers. They denied anything that could not be proven. I determined never to become a skeptic, because it might destroy my faith in God. On the other hand, my faith was already crumbling.

I decided to visit my Grandma for a week-long vacation to get away from my parents. That vacation turned into a summer, the best summer of my life to that point. During that stay, I met other normal 20-year-olds who showed me what it was like to live in the real world. They taught me how to let loose and enjoy myself. After that terrific summer with my grandmother, I felt guilty about my "heathen lifestyle." I moved back in with my parents and rejoined Chicago Tabernacle, as much as I internally disagreed with their doctrine and practices.

After a traumatic experience at Chicago Tabernacle, where I was declared to be mentally ill because I questioned my faith, I left that church for the final time. I dropped out of church completely while I re-assessed my belief system, but I continued "walking with God" through prayer and personal Bible study

Dropping My Church

Three churches down, and I was discouraged I would never find another good church. First Baptist Church: too much of a cult. Brooklyn Tabernacle: too feeling-oriented. Chicago Tabernacle: too authoritarian. Was my discernment lacking? If I could not determine God's will for my own life, had I simply fallen prey to Satan? I was confused and alone. I still felt traumatized every time I walked into a church building. I only wanted to be anonymous and never again a "core member" of a church.

I began approaching religious belief with a cavalier attitude. I wanted facts. I wanted evidence. I wanted proof. That's all I asked. Notice that I had made a shift in my thinking from my earlier position. I wanted substantiated facts, not simply a make-believe promise made by well-meaning religious people that God was always there for me.

Then, it happened. I had an epiphany. I realized that "the voice of God" was just my own intuition. I was the one manipulating that voice to align with the scriptures and sermons. The Holy Spirit did not exist.

I asked myself, "Why do billions of people still believe in various gods for whom there is no corroborative evidence?" I still held the assumption that there must be something to religion since billions adhered to some type of system. I researched the origins of religion through anthropology. It held many of the answers I was searching for. Religion, it seemed, came to be through an evolutionary adaptation to our environment.

Before arriving at my final conclusions about religion, there was one church I had not explored. The world's largest religion: Catholicism.

Catholic Last Resort

Still, I desperately wanted to believe in God. I began attending weekly mass at a local parish. I enjoyed the solemnity and sacredness of the services, a stark departure from my Baptist and Charismatic experiences. After a few months of attendance, I met with the priests about joining the Church. It was not as simple as walking the aisle and getting baptized (Baptist) or speaking in tongues at the altar (Charismatic). Catholicism required several months of weekly RCIA (Rite of Christian Initiation of Adults) classes to become a member. I signed up for the next available classes.

During those classes, I struggled internally. If I resisted and blindly embraced Catholicism, I hoped the doubts would vanish. I wanted to again feel that warm, bubbly "I'm in love with Jesus" delusion.

Halfway through the program, I was done. I could not force myself to fake belief. The teachings of the Church were not adding up. The teachings that did not add up for me were: the Messiah as the One God; the Holy Sacrament turning into the body/blood of Christ; the innate sinful nature of man; the priest hierarchy... those are just a few. My last chance for belief in God was gone. Without a god to believe in, what was the meaning of life? Why was I here? For the first 23 years of my life, I had lived in a world of virtual reality; of religion. Now what?

Coming Out Atheist

After a few months of intense study about atheism and skepticism, I realized that I no longer believed in God. The evidence did not add up. The Bible was not inerrant. Jesus may not have even existed. I could deny it no longer: I was an atheist.

Coming out. Those two words petrified me. If I even breathed the word "atheist" to my friends and family, I would be shunned.

I then began reading *The Artist's Way* by Julia Cameron, more for my writing ambitions than establishing my newfound freedom from religion. Still, this book played a vital role in my coming out as an atheist. Through the exercises in the book, I realized my own identity, apart from any spiritual calling. A part of this course was 'moring pages' (see Julia Cameron's book for more on this), three pages of stream of consciousness writing. I used this time to explore my refashioned psyche. Each word I jotted down was like another drop of soothing balm on my religiously molested wounds. True healing began here. Later, I discovered that I was working through Religious Trauma Disorder. [15] The consequences of RTS often mimic the symptoms of post-traumatic stress disorder.

---

[15]Winell, Marlene. "Religious Trauma Syndrome," http://www.journeyfree.org. Retrieved: December 1, 2012.

It was time. I had a choice to make. I could ally with courage and embrace my atheism. The choice was mine this time. I was no longer dependent upon my parents for financial stability or my church for community. After several weeks of silent wrestling, I came out of the closet through a post on Facebook. This act had consequences. My mom, who had just been diagnosed as bipolar, sunk into depression. Many of my religious family members sent emails saying that they were praying for me along with lists of Christian apologetics books. They assumed my atheism was due to my negative experiences with religion. They refused to accept as valid any alternate explanation. How could I have abandoned God?

Living After Faith

Life after faith. I thought it impossible to live a meaningful life without a god dictating my every move. Now, with newfound unbelief, I embrace life beyond the scope of my experience as a Christian. Life is finite, each day to be treasured. I no longer fear death or the flames of hell. Death is inevitable and final, but I can accept that reality. I have never felt the thrill of being alive, as I do now. I only wish that more people could experience this freedom to think for themselves, without fear.

Looking back upon my journey, I am amazed that I survived psychologically without a mental professional, something I would recommend to those leaving any type of restrictive group. I escaped childhood indoctrination, forsook the cultic group, and emerged into a healthy and happy atheist. My ambition is to live the life of a good atheist, to demonstrate to my family and friends that it's possible. It's only been two years since I came out, but even my mom has commented that I'm still a nice person, nothing like her perception of a militant atheist.

Was the journey easy? Not at all. At the time, I risked everything to leave faith. The cost was more than most Christians would be willing to lose. Would I do it all over again knowing what I know now? Without a doubt. Deconversion is a painful process, but worthwhile for the person seeking truth based upon evidence. Christian or non-Christian, we all have a responsibility to examine the evidence and make a choice. Ultimately, that choice is up to you.

For me, I feel that deconversion opened a new door. Once I realized that I no longer believed, that was the end of that book for me. It felt settled, like I no longer needed to bandy around these God Questions any longer. Since that time, my life has moved on. And I'm all the better for it.

12

NO CROSS NO CRESCENT

A "Miraculous" Journey

From Devout Muslim to Outspoken Atheist

HOW DID I COME TO BE WHO I AM TODAY? THERE ARE quite A few among us who grow up to be the exact antithesis of what we are expected to be. Hence not fulfilling the expectations of family and community is not so rare; people like me end up being "family disappointments" (regardless of our personal and professional achievements otherwise). It just makes us the black sheep that many of us feel comfortable being. I have met countless dissenters from communities that traditionally view faith as a matter of identity and, as such, renouncing it carries a hefty price tag (Mormons and African Americans are easy examples to cite). And yet, among Muslims, and when it comes to religion, this is fairly uncommon (even though there are encouraging indications that things may finally be changing, even among as conservative communities as the Iraqis and the Palestinians). The reason for this is simple: Islam has a no-nonsense, my way-or-the highway answer to dissent—comply or die.

And so the story begins—but with details concerning time and place omitted. That is due to the simple fact that I still have family back "home," where, like much of Islamic world, harassments, and even hostage takings in the service of enforcing conformity are by no means uncommon.

(An aside before I begin: While the following is about Islam, I am sure many ex-Christians, particularly those raised in more conservative and fundamentalist traditions, won't miss the parallels).

Growing Up In a Conservative Muslim Environment

"The problem with Islamic fundamentalism are the fundamentals of Islam" –Sam Harris

As I look back at my early life, prayer and devotion are among the first things I remember. My family wouldn't be considered particularly religious, and yet there were many "fundamentals" that were never to be questioned: the infallibility of the Koran and its miraculous nature; the prophet's divine revelations and their everlasting relevance for all mankind; the nature of human existence (as a miracle of God, of course); the eternal afterlife (indeed, with rather vivid imagery of Islamic hell's revolting minutiae), and sanctity of words and deeds of the prophet and the saints.

While faith was never the top issue in the minds of my parents, my maternal grandfather was very pious. He prayed five times a day facing Mecca, according to the teachings of Islam. Through him, I learned how to pray (which is actually a fairly complex ritual and takes a good bit of effort on the part of such a young mind), and to memorize some of the shorter chapters of the Koran. (At the time, the devotion brought great joy; these days, the memory is unpleasantly chilling, and to me, borders on abuse).

Granted, like most believers, my family read the scriptures very selectively. And hence, when I was young, I didn't know much about what the Koran said; I just "knew" it was the word of God, and everything it said was true.

But as I grew up, came the age of the fire-breathing clergy, with a religious awakening like none other; and all the gory, violent parts of the Koran that everyone used to ignore conveniently were suddenly being preached from every pulpit. It was in my early teen years that I "learned" how terrible Jews were for dismissing Mohammad as a prophet; that they had been lying and somehow distorting their own scripture so that they didn't have to convert; that God was somehow everywhere at once, and yet his apostle Mohammad had to ride a flying donkey to meet him; that "Shirk" (literally "partnership"), meaning the belief that there is any creator other than the one and only God, was the biggest sin (hence, for instance, no chance that he could ever have had a son); and that God had an obsessive and sadistic imagination about how He was going to torment everyone whomsoever doubted any bit of this orthodoxy, forever and ever.

I had never doubted my own faithfulness—until the first hit. That was when I read William Shirer's *The Rise and Fall of the Third Reich*. The part that shook my faith was learning about how Hitler extremely narrowly survived the assassination attempt against him (dramatized in the 2008 movie *Valkyrie*) ten months prior to the end of the War, which would have saved millions of lives (not to mention, quite likely, averting the suffering of millions more as a result of the division of Europe during the Cold War). I remember his radio address after its failure: "I see the Hand of the Providence in my survival." Now, this carried an extremely familiar tone, since in my living environment, attribution of the mundane to the miraculous was a dime a dozen. Hitler's survival, if anything, was even more improbable and dramatic than many of the "miracle" stories I heard every day. So, was I supposed to believe Hitler was wrong? And if so, how would I know which survival miracle claims were "true" and which were mere accidents?

With the growth of religious fervor and the ubiquity of scriptural quotes, I found myself confronted with what the Koran actually said. The more of it I read, the less sense it made. But what made even less sense was the clergy's apologetics trying to make it more palatable.

Every single chapter of the Koran (except one) starts with the following refrain: "In the name of God, the beneficent, the merciful." You see, the problem for me started right there, quite literally. That God, in his boundless mercy and love, wrote not just "a book," but "The Book" that would last thousands of years and made it brimming with insults, threats, and glorifications of his past genocides, from cover to cover.

In addition to some of the biblical mass murders quoted more or less authentically in the Koran (such as the Great Flood), there are a few more stories in the Koran describing tribes (such Ad and Thamud) who failed to convert despite being preached to by God's prophets, and paid the ultimate price for doing so. While there is absolutely no archaeological evidence that they ever existed, the point was quite clear: God is not the one to play games when it comes to the contents of your conscience. You'll believe what you are told to, or else.

Aside from God gloating about his past feats, his "promises" for the future were even more colorful, and belief-defying at once. While there are countless example of what God has in store for you if you fail to toe the line, I have to say this is my favorite example:

Lo! Those who disbelieve Our revelations, We shall expose them to the Fire. As often as their skins are consumed We shall exchange them for fresh skins that they may taste the torment. Lo! Allah is ever Mighty, Wise. (Koran 4:56).

Sure, without the wisdom of God, who would have thought of somehow growing your skin back once it's burned already, such that they can burn it again?

Just for your entertainment, here is another one:

Then We sent our messengers one after another. Whenever its messenger came unto a nation they denied him; so We caused them to follow one another (to disaster) and We made them bywords. A far removal for folk who believe not! (23:44).

See, God doesn't mince words. On the other hand, he does make mincemeat of nations, one right after the next, and makes examples of them, for failure to listen to His prophets.

And then, there were the apologetics. For "starters," the clergy would tell you that the apparent disconnect between the title of Koranic chapters and their actual content is resolved by looking closely at the phrase "the beneficent, the merciful." Supposedly, "beneficent" is something that applies to everyone, but "merciful" shall apply to true believers only. How is one expected to draw that conclusion by reading the title? Your guess is as good as mine. But the one I liked best: it is not God tormenting disbelievers; it is the disbelievers doing that unto themselves:

195

Lo! Allah wrongeth not mankind in aught; but mankind
wrong themselves. (10:44).

Now, how does that sound any different than any domestic
abuser's favorite excuse "she asked for it"?

But the clergy had no monopoly over unconvincing
apologetics. My fellow citizens disappointed me the most. Very
few were willing to admit that the cruelties they were witnessing
for the first time in their lives had anything to do with the faith
they had grown up with. It had to have everything to do with the
clergy's "perversion" of the faith, not the faith itself. It left me
stunned at how a layperson, never having studied religion, could
claim he understood it better than a man in a funny robe who
had "earned" the right to wear it through dedicating his entire
life to the matter. I had to conclude that most people were
simply making up their own version of the faith. And if everyone
was entitled to his/her own version, then there could be no
"true" version.

The last group that I think deserve mention here were the
"moderate" clergy. While this fairly small group condemned the
excesses of the overwhelming majority of their colleagues, the
way they went about doing so always smacked of dishonesty. For
example, they would discuss cases of amputations or stonings in
the context of a religious rule under very specific circumstances,
and then they would accuse their colleagues of implementing
them too freely without fulfilling all the requirements (an Islamic
version, if you will, of "let he who has not sinned cast the first
stone"). What felt dishonest to me about this was that while, like
any decency human being, they found scenes of public flogging,
limb amputations, and other physical Islamic penalties revolting,
they would never go so far as to admit that openly, and were
only willing to stop them through obscure technicalities. Once
again, the story had a familiar tone: to protect religion from

criticism, all lies, distortions, and mental contortions were justifiable. Because no one dared touch the elephant in the room with a ten-foot pole.

All the unanswered questions and, perhaps even more, the lame attempts at answering them that I have already mentioned, took a heavy toll on my faith. Like most people living in theocracies, however, I found myself living a double life, paying lip service to the glorification of faith in public (which was not just an expectation, but a requirement) while loathing it deep down. I started to feel like a hypocrite, and hated myself for being one. When I was still very young, questioning the faith provoked plenty of mental anguish, or led to what may be called a "crisis of faith." In fact, having a questioning mind and seeking better answers when you are not satisfied with you are told is no crisis. For believers though, it very well can be. For if you have been spoon-fed to believe in a literal hell during your formative years, your perception of it is just as real as if you knew about it from personal experience. And I did fear damnations, but once questions arose, they wouldn't simply disappear because they were inconvenient.

I reasoned that if God was going to send me to hell for being honest (at least to myself), then I could not worship this God anyway. And the "bigger picture" offered by Islam became more absurd by the day: "We give you the "gift" of life, but if you stray from the path We will torment you forever and ever." Really? When did I agree to these terms? Why wasn't I ever consulted about whether I was interested in the "gift" in the first place? Having started as all merciful and benevolent, God came to look like a sadistic psycho, and life itself like a horror movie.

As I grew older, the hellfire fears started to disappear. On the other hand, I became more and more conscious of how different I was from everyone else. I woke up to the fact that the society around me was overwhelmingly religious, and I could not even attend a physics lecture or read my college handouts without coming across some scriptural reference. While I felt like a fish out of water, going back was simply not an option.

At home, growing distant from the faith did not land me in a lot of trouble, but led to a good deal of nuisance. My mother, for instance, didn't often pray herself, but would have loved to see me behaving like I did back in my younger years when I regularly prayed, and spent more time reading the scripture; this at a time when I had to dedicate my time to academic achievements. It was tolerable, but certainly not helpful. As for my grandfather, I sometimes thank the Flying Spaghetti Monster that I didn't spend a good deal of time with him beyond my very early years, or else breaking free would have been much, much harder. While I never personally confronted him on his beliefs, he continued to urge me to come back to the faith well into my early adulthood. I never confronted him, and felt that discussing the matter with him was a sheer waste of time. For instance, I never forgot the horror in his eyes when my mother brought up a very mild criticism of the scripture (that it was vague and lent itself to different interpretations, leading to the appearance of many different sects and denominations). To him, it was heresy even to entertain the thought that the Koran could be anything but absolutely perfect. Such minor instances at home only confirmed to me that I was even lonelier than I thought. Hoping to get out of that environment was the only thing keeping me going, even though, in retrospect, I had it easier than many of my ex-Muslim friends of today, who were beaten (in some instances quite literally) into praying at home.

By the time I reached my twenties I had lost my faith (for the most part), and while I didn't know how I might identify my beliefs (in a safe situation), I sometimes identified with Voltaire's deistic philosophy. Which, in hindsight I should say, both

Voltaire and I may have been excused for, for not knowing about Darwinian evolution.

But there was still a nagging doubt in my head: how about the Koran's "scientific miracle" claims?

The Opportunity to Grow
Through Learning and Self Improvement

Coming to the US brought with it daunting challenges. As a new arrival, I had to put questions about religion and philosophy on the back burner for a number of years, as I had more pressing issues on my mind. But the Genie stayed out of the bottle all this time, and grabbed my attention not too long after I felt a bit settled. As I went back to questions about faith, I found one question most pressing: what about Koranic "miracle" claims?

A good many such claims are absurd on their face. One that is particularly hard to swallow is the "argument from aesthetics": it is said that Koranic style is so unique in its beauty and so unparalleled in its tone, is so outstandingly inimitable, that in all the centuries and among speakers of all languages, no one has ever been able to write anything mimicking a single chapter of it. It cannot humanly be done because it is divine:

> And this Qur'an is not such as could ever be invented in despite of Allah; but it is a confirmation of that which was before it and an exposition of that which is decreed for mankind - Therein is no doubt - from the Lord of the Worlds. Or say they: He hath invented it? Say: Then bring a surah [chapter] like unto it, and call [for help] on all ye can besides Allah, if ye are truthful. (Koran 10:37-38).

One has to think hard to come up with more bizarre "evidence" for divinity than this. For starters, no non-Arabic speaker (say, hundreds of millions of Pakistani or Indonesian Muslims) can investigate the claim about the Koran's uniqueness in Arabic, let alone in other languages. Hence, they are supposed to base their faith on claims made by humans, or more specifically, their Arabic-speaking fellow Muslims, who can hardly be considered unbiased. And a book that is but insults, threats and glorifications of genocide can hardly be considered a masterpiece in its aesthetic appeal, no matter how musical it sounds when read out loud (especially if you are among the would-be victims). And as for the inimitability challenge, there has been no shortage of responses—only that not many are investigated by Islamic scholars. For instance, look at one of the shorter chapters, 111, Palm Fiber:

The power of Abu Lahab will perish, and he will perish.
His wealth and gains will not exempt him.
He will be plunged in flaming Fire,
And his wife, the wood-carrier,
Will have upon her neck a halter of palm-fibre.

Now compare it to the following imitation, the likes of which are not rare if you do a Google search:

In the name of Marvin, most-merciful, all-compassionate:
Damn both hands of my neighbor Sam; damn him!
His money and children will not save him!
He will be burnt in a blazing flame –
Sam and his dame, who is also to blame.
As she was carrying wood to her home,

She put some thorns in the path where I roam.
So she shall suffer a torment most dire,
Dangling in hell from a noose of palm-fibre.[16]

Which one is better? Depends, among other things, on whether you approve of a hint of levity in (supposedly) a message for all times and all humanity, missing entirely from the glum book that is the Koran.

But there is one claim to the divinity of the Koran that is harder to crack—that is, until you look at it a bit more closely, and censorship has not blocked access to all rebuttals, which can be fairly easy to find on an unrestricted internet. That would be the claim to scientific "predictions" in the Koran. In reality, no such things exist. It is uncontroversial that there has been not a single scientific discovery based on Koranic guides. Nowhere does God tell humans to investigate the world around them empirically, and nowhere does it predict what they would find; and nowhere does it give them instruction on how to make a rudimentary scientific device like a microscope (which the ancients certainly could have done if they had the knowhow). Rather, this is how it works: scientists make discoveries entirely independent of the Koran, and then apologists jump into the fray and claim it as a Koranic prediction based on their interpretation on some vague-sounding verses (no word on why no one ever saw it coming beforehand, if that is what the Koran meant all along). Aside from this, why should anyone take the Koran seriously as a book with "scientific prophecies," given

[16] Skeptics' Annotated Bible Discussion Board, Surah 10. http://sabdiscussionboard.yuku.com/topic/2939#.UypWQZ_n8sl, Accessed March 2014

that the Koran parrots long debunked biblical fantasies such as the creation of Adam and Eve, or the fairy tale of Noah's Flood?

But what doesn't help the matter is that some Western, non-Muslim scientists, for reasons that are entirely unknown to me, have given credence to some such claims. And this is perhaps the most flagrant example of such ignorance, if not downright dishonesty.[17]

> In the early 1980s, Prof. Keith Moore, formerly an anatomist at the University of Toronto, Canada produced a special edition of his embryology textbook, the standard version of which has been widely used in medical schools around the world. Apparently when he first read what the Qur'an had to say about the development of the human embryo he was "astonished by the accuracy of the statements that were recorded in the 7th century AD, before the science of embryology was established".

This "scientific prophecy" is based on the following:

> Verily We created man from a product of wet earth; Then placed him as a drop (of seed) in a safe lodging; Then fashioned We the drop a clot, then fashioned We the clot a little lump, then fashioned We the little lump bones, then clothed the bones with flesh, and then produced it as another creation. So blessed be Allah, the Best of creators!". (23:13-14)

---

[17] Answering Islam, Embryology of the Qur'an,
http://www.answering-islam.org/Quran/Science/embryo.html,
Accessed March 2014

It has been utterly debunked on numerous occasions, including during the debate between Western Islamic apologist Hamza Tzortzis and biologist PZ Myers.[18] It is entertaining to watch such debates to see the liberties Muslim apologists take with logic (for instance, mistranslating a word to mean "leech" and then claiming it physically resembles a human embryo, which it doesn't, but kudos to Mr Tzortzis for being so "creative"). But the only claim made in the quoted verses that (supposedly) could not have been written by an ignorant 7th century man is the "staged development" of human embryo, only that the Koran gets it wrong:[19]

The final stage of human development which the Qur'an describes is the creation of bones, and the clothing of bones with flesh. However, according to modern embryologists including Prof. Moore [modern anatomist turned Islamic apologist!] , the tissue from which bone originates, known as mesoderm, is the same tissue as that from which muscle ("flesh") develops . Thus bone and muscles begin to develop simultaneously, rather than sequentially. Whereas however most of the muscle tissue that we have is laid down before birth, bones continue to develop and calcify (strengthen with calcium) right into one's teenage years. So far from bones being clothed with flesh, it would be more accurate if the Qur'an had said that muscles started to develop at the same time as bones, but completed their development earlier. The idea that bones are clothed with flesh is not only

---

[18] Richard Dawkins, PZ Myers, AronRa and Hamza Tzortzis at Atheist Convention, http://youtu.be/3T5Pm7qLH50, Accessed March 2014

[19] Answering Islam, Embryology of the Qur'an, http://www.answering-islam.org/Quran/Science/embryo.html, Accessed March 2014

scientifically completely false, but is directly copied from the ancient Greek doctor Galen...

I continued to struggle with the veracity of such claims long after I had renounced everything else about Islam. But it took leaving my home country (hence, having access to necessary resources) to break the remaining chains. At this point, there was no going back, and I didn't hesitate to tell my family that I felt Islam was a lie, and it had ruined many years of my life. Afterwards, however, I was pretty amused to be confronted with "Pascal's wager" by conservative Christians—given that I had already been bullied by the same sort of argument to believe or else, only I was supposed to believe something very different the first time.

My family in my country of birth did not particularly care about my views, or my "eternal soul," but they felt it was over the top when I went out of my way blogging about Islam. But I was not going to shut myself up about something I had been forbidden from talking about for many decades, even though I had to write anonymously, for it is by no means beyond Islamic rulers to harass the families of anyone who voices dissent against Islam. My US family were a different matter, though: while they had never been practicing Muslims, they hadn't been hurt by Islam like me either, and they were clinging to it as a matter of identity. As a result, after some bitter disputes, I ended up splitting with most of them, which I have never regretted.

Conclusion: A Call to Action

Muslims make up over a fifth of humanity. Western secularists and humanists cannot remain neutral in the face of ignorance and suffering of humanity, for no reason but accidents of birth. There is no question that an Islamic Enlightenment is long overdue. However, it is futile to expect this to come from Muslim-majority countries, many of which have harsh laws against freedom of conscience. It has to start in the Western world; only then can we expect it to spread to Muslim majority nations. And Western secularists have a unique opportunity to help that happen.

I have been in touch with a good many ex-Muslims like myself, and I freely admit that my story does not represent the challenges faced by many of them. There are numerous questioning Muslims in Western Islamic communities. Intellectual challenges make but a small part of the obstacles many of them face before they can break free: from financial dependence on their communities, to not wishing to hurt the feelings of their families, to thinking they need Islam to make them distinct and give them an "identity." And they are not going to come forward if such needs are not answered by secularists in their countries of residence. While some organizations such as the Council of Ex Muslims of Britain have done a splendid job of trying to be an intellectual and communal refuge for questioning and ex-Muslims, there is indeed much, much more to be done.

In my adopted home country, the US, I see secularist organizations such as American Atheists or the Freedom From Religion Foundation fight for separation of church and state, and I commend them for what they do. But I also feel that there is a bigger picture they are missing. The image of atheism to date has been one with very little diversity, and near total exclusion of minorities, Muslims included. You only need to take a look at pictures of "New Atheist" authors. This elitist image is staring at us, quite literally, in the face. If humanism is ever to become a movement for humanity and not just those belonging to a certain gender or ethnicity, secularist organizations need to reach out to, and offer their support for minorities leaving faith behind so that they can make a safe and welcoming environment for our new "brethren," answer their questions, and assure them that secularism can give them both a community and an identity.

13

REBECCA BRADLEY

The God-Shaped Hole

TECHNICALLY, I NEVER LOST MY FAITH, SINCE I NEVER had any faith to lose. I grew up able to walk the walk and talk the talk, but my heart was never in it, and *it* was never in my heart. Born into a fundamentalist evangelical cover-to-cover-Bible-believing born-again Christian family, with five saved siblings and adorable parents positively glowing with radiant faith, I still somehow managed to miss out on the whole faith thing.

It was not for want of opportunity, though, in the theoretically formative years. Some of my strongest early memories are set in the now-defunct People's Fellowship Tabernacle, Vancouver, an independent fundamentalist church set up by a hardliner who went solo after splitting from the Southern Baptist Convention in the 1940s, on doctrinal grounds. His biggest sticking point, it seems, was that he was not merely a Bible literalist; he was adamant that the King James Version was the only translation directly inspired by God, while all other translations were part of a satanic plot to destroy the true remnant church from the inside. He was also my uncle by marriage, affable enough at extended-family functions, but a terror behind the pulpit.

It took me a long time to work out that the PFT was the next thing to a religious cult, though in a pretty benign form. Uncle Mark, a graduate of "Bible Bill" Aberhart's Prophetic Bible Institute in Calgary, saw the Book of Revelation as an accurate forecast of tomorrow's news; that is, he could be relied upon to make a one-to-one match between the headlines and some dire end-times prophecy on any given day. It was the sixties, the height of the Cold War, so of course the Soviet Union, Israel, the Pope, the US, and Mao Tse-Tung ("the Yellow Peril") all had their parts to play in God's apocalyptic melodrama. We were Pre-Tribs, meaning the Rapture was expected to take place before the Tribulation, so—with all the signs of the Second Coming clearly spelled out in the daily papers—we could expect to be whisked into the safety of heaven "in the twinkling of an eye" at any moment.

Except, of course, I could expect no such thing, because I had never been born again. As a small child, I had listened with interest to the Sunday school stories and sucked up the hymns like a thirsty sponge, but I had learned to let the sermons wash over me like so much white noise. Crucially, however, I had also been the faintly embarrassed observer of many, many iterations of that powerful rite of conversion, the classic *altar call*. For those of you who have never experienced a revival meeting or a Sunday evening service in an evangelical church, an altar call is the part of the program where the minister invites any who feel under conviction of sin to come to the front and publicly accept Jesus into their hearts, or reconfirm their existing commitment, or simply repent of their sins. (Note: there is rarely an actual altar.) But that bare description does no justice to the psychodrama of the event.

No evangelist worth his thank offering will simply issue the sacred invitation in the same manner as he would announce, say, a coffee social in the church basement after the service. The ground will be prepared with a sermon designed to make you feel frightened and unworthy: all of us are sinners, wicked to the core, fully deserving of the eternal hellfire which God has prepared for our punishment. And there is no hiding from it, because God sees your every deed, and knows every tiny, dirty secret of your heart. He writes it all down, too. Then, when you are properly quaking with guilt and fear, the emphasis shifts from the stern God who hates sin, to the gentle Jesus who loves the sinner. That is the segue to the actual altar call. The congregation rises and sings softly in prayer mode, eyes closed, heads bent, while the preacher does a kind of voice-over: *Come! Come to Jesus! Come now, before it is too late!* The song is almost invariably *Just as I Am.*

Just as I am, without one plea,
but that thy blood was shed for me,
and that thou bidst me come to thee,
O Lamb of God, I come, I come.

Now, altar calls in some churches can apparently get very exciting, especially with Pentecostals and Holy Rollers and televangelists and such. But my Uncle Mark held that the "gifts of the spirit"—things like faith healing, speaking in tongues, and dancing in the spirit—had been a limited-time offer, which expired in the age of the Apostles. We were now in the Dispensation of Faith, he said, and people who spoke in tongues etc. nowadays were being duped by the devil, and opening themselves up to a Satanic takeover. Hence, even the congregational shouts of *Hallelujah!* and *Praise the Lord!* had to be fairly restrained. This was a little hard on the old Pentecostal lags in the PFT flock, who still loved a bit of holy bellowing now and then. But the PFT altar calls were not without drama of their own kind.

Picture the congregation swaying gently to the strains of the hymn, eyes shut, one large temporary organism in a kind of ecstatic communal trance. Here and there in the pews, though, a few celebrants would be doing a bad job of restraining their sobs and holding back their tears. The song would go on. The floodgates would open. Eventually, five or six sinners would totter weeping up the aisle, where Uncle Mark would greet them joyously and kneel with them in prayer. When they turned and testified to the still-crooning congregation about the Lord's goodness and the sweetness of surrender, the old Pentecostal lags would be permitted a few hallelujahs. On especially good nights, the deacons would help out with the overflow at the nonexistent altar. At last, Uncle Mark would end the proceedings with a long—often very long—parting blessing.

Now, I was never one of those who tottered up the aisle to be prayed over, though other children and teenagers did. What I remember best is singing along like a good little Christian, but *with my eyes open*—just open a slit, of course, just enough so I could observe the people around me. It had to be surreptitious because, even if God couldn't see me peeking, Uncle Mark might. And what I mostly felt, beyond bored and tired, was *left out*. Excluded. All around me, everybody, including my family, appeared to be united by some powerful emotion that I had no part in. I felt nothing, neither the shared emotion, nor the presence of God, though Uncle Mark confidently assured us the deity was both present, and taking a lively interest in the proceedings. And I did not feel too bad about being an outsider, either, because (though it sounds awful to admit it) the whole business struck me as more than a bit silly.

This, naturally, had to be kept to myself. For one thing, an honest reaction would have been plain rude; worse, much worse, it would catch me up in the loving but inexorable playing out of the grownups' concern for my immortal soul. It would get me wept over and prayed over; I would be testified to, fussed at, grieved for, conferred about, and spiritually counselled. No, I was not about to let myself in for that.

I did have one ironic advantage. Nobody thought to ask why I never answered the altar call because, quite fortuitously, I had armored myself against it with something that happened when I was five. I had been hearing about "asking Jesus into your heart" for as long as I could understand words, and thought I might as well give it a try one day, to see what happened. Nothing happened. I was unimpressed. I started to tell my mother, actually to complain, but her outburst of joy at the words "I asked Jesus into my heart" stopped me cold. Even at five years old, I could see when silence was golden. At the time, allowing her to believe I was born again was very much better than disappointing her with the honest truth. And how the wicked prosper! That little lie-by-omission saved me a pile of trouble later on, as it was assumed I would not need to be "led to the Lord." Hence, no pressure at the altar calls, and no parental anxiety about the state of my soul.

My tactful silence on the matter lasted until I left home at twenty. Meantime, I walked the walk and talked the talk, even with nonreligious friends—though my deception continued to be mainly by omission rather than by actively proclaiming a salvation that had not occurred. Awkward questions occasionally popped out—the result in one case was that Uncle Mark took out a subscription to the Institute for Creation Research newsletter on my behalf—but generally I pottered along quite happily through a loved and secure childhood, keeping my secret safe.

But Uncle Mark's hellfire sermons were not entirely without effect. It is fairly straightforward to admit to yourself that you do not find God to be a credible proposition. It is not so easy to be sure that you will not be punished for it. What if I was wrong? That hellfire thing sounded mighty unpleasant. I also had a few bad moments now and then when I came home to an empty house, and became worried that everyone else had been Raptured away while I was out. But the more I learned about what other sects, cults, and religions believed, all with an assurance and fervor equal to that of Uncle Mark and my parents, the better I was able to put my family's beliefs into perspective. When I left home, I quietly put the pretense away forever.

Now, I've compared notes with other atheists from a similar background—you often find a little knot of us at atheist/skeptic conferences, quizzing each other merrily on Bible trivia and the Baptist hymnal—and many of them had experiences similar to mine: early realization that they did not believe, years of tactfully keeping shtum about it, and eventual disengagement without much fuss or drama. Few feel embittered, or self-identify as "survivors," unless the church they left was particularly cultish or oppressive. None felt any urge to replace one ideology with another. Clearly, we were the lucky ones.

The situation now? My parents are no longer an issue; my father is dead, my mother deep in dementia. My sibs, who still hold to the faith, know perfectly well that I am an atheist, and wish that I weren't, but it has not poisoned our relationships. We love and amuse each other, and live virtually identical lifestyles, except that I am free to sleep in longer on Sunday mornings. They have all moved away from hardline fundamentalism to a degree that would shock our late Uncle Mark; in fact, they are typical of what many hardline atheists regard as more dangerous than the fundie lunatic fringe: liberal, educated Christians, socially responsible, ecologically aware, intelligent, charitable, kindly, and open to diversity. In short, the sort of Christians who give religion a good name.

For a long time, my question has been: why me? Out of six similarly nurtured children, why did one of us drop the baggage and amble away, while the rest continued in the faith? Contrary to some of the hardline atheist rhetoric, my siblings and a great many other religious people are not stupid, irrational, brainwashed, delusional, fanatical, or anti-science. And yet they believe.

Long discussions with one sister have been somewhat illuminating. Like me, she found the altar calls embarrassing and manipulative. Like me, she failed to feel the presence of God that the rest of the celebrants apparently felt. Like me, she recognized the unbelievable nature of much of what we were expected to believe. But she drew a different conclusion from mine: God was up there, all right, and her doubts were no more than a sign of her wickedness and lack of worth, not to mention her arrogance and pride. She kept on struggling well into her twenties, until she could convince herself that some things were beyond mortal comprehension, so it did not matter if they made no sense to her—as long as they made sense to God, the universe would unfold as it should. A critical difference between us was that she, by her own account, had the proverbial "God-shaped hole" in her life, whereas I did not. She felt she *needed* God to be there, or life would have no meaning. For my part, I had many questions about the universe, but the meaning of life was never one of them. So what about that God-shaped hole?

I had a kind of epiphany about it a few years ago. That sister and I had been having a long email debate about religion, frustrating because I could not understand how such a bright, thoughtful woman could believe such palpably unreasonable things. Inconceivable! Then she began annoying me with one of those canards that Christians often apply to atheists: that I was only an atheist because I was angry with God. With gritted teeth, I was wrestling with how to explain to her that I could not be angry at somebody else's imaginary friend. Then it hit me. She found my unbelief as unimaginable as I found her faith. No God? Inconceivable! Literally. I had always discounted the

"God-shaped hole" as being no more than an especially irritating bit of Christian rhetoric, never having had one myself, but I began to wonder whether it might be a genuine phenomenon—for *some people.*

Since then, I have been amassing material about the "god-shaped hole," which has led me through many byways and thought experiments into a nifty collection of charismatic cult messiahs, dictators, politicians, and gurus, many of them apparently psychopathic. The common thread is that people follow them eagerly, often at great personal cost, and often in great numbers, while others are immune to their charisma. The followers frequently explain the attraction in much the same words as my sister described her struggle to find God, in terms of filling a void and providing meaning to a life that otherwise seems empty and directionless. But it looks to me as if the void has been misnamed: it is an X-shaped hole, where X can stand for any ideology. Here are my modest proposals about this strange compulsion to believe, presented as rank speculation for the reader's amusement:

1) Most humans have a hardwired tendency to "follow the leader," reflecting the hardwired power hierarchies of our hominine ancestors and relatives. Think silverback gorillas, alpha chimps, and glorious leaders. The human variant of a chimp troop would look an awful lot like a cult. The hardwired imperative to imprint upon a charismatic leader would look an awful lot like a "god-shaped hole." As a pattern shared with our fellow great apes, this would be a primitive rather than a derived trait, predating the development of big brains. However, our big brains would allow bells and whistles like charisma and spirituality to be co-opted into

what is essentially a matter of simple dominance.

2) The tendency is heritable, but variable. A minority of humans may be born without the imperative to imprint on a charismatic leader— that is, without the "X-shaped hole." The trait has nothing to do with intelligence or empathy, but I suspect the lack of a capability for self-transcendence is involved.

3) Studies of the heritability of religiosity are looking in slightly the wrong place. Spirituality is a red herring. The "X-shaped hole" is fundamentally about power and hierarchy, not spirituality. It can be as easily filled by political as spiritual ideologies, or by sports affiliation, or brand loyalty, or even a particular flavor of atheism. Social identity theory and the concept of collective narcissism could go a long way in sorting out some knotty questions in evolutionary psychology.

My own journey was a simpler and easier one than most. I never felt an impulse to believe, or to call on supernatural help, even at the worst of times. I had no great struggle to lose God or to find an overarching meaning to my existence, no terrible guilt regarding my unbelief. In fact, the most pernicious lines I remember from all those altar calls were the ones that urged us to turn off our brains, ignore the contradictions and barbarities and talking snakes, forget about asking questions or even applying commonsense, and simply believe, with the faith of a little child. Well, not *this* little child. But I wonder how much of my immunity was simply the luck of the draw.

If, as I suspect, the X-shaped hole is bred into the greater part of humanity, then we are stuck with its ramifications. However, this would not necessarily be a reason to despair—it would depend on what our fellow humans chose to fill that void with. Not all the monsters are on the side of religion. I have seen some atheists with as gaping a void as any Bible-thumping fundamentalist, filled to the brim with malignant ideologies. I have seen some people of faith whose hopes for the world are essentially secular, and identical to my own. Personally speaking, in a world as perilously poised as this one, I would not reject potential allies solely on the grounds that they answered an altar call that I am unequipped to hear.

14

MIKE DOOLITTLE

A Goat Among Sheep

I WAS FOURTEEN, AND I WAS ANGRY AT MY FATHER. WE'D HAD what to this day remains the biggest fight we'd ever had. It's been so long that I can't even remember what the fight was about. Like many teenagers, I was prone to testing the patience of my parents, but this fight was unusually intemperate. I remember sitting on the couch, my father standing ominously over me as we shouted at each other. I tried to leave, but he pushed me down. Aside from a light spanking when I was very young, my father had never laid a hand on me. I was in disbelief. While today I have a wonderful relationship with both my parents, that moment stands out to me as a time of deep division between us. I don't remember the rest of that day, but I do remember that I spent the next couple of weeks grounded.

My brother, three years my senior, had been attending an evangelical youth church. He was clearly becoming more devout. He would occasionally provoke me into arguing with him, challenging my commitment as a "true" Christian. I generally found the arguments aggravating rather than enlightening and found his piety more smug than admirable, but when he offered to let me tag along to a service, I could hardly refuse. Still angry at my parents and eager to get out of the house, a church function presented the perfect opportunity to plead for an exception to my punishment—one which my religiously-inclined parents graciously granted me.

Most of my life, my family and I were "twice a year" Christians. When we moved from Milwaukee to Tulsa in the mid-80s, my parents, who had been regularly attending a Lutheran church in Milwaukee, had trouble finding a new church to call their own. Eventually, they just let it fall by the wayside. As I entered my adolescence, my mother expressed regret that she and my father had not been more diligent getting my brother and I involved in church. Upon moving to a new house in the early 90s, they joined a large Presbyterian church down the street and began attending regularly. I tagged along every once in a while, but didn't make it a regular habit. My parents had even tried to get me to go to Confirmation classes, of which I attended one before employing my full arsenal of teenage rebellion and absolutely refusing to return. Suffice to say I had some sentimental attachment to Christianity. I was certainly not devout, but I most definitely believed in God, in Jesus, in the truth of the Bible and viewed the church as an institution of moral guidance. So that night in 1994, when I tagged along with my brother to his youth service, the stage had been set for what was to come.

Upon arriving at the church—little more than an unassuming community center, nothing at all like the towering cathedrals to which I was accustomed—my brother and I participated in a small Bible study group. The group was called "Hellfighters." They even had their own t-shirts. After about an hour of Bible study, we congregated in the main room for the service. The sermon was delivered by a guy wearing a t-shirt and jeans—these were the early days of the "contemporary" service style that has become ubiquitous over the last couple of decades and, at the time, it was a refreshing departure from the stodgy, formal services I had always associated with church attendance. After the short sermon, we began "worship." Another t-shirt-and-jeans clad guy started playing atmospheric music on his keyboard. People closed their eyes, held their hands up, and prayed. Some mumbled, some prayed aloud. Some laughed or cried. Some babbled incoherently—something I'd soon learn was called "speaking in tongues."

The pastor did what's popularly known as an "altar call." He invited us to come down to the front to be prayed for and to be absolved of our wrongdoings in front of the congregation. Feeling guilt over my ornery and disrespectful behavior toward my father, I marched to the front without hesitation. The pastor put his hands on people, who suddenly fell to the floor. When he got to me, I followed suit; it was as though I lost control of my body and simply could not stand up. I lay there for a good twenty minutes, face down, praying and crying. From that moment on, nothing in my life was the same.

In the weeks following I learned about God. I learned about the Holy Spirit and how God works through people. He lets us communicate with him in, as the Bible says, the "tongues of men and angels." He gives us visions and prophecies. He even heals us from our afflictions. But most of all, through the sacrifice of his son Jesus, he absolves us of our sins—our transgressions against him. And those who fail to embrace that forgiveness are surely doomed, for as Jesus said, "I am the way, the truth and the life. No one comes to the Father except through me." I felt tremendous joy in that forgiveness, knowing that no matter how much I had messed up, God still loved me and had given his only son so that I could be saved. What a profound sacrifice.

I began attending church functions with such regularity that they became the central focus of my social life. At one point, I counted five of seven nights of the week as church functions. Monday was a discipleship with a church leader and some students. Wednesday was a youth service. Thursday was a large-group discipleship, where we met at someone's house for prayer and Bible study. Friday was the "Powerhouse," a sort of hangout for teens with live music and a small service. Saturday was the Hellfighters service, and Sunday was the main service of the parent church, a large evangelical church in South Tulsa.

During high school, I carried two Bibles with me. I felt disconnected from my friends there, whom I viewed as "worldly," succumbing to the pressures of sex and drugs while I strove for something more meaningful. A few friends and I held Bible studies together during our lunch breaks. I regularly shared my faith with my friends, trying to convince them that I had found a deeper, more enriching way of life than they were living. What could be more enriching than being connected to the Creator of all things? This undoubtedly annoyed some of my friends, but I didn't care. I knew that I was looking out for their better interest—their eternal salvation. I wanted them to confess their sins and ask God into their hearts as I had. Surely they would be far happier, as I certainly was. I even took to the streets with my fellow Hellfighters to hand out "tracts" to complete strangers and invite them to be saved. That was the amazing thing about being "saved" —you couldn't *help* but want to spread the good news—and spread the good news I did.

I was living the life of a full-blown evangelical Christian, and I was very happy. There were still problems in the church, such as social cliques and a sort of "piety competition" in which we were all eager to demonstrate the fervor of our faith by showing off our knowledge of scripture, subtly boasting of our time spent in prayer or how many people we had led to Christ, and showing ourselves swept up in the power of the Holy Spirit during services. I had come a long way, and it seemed like nothing could stop me. But doubt is a powerful thing.

Before I discuss my deconversion, I'd be remiss if I didn't address one common objection with respect to faith. Some people have assumed that it's simply not possible for a "true" Christian to deconvert, therefore, I must not have really been a Christian. Perhaps the churches I attended weren't properly Biblical, or perhaps I wasn't truly "saved," or perhaps I wasn't truly devout. I have heard them all. This is a sort of *No True Scotsman* fallacy. However, in my mind, my heart, my family, and my community, I was by all definitions a devout Christian. I believed I had felt God's presence, witnessed miracles, heard prophecies, heard God's instructive voice, and seen lives transformed by the power of the Holy Spirit. If I was not a "true" Christian, I can't imagine what it takes to satisfactorily fit that definition.

As the years went by during my evangelical fervor, certain conundrums popped into my head about the nature of my faith. No single question, in itself, would be nearly enough to cause my faith to waver. Like most, I simply attributed my cognitive dissonance[20] to my own ignorance. It would have been extremely presumptuous to assume I knew something my church leaders didn't. Surely, I reasoned, someone else could answer the questions that were bothering me—my neighbor in the seat next to me, my pastor, or maybe even my discipleship leader. And yet, unanswered questions accumulated and, over time, began to cause me great distress.

---

[20] The idea that if we have two dissonant, disharmonious, ideas or beliefs in our heads (the belief that prayer works, and evidence that it doesn't) then the brain feels it must harmonize them. As such, it invents ways to knit them together (you can't test God), or reject the lesser idea or belief (the test must have been badly conducted).

I also began to feel a bit detached from the behavior of my fellow congregants. One night, we were at a local mall to "witness." We'd been there for a while when we saw a young girl fall and hurt her ankle. The older kids with me decided it would be a perfect time to demonstrate the healing power of Christ. So they approached the panicking mother and began to preach to her, and asked if she wanted them to pray over her daughter. Unsurprisingly, she reacted angrily, shouting, "Do you MIND?!" A security guard asked us to leave, and afterwards we stood around in the parking lot talking about the incident. Everyone else seemed baffled that the mother didn't take the opportunity to be prayed for. I stood silently, questioning whether it had been the right move. Despite my faith, my gut told me it had been in poor taste. We had to *invite* people to our faith, not exploit their fears, pressure them or coerce them.

Around this time, I also grew tired of the social cliques and the "piety competition." When I joined the church, I was accepted unconditionally, and everyone was very friendly. But over time, it began to feel just like high school. There were crushes, relationships, cool kids and not-so-cool kids, and petty drama. It didn't seem like these kids were all that much better than my friends at school, who I had looked down upon as I had become more involved in the church. The displays of piety, then, started to seem more hypocritical than anything else. People waved their hands in the air and spoke in tongues, fell to the floor, and praised God. But in the big picture, they didn't behave all that differently from anyone else I knew, save perhaps for the stringent self-inflicted prohibitions against sex and drugs, which of course weren't always followed or, in the former case, led to hasty teenage marriages (most of those couples, to my knowledge, are now divorced).

This led me to feel increasingly detached from the church community. But I still had a strong personal faith and, despite the human failings of those around me, I believed that great opportunities for church leadership lay before me. I thought about going to seminary and becoming a pastor. I believed that the church leaders, both those close to me and those I saw on television, possessed a deeper relationship with God than I could ever hope to achieve, unless I began tackling those tough questions and really began to *understand* my faith. It was no longer enough for me to go through the motions. I wanted to really understand *why* I believed what I believed, to understand theology and philosophy, and to learn the Bible inside and out.

Some of the questions that spurred this thirst for knowledge were fairly simple:

> Why does God bless those of us who already have so much? What about the poor, the starving, the destitute in the world? Why would we thank God for the "bounty" of food on our table while millions of people—including helpless children like the ones we see on UNICEF ads—starve to death? What is God doing to help them? And, most importantly, why are they suffering so much in the first place?

> Why are there so many religions? If God loves everyone equally, why would he "choose" the tribes of Israel to reveal the one true faith, while essentially leaving the rest of the world to its own devices—especially when the stakes are so high? Will those people go to hell just because they haven't heard of Jesus? And even if they've met missionaries, how could we expect someone to just abandon the beliefs they were raised with? If someone refuses, do they go to hell just for being wrong?

I feel that it's important to emphasize that none of these questions were catalysts for my deconversion, at least not directly. They simply spurred inquiry. Being somewhat detached from my church community, I was no longer content to ignore my cognitive dissonance and continue assuming that someone smarter than me probably has the answer. It was time I got some answers for myself. If I didn't, so I reasoned, I could never be the man of God I wanted to be.

Thus began a long inquiry into theology, philosophy, history, and comparative religion. I had been warned not to read books by non-Christians; they were "of the devil" and would lead me away from God. But I reasoned that if Christianity were the rock I believed it to be, I had nothing to fear. I would study Christianity *and* I would study other religions, even objections against religion, entirely; then, I could see the truth of Christianity for myself instead of taking other people's word for it.

I was a bit surprised, then, to find that virtually all the other major religions shared the basic humanitarian values of my own. Religions had different ideas about what God is, how we interact with God, what happens to us when we die, and what types of rituals we should perform. But the basic values of kindness, compassion, and selflessness weren't unique to my religion—nor was the reverence for God any less sincere. As I read philosophy of Shintoism, for example, I was struck by how much I had in common with its followers, and how strongly their values echoed my own. This seemed at odds with the idea I had always held—that all these other religions were, if not abjectly evil, certainly deficient in some way. More conservative members of my church said other religions, often even mainstream Christian denominations, were attempts by the devil to lead people away from the true faith. More liberal believers didn't necessarily think other religions were bad, but they certainly thought that Christianity was the "most right" path to God—that, ultimately, believers from all faiths would answer to and be judged by the god of Christianity.

Continuing on with my inquiry, I studied the writings of C.S. Lewis and of modern theologians like R.C. Sproul. I read books by Rabbi Harold Kushner, whose liberal theology seemed remarkably sensible. But most of all, I studied the Bible. I read the Old Testament in great detail, and in studying the New Testament I paid special attention to the book of Hebrews, since it essentially explains how Christianity works—why Jesus died and was resurrected, and how it's connected to the Mosaic covenant of the Old Testament. I even struck up regular conversations with a Baptist minister, a chaplain who had been a co-worker with my mother, about biblical matters.

Unfortunately, all this study did little to ease my concerns. In fact, it just made things worse. It seemed like for every answer that I heard or every rationalization I could conjure up, more questions just piled on. But there was something more insidious that bothered me greatly. While many theologians seemed to be able to conjure up rationalizations for some of the tougher questions—like why a God who loves all his creation equally would choose to reveal his one true religion only to a small culture in the Bronze Age Middle East—no one seemed to have any way of objectively knowing whether their rationalizations were correct. It seemed like, with enough creativity, just about any conundrum could be conveniently resolved. Not only did the answers usually just raise more questions, but I also began to realize that *sounding plausible* and *being true* are not the same thing. Just because an explanation appears to make sense doesn't mean it's actually correct. How do we *know* our beliefs are true?

It wasn't enough for me just to defer to "a matter of faith." In my conversations with the Baptist minister, I queried as to why God would have allowed so many false religions to flourish, instead of telling *everyone* the truth at the outset. He simply responded that our faith could be "true for us," that there could be plenty of other ways to connect with God. This rang hollow to me. The claims in the Bible—like "I am the way, the truth and the life"—are either true or not. What sense does it make to say that something can be true for me, but not true for anyone else? The events in the Bible either happened as described, or they did not. We may be entitled to our own opinions, but we're not entitled to our own facts. There is simply no getting around the fact that all the world's religions make conflicting claims about God. They can all be wrong, but they certainly cannot all be right. The question is, how can we sort through this mess?

This confusing time served as a primer for what I now consider to be very important ideas about *epistemology*. In philosophy, epistemology deals with what we are capable of knowing—how do we really know what we claim to know? At this point, the importance of evidence was becoming relevant to me. "Faith" was not good enough, because as long as we defer to something "as a matter of faith," there's nothing to stop us from making up and subsequently believing whatever we want. If we take that path, how could we ever distinguish between what is really true and what we merely *wish* to be true?

These thoughts culminated with my deconversion from Christianity at the age of nineteen. It wasn't, as many often assume it was, a sudden rebellion against my faith. Rather, it was a gradual, heartbreaking process of disillusionment. Things which had seemed so certain to me for years now seemed filled with affronts to logic so vast that they couldn't be ignored. Christianity had not only been central to my social and familial life, but it was an important part of my personal identity. It had given my life a sense of purpose, a sense of strength when I was down, and a sense that I belonged to something greater than myself.

Because of these deep emotional attachments, deconversion was extremely difficult. For someone who has spent their entire life as a believer, it's not a particularly desirable process. I didn't want to feel alienated from my friends and family, or to feel like all the beliefs to which I'd fervently committed myself had been lies. Why would anyone want such a thing? I spent my last several months as a Christian studying incessantly, desperately trying to make sense of beliefs that now seemed as foreign and absurd to me as other religions had seemed when I was a fully committed Christian. But after a time, I had to face the truth: I could no longer believe what I had believed, and call myself a Christian. How would I go on? What would I believe? I didn't know. This was many years before the modern atheist community, before Richard Dawkins wrote *The God Delusion* and the atheist blogosphere was alive and vibrant. I felt like an outsider, irreparably separated from my friends and family in an important way. I had no one to turn to, and no one I could even talk with about my loss of faith. As a Christian, I had often been told that there is nothing wrong with doubt. But Christians only seem to believe that doubt is acceptable when it is transient—an obstacle to be overcome as faith is renewed and strengthened. When doubt leads you from the flock, it's not looked upon so forgivingly.

I had not completely given up my faith, however. I still believed in some kind of vague conception of God; I believed that there was a God who made us, who was responsible for the good in us, who created the universe and acted as a moral compass within us. I called myself a "theistic agnostic." For the next several years I attended college and, for the most part, put my theology on the backburner. I found that life outside the church wasn't so bad after all, and in college I made many friends who shared my agnosticism. But in time, even my vaguely defined theism fell apart after I subjected it to the same kind of scrutiny to which I had subjected my Christian beliefs many years before. And by the age of twenty-eight, after having read Stephen Hawking's *A Brief History of Time*, I had become a full-fledged atheist. I've often struggled to give a concise explanation of why I am an atheist, but I think I've come close: to me, everything about the world simply makes much more sense with God out of the picture. The indiscriminate suffering in nature, our insignificance in a vast and hostile universe, the brutality of evolution, the great questions of scientific inquiry— at no point does "God" even enter the equation as a necessary or valid explanatory mechanism. Even if God does exist, he's utterly irrelevant to our understanding of the world. And, as I've become fond of saying, the only thing worse than a God who does not exist is one who might as well not exist.

15

BRUCE GERENCSER

Recounting Nearly Three Decades of Service to the Church

Dear Lord Jesus,

I know I am a sinner. I know you died on the cross for my sins. Please forgive me of my sin and come into my heart and save me. In Jesus' name, Amen.

And so it began.

IN 1962 MY FATHER MOVED US FROM BRYAN, OHIO TO SAN Diego, California. My father grew up on a hundred-acre farm and was the youngest of six children. Dirt poor, he was always looking to strike it rich, which meant, in his mind, California was the place to be if one wanted to make their mark in life. When my father died decades later, he was still looking for the Mother Lode.

As an infant, my parents had me baptized at the Episcopal Church in Bryan, Ohio. My mother had a Lutheran background.

I do not know what my father's religious background was. When we moved to San Diego, our family began attending Scott Memorial Baptist Church.

My parents were actively involved in right-wing politics in the 1960s as well as being members of the John Birch Society. My mother actively worked in Barry Goldwater's 1964 presidential campaign. Their right-wing political ideology fit well with their right-wing religious ideology. In the summer of 1970 our family moved from Deshler, Ohio to Findlay, Ohio. Here, my father sold vacuum cleaners for Kirby while my mother continued to be deeply involved in right-wing politics. She worked as a volunteer for George Wallace. Wallace ran as a Democratic Party candidate for President in 1972.

In the spring of seventy-two, my parents divorced. A short time later, my mother married her first cousin, a recent parolee from prison, and my father married a nineteen-year-old girl with a newborn child. My sister and I lived with my father, whereas my brother moved in with my mother.

We attended Church every time the doors were open. I mean EVERY time. Our family attended upwards of two hundred plus services a year (Sunday school, Sunday Mornings, Sunday nights, Wednesdays, youth meetings, youth rallies, revivals, Bible conferences, and mission conferences).

My father went into business with a man in the Church and they started a hobby store called *G and B Trains*. The business folded a few years later when my father and his partner got into a dispute over money.

At fifteen years old, I made a public profession of faith in Jesus Christ. At an Al Lacy revival meeting, I went forward during the invitation and prayed the sinner's prayer. I was baptized by immersion the following Sunday. Several weeks later, I informed the Church that I felt I was being called to preach. In the early months of 1973, my father suddenly announced we were moving to Tucson, Arizona. We immediately packed up, had an auction, and moved. Later on I found out that creditors were after my father. Another few days and we wouldn't have had a car to make the trip in. They eventually tracked my father down and repossessed the car.

Shortly thereafter, in the summer of 1973, Bruce Turner, the youth pastor at Trinity Baptist Church, became like a surrogate father to me. I have no doubt that my life would not have turned out as well as it did if it had not been for him. While I am quite certain Bruce is not at all pleased with where I am in my life today, I still owe him a great deal of gratitude for all that he did for me. The years I attended Trinity Baptist Church in Findlay Ohio were instrumental in defining who I would become as an adult, and later as a Baptist pastor.

As with most Independent Baptist Churches, Trinity had a large, thriving Youth Group. The Church was large enough that the Junior High and High School students each had their own group. On Sunday morning Bruce Turner taught the Senior High Sunday School class. Bruce taught typical Independent Baptist stuff: Get saved, and don't do … so on and so forth.

After Sunday night service, the Senior High students met for youth group. This was the place where it all happened. The camaraderie. The hook-ups. The food, fun, and fellowship. We would often go out after youth group and hang out at one of the local fast food restaurants. I have nothing but fond memories of youth group. I dated a lot. I broke up a lot. I had lots of friends. The youth group was the social hub of my life. Everything revolved around the youth group.

One summer the Church held what they called a Super Summer Bible Rally. An older couple and their sixteen-year-old daughter, named Charlotte, came to the Church and held the Bible Rally. Each night, five hundred children would pack the auditorium to be taught "the Gospel."

Needless to say, I was smitten with Charlotte. She was my first love. We had a whirlwind five-day romance and then carried on a long-distance romance after that. She lived in Troy, Ohio, which was over ninety miles south of Findlay. We wrote letters and talked on the phone. It was "true love."

Later in the year the church Charlotte attended was showing the film "A Thief in the Night". I talked Bruce Turner into taking the youth group to the Troy Baptist Temple to see the film. Of course what I really wanted was to see Charlotte.

After the film was over, we headed back out to the Church bus. It was time for Charlotte and I to say goodbye. Public displays of affection were considered a no-no. Bruce Turner told me, "I am going to turn my back for a moment. You say goodbye." He turned his back, we kissed, and that was the last time we would see each other. A few months later our long-distance romance ended when we found real, close-to-home flesh and blood people to love. For me, that's what made youth group so great, an endless pool of girls.

Underneath the surface of the happy-go-lucky youth group were kids with a lot of personal troubles. In the 1970's there was a lot of premarital sex going on. Alcohol and drug use was common. Girls got pregnant. In spite of all the moralistic preaching and rules, kids did what kids have always done. Experiment. Test boundaries. Make bad decisions; sometimes making decisions that scarred them for the rest of their lives.

The Church did little to help those who fell into "sin". Get saved, get right. That's how most everything was handled. Kids with lives spiraling out of control often spiraled right out of the church and out of the youth group. It wasn't for them.

On the other hand, I bought what Trinity was selling. I ate the whole enchilada. I am not a person that does anything halfway. If I am going to embrace a belief system, a way of life, then I am going to go all the way.

I didn't smoke, drink, cuss, or chew tobacco. I didn't go to movies. I didn't wear my hair long. I didn't listen to rock music. I was a virgin up until my wedding day. I carried my Bible to school every day. I handed out tracts in school. I wrote English papers about the Baptist Church. I challenged my biology teacher on his teaching of evolution.

I was a good Baptist boy. I considered it a test of my "virtue," of my Christian character, to withstand my friends' sinful behaviors—such as smoking and going to the movies. In addition to all this, I saw that the very same people who told us to live a certain way were having a hard time doing it themselves. Adultery was a big problem in the Church. Several Church staff members got caught up in adulterous affairs and had to resign from the Church. One of the things that troubled me the most, however, was the level of child abuse that regularly went on.

Up to now the things I was taught by the preachers were innocuous at best. However, what follows was not so harmless. What follows harmed me greatly, and I deal with the consequences of it to this day. I have spent hours in counseling trying to overcome the damage done to me by the teachings I received.

The preachers taught me a rule-based Christianity. This is commonly called legalism. While the preachers taught salvation by grace, what I understood from their preaching was that in order to be a real Christian you had to follow the rules. The preachers were dispensationalists. They taught we were no longer under the law, we were under grace. Instead of adopting the law of the Bible the preachers frequently invented their own. They would claim their laws (also called standards) were from the Bible but it seemed every preacher had a different set of rules and laws.

It seemed there was a rule for everything. Dress code. Hair code. Music code. Dating code. Family code. Everything was judged according to the rules, the standards of the Church.

I wasn't allowed to go to dances, square dance in gym class, listen to secular music, have long hair, wear worldly clothing, date non-Baptist girls, or sing secular songs in choir. The world was evil, the flesh was evil. Only in the teachings of the Bible, only in Jesus could a person find meaning, purpose, and direction in life.

All of these experiences shaped my view of the world.

A week before the end of my junior year of school, I left Findlay and moved back home with my Mom. My Mom, long plagued with mental problems, needed me to return home. It was very hard for me to leave Findlay and Trinity Baptist Church, but my Mom and siblings desperately needed me. Sadly enough, a few months later, my mother ended up in the state mental hospital in Toledo for psychiatric care.

When I went to enroll at Bryan High School for my senior year, I was informed that Findlay High School denied me credit for my entire junior year. I had missed taking my finals and I would have to retake eleventh grade all over again. Instead of fighting over my credits I dropped out of school (thirty years later I would go on to take the GED exam. I am now a high school graduate).

In 1976, I decided it was time to act on my call to the ministry by enrolling in a Bible college. Originally I planned to attend Briarcrest Bible College in Caronport, Saskatchewan, Canada. But I could not meet the financial requirements for crossing the border so I looked for a college in the U.S.

Grandpa and Grandma Tieken lived in Waterford, Michigan. Grandpa operated an aircraft engine repair shop at the Pontiac Airport. Grandpa and Grandma suggested that I come and visit the Midwestern Baptist College. So, in the spring of 1976, I made a trip to Pontiac, Michigan to check out Midwestern Baptist College. I was impressed so I submitted an application for enrollment and I was accepted as a new student.

Since I was a high school dropout, Midwestern accepted me as a provisional student. If I completed one year of college successfully, they would then grant me regular student status.

At Midwestern, a four-year unaccredited, Premillennial Baptist College, the primary purpose was to train preachers. Women who attended Midwestern were primarily there to look for a husband (aka a "Mrs. Degree"). The theology and methodology that I would use in the ministry over the next twenty-five years was cultivated during my time at Midwestern.

As an unaccredited college, the credits I earned at Midwestern were basically worthless, unless I wanted to transfer to another Bible College. Many young people go off to Bible Colleges every year with grand plans of getting a Christian college education. Four years later they get a degree. Ten years later they find out their degree is worthless.

As an unaccredited college, Midwestern offered no student aid. Most every student that attended Midwestern had to work a part-time or full-time job. Many young men found jobs at local auto manufacturing plants. The auto plants paid *great* wages. In fact the wages were so good that many young men, four years later, upon graduating from Midwestern, would not leave the good wages at the auto plant for the poor wages of the pastorate. They were the smart ones.

I often tell people that I made the Dean's list quite often at Midwestern. What I don't tell them is that it was the Dean's disciplinary list that I so frequently made!

One time I was written up for borrowing. Yes, *borrowing*. Midwestern had a rule against borrowing. One winter day I borrowed my fiancé's winter parka. It was a unisex parka. Evidently my roommate saw me borrow the parka and he wrote me up. I had to appear before the disciplinary committee to answer for the sin of borrowing. I tried quoting the Bible in my defense. Matthew 5:42 says, "Give to him that asketh thee, and from him that would borrow of thee turn not thou away."

Of course, the committee was not interested in what the Bible had to say. All that mattered is that I'd broken the rules.

This wasn't the first time I'd be in trouble with the disciplinary committee either. Another time I was written up for breaking the 'six-inch rule'. The six-inch rule was a rule meant to keep unmarried men and women from getting too close to each other (physically). Six inches is about the width of a songbook or a Bible and unmarried students of the opposite sex were not allowed to be closer than a songbook or a Bible from each other.

As a student on the college basketball team, my trouble all began when, during practice, I severely dislocated my finger. I was rushed to the emergency room and the doctor was able to fix the dislocation.

At Midwestern, however, every male student was required to dress like a gentlemen and we were to wear neckties whenever attending class. Due to my basketball injury, I found it very difficult to tie a tie with one hand, so one day I asked my fiancé to tie my tie for me. In doing so we broke the six-inch rule. Someone anonymously turned us in for breaking the six-inch rule and we had to appear before the disciplinary committee to answer the charges against us.

We each received twenty-five demerits and were warned that if we broke the six-inch rule again we would be expelled from school.

Most students tried to adhere to the rules for a while. Some, like my fiancé and I, kept the six-inch rule religiously until we went home for our first Christmas break. While home on Christmas break we were allowed to act like normal young couples who were in love. We held hands, kissed, necked, and pretty much acted like any other infatuated couples.

Once the genie was out of the bottle though, it was impossible to put her back in. When we returned to Midwestern we realized we could not continue to keep the ridiculous six-inch rule. So for the next eighteen months we sought out couples to double date with that shared the same view of the six-inch rule as we did. As you can imagine, we had to be very careful. Choose the wrong couple to double date with and you might end up getting expelled from school.

Restrictive rules, like the six-inch rule, put the dormitory students in a position where they had to lie and cheat just to be able to behave like other ordinary people.

We were children of the 70's. Rock'n'roll, free love, muskrat love, and political and social upheaval. But the key thing that differentiated us from our counterparts in the outside world was that we all came from independent Baptist churches that preached against most everything that was going on in America at the time.

My wife and I were both virgins when we married. I've often said that if we had waited much longer I doubt we would have lasted. The sexual pressure placed on us by the college rules, and our independent Baptist upbringing, was insufferable. Even the natural release of masturbation was considered a sin. Needless to say, most men in the dormitory "whacked off." One can't help but wonder what took place on the women's floor of the dormitory.

At Midwestern we were taught to be sexually dysfunctional, so it should come as no surprise that many of the students had problems after they married. The only training and teaching on sexual matters we received came from the pulpit and from a well-marked, dog-eared copy of the Christian sex classic, *The Act of Marriage*. It took my wife and I many years to break free from the sexual dysfunction that we were taught. Both of us would say that the sexual relationship we have today without God (i.e., without that bizarre threesome) is far healthier and a thousand times better.

In retrospect, I can now see how oppressive the rules were, but like the good Baptist boy that I was, I adapted to the rules and learned to work around the rules that I couldn't manage.

I have come to see that Midwestern did not exist for the purpose of giving me an education. It's no secret that the academics at Midwestern were very substandard, as it existed for the purpose of indoctrinating me in the Fundamentalist, Independent Baptist faith, not educating me about the world with real world knowledge.

Difference and dissent were quashed. Curiosity about the world was shot down. Troublemakers were thrown out. Academic freedom did not exist. Either a teacher taught the party line or they were fired.

Learning to evangelize was a key part of the training I received at Midwestern Baptist College. The Bible says that, "he who winneth souls is wise" (Proverbs 11:30). Soul-winning was preached on a regular basis.

A few years into the ministry, I realized that the education I received at Midwestern was academically inferior to other, accredited, universities. As such, I began to buy books and started the long, arduous task of learning the Bible. Over the years I ended up with a library of over thousand theological books. More than once someone would come into my study, and upon seeing the books, ask me if I actually read all of them. The answer was a resounding, "Yes." What learning I now possess I do not owe to Midwestern.

For the first ten years of my time in the ministry, I practiced and followed the soul-winning techniques that I was taught at Midwestern Baptist College. The results were quite impressive.

Large numbers of people attended the churches I pastored. Every week someone new was professing faith in Christ. Yet, it seemed we turned a lot of people over. They would get saved, baptized, and attend church for a while, but by and large, in a short time they were no longer attending the church.

Over time I learned that this was not a good way, nor a mature way, to build a church.

In July of 1978 I married Polly. Shortly after, Polly and I set up house in an upstairs apartment in Pontiac. We both worked and attended College full-time. Six weeks after we were married we found out Polly was pregnant. Six months later, having lost my job, we withdrew from Midwestern and moved to the NW Ohio community of Bryan.

When we withdrew from Midwestern, teachers and friends alike told us that we were disobeying God and that we would never do anything for God with our lives. We were quitters and if there is one thing we learned from virtually every chapel speaker is that God doesn't accept quitters. We made up our mind that we were going to be the exception and for the next twenty-five years we were anything but quitters.

In late 1981, I joined with my father-in-law to plant a new church in Buckeye Lake, Ohio. I served as assistant pastor of Emmanuel Baptist Church until the spring of 1983. In April of 1983 I was ordained by the Church and I left a few months later to start a new Independent Baptist Church in Somerset, Ohio.

I pastored the Somerset Baptist Church from 1983 to 1994. During my time in Somerset, the church grew numerically and over the course of nearly twelve years, six hundred people made public professions of faith.

In the spring of 1994 I left Somerset Baptist Church to become the co-pastor of Community Baptist Church in Elmendorf, Texas. During my time at Community I helped to establish the church's evangelistic outreach and started two new

Baptist churches in nearby communities. I also helped the church set up a Christian school.

Due to a personal conflict with my co-pastor I resigned as pastor of Community and moved back to Ohio. The fallout of this move was swift and severe. The church excommunicated me and to this day they consider me an unsaved publican and heathen (cf. Matthew 18:17). In a blink of the eye my good name and reputation were dragged through the mud. For the first time in my life I felt abused and vulnerable. For the first time in my life I wondered, "Is this how Christianity is supposed to be?"

For the next eight years I would pastor two more churches in Ohio. During this time my theology began to shift from fundamentalist Calvinism to a kinder, gentler form of Christianity. When I left Our Father's House in West Unity, Ohio in 2002, I left as a progressive Christian, still committed to Christian orthodoxy but no longer a card-carrying member of the religious-right.

In 2003, I moved to Clare, Michigan to pastor a small Southern Baptist church. This move was a mistake on my part. By this time, I was tired of the constant stress of the ministry. I was tired of all the in-fighting and doctrinal wrangling. I told the church I was not a fighter and that if there was any fighting I wouldn't be their pastor. Evidently they didn't believe me because after seven months fighting broke out and, true to my word, I left the church.

As I look back on it now I see that my relationship with the Christian church was much like having a mistress. With God in my heart, and the Bible in my hands, I was willing to sacrifice my family, health, and financial well-being for my mistress. She took all that I gave her and always demanded more.

It was at this juncture in my life that I first began to question my Christian faith. For almost fifty years I didn't have a single doubt. I was a true-blue believer. I believed every jot and tittle of the Bible. It was the inerrant, inspired, and infallible Word of God. By faith, I believed Jesus was my Lord and Savior and I knew that whatever happened in my life was for my good. No matter how hard life was, no matter how difficult the ministry was, I had to remain faithful. After all, the Bible said, "he that endureth to the end shall be saved." (Matthew 24:13)

This kind of thinking no longer was enough for me. I had a lifetime of church experience. I had seen the monster from the inside. I knew all its ugly secrets. I had experienced years of conflict with disgruntled church members and I-am-more-right-than-you fellow pastors. Years of constant conflict took their toll mentally, emotionally, and physically. Ultimately I decided that I could no longer be a pastor.

For about four years my wife and I embarked on a journey to find a find a Christian church that took seriously the Bible and the teachings of Jesus. Finally, we came to the conclusion that regardless of the name on the door every church was pretty much the same and that, for the most part, no church took the Bible and the teachings of Christ seriously. We realized American Christianity had become a cultural name-only religion, a religion of political power, empty of any real spiritual power.

In November of 2008, my wife and I attended church for the last time. I was still a Christian then, believing the orthodox teachings of the church, but I no longer believed the American Christian church was relevant and I thought the church was out-of-touch with needs of the average person.

My politics had changed dramatically over the course of my adult life. When my wife and I married in 1978, I was a card-carrying member of the Republican Party—God's Only Party™. I was a homophobic, anti-abortionist with a racist hangover from being raised in a John Birch Society-inclined family. By the time I left the Christian church in 2008, my political beliefs had dramatically shifted leftward.

I left the Republican Party and became a registered Democrat. I voted for Barack Obama in 2008, the first Democrat I had voted for since Jimmy Carter in 1976, and I had become a pro-choice, pro- marriage equality, anti-death penalty, pacifistic socialist.

I am often asked, "When was the moment that I knew I no longer believed in God?" I wish it was as simple as stating a date, time, and place. But like most important things in life, it is just not that easy.

My turn away from God began, ever so slowly, in my disaffection with the Christian church and my move towards liberal political views. I began to evaluate how I had spent my life and the things I said I believed. I always prided myself in being willing to believe the truth wherever I found it. Little did I know my commitment to truth would lead me out of the truth I had held dear for almost five decades.

Instrumental in my defection from the Christian faith was my seeking out a counselor to talk to. This was a hard decision for me to make. By my saying I need to talk to someone, I was saying that I need help, that I didn't have all the answers.

Finding someone to talk to was not easy either. First, I lived in a small, close-knit rural area. Everyone knows your business. I feared being found-out by a Christian friend, family member, or former parishioner. Most of the counselors in my community were Christian "the Bible has all the answers" type counselors. Fortunately, I stumbled upon a counselor who was a liberal Episcopalian, a man who had as many questions as I did. Over time, he helped me to unpeel the onion of my life. He helped me to take a hard look at my life and most of all he helped me embrace who I really was.

Over the course of many years in the ministry I had been swallowed up by the church and the ministry. I lived according to the JOY acronym, Jesus First, Others Second, Yourself Last.

By living my life this way, I lost all connection with who I really was. I buried my emotions, but with the help of my counselor, I started reconnecting with the real Bruce Gerencser. I learned it was OK to have emotions and that being angry was a normal part of the human experience.

And boy was I angry. I was angry over a wasted life. I was angry over what I had done to my wife and children. I was angry over the financial hole that I put us in. I was angry over the physical problems that I now had. I was just plain angry over most everything.

At this juncture in my life I met a man who was a former Charismatic pastor. He too had been in the ministry for twenty plus years. Like me, he had been misused and abused. Like meeting my counselor, he became an important part of eventual defection from Christianity.

We'd get together fairly often to talk about the Bible, the ministry, politics, and the like. We allowed each other to shout, complain, and bitch at will. Although my friend Jim was an agnostic, I was not, but I knew I was headed in that direction. Through counseling and my time with Jim, I was starting to have a lot of questions about Christianity itself.

I did what I always did when I had questions: I read books, websites, and magazines. I began to research outside the safe confines of Christian orthodoxy. I read books written by authors like Bart Ehrman, Robert M Price, Richard Wright, Richard Dawkins and the late Christopher Hitchens.

Doctrine by doctrine, I began to reevaluate what I believed. The more I read and studied, the more questions I had. Was the Bible inspired by God? Was the Bible without error? My fall from the grace hinged on these two issues.

Over the course of my gradual deconversion, I've come to the conclusion that the Bible is not inspired by God and that it is an errant text. At best, the Bible is a spiritual guide and a book of mythical stories written by men thousands of years ago. It is not a book that is overly relevant to the world that we live in today.

There is wisdom to be gained from reading the Bible, sure, but it isn't exactly a book anyone can govern their life by. Bible stories make for great reading, but that's about it. They offer very little in the way of real practical wisdom for moderns in the 21st-century.

Once the Bible lost its authority over me the Christian house quickly came tumbling down. I came to see that the Christian church's attempt to prop up the Bible was a house of cards. Instead of confronting the fallibility of the text and the many errors within it, the Christian church has instead developed convoluted and often humorous explanations for the perceived errors and contradictions contained in the Bible.

The Biblical historian and theologian Robert M. Price said that once a person stops believing the Bible is the Word of God they are on a slippery slope where there is no stopping place. That's where I found myself. For a time I was content to call myself a progressive, liberal Christian. As I continued to slide down the slippery slope, I thought that maybe Universalism was the answer. And quite frankly, if I was going to have any religion at all it would be Universalism. But, at the end of the day, Universalism did not satisfy me and I came to a place where it was time to stop calling myself a Christian.

I believe the word Christian means something. In fact I believe it means something more than a lot of Christians seem to think. To be a Christian means you believe the Bible to be the word of God. To be a Christian means you embrace the beliefs and teachings of the Christian faith. Since I do not believe the Bible to be the Word of God, and I no longer embrace the beliefs and teachings of the Christian faith, I am no longer a Christian.

My full deconversion came at the moment where I finally admitted to myself that I no longer believed the Bible to be the word of God. As I have often said, it really is all about the Bible.

For two or so years after my loss of faith, I self-identified as an agnostic. Even today, when it comes to the ultimate "Does God exist?" question, I am agnostic. I am, based on the evidence at hand, quite certain than none of humankind's gods are at all real. Might there yet be a god that reveals itself to us? Sure, that's possible, and for this reason I am an agnostic. However, I seriously doubt any god exists, so I live my day-to-day life as if god does not exist. In 2010 I decided to publicly declare that I was an atheist.

Some of you might ask how it is possible that my Christian life so quickly unraveled. Yet, in no time at all, it unraveled none-the-less. Some might even suggest that I had some character or mental flaw that caused my deconversion. My counselor told me it is quite rare for a man of my training and experience to walk away from it all, especially at the ripe ole age of fifty. All I know is that I once was saved and now I am not. I was once a follower of Jesus and now I am not.

When I was five years old, my Christian, right-wing, mother, taught me to read. She taught me to be passionate about what I believed. She instilled in me a love for truth. I want to think she would understand why her pastor son, the son whom she was always so proud of, has since become an atheist. While she might not understand how I came to such a conclusion, she would know that I had done my homework and that I had embraced the hard-won truth.

16

BETH ANN ERICKSON

Six Dangerous Words

I BLAME THE QUESTIONS. THOSE F—ING QUESTIONS. THE G-D questions.

I should apologize. Utilizing curse words before I even begin my story shows a marked lack of vocabulary. But sometimes swearing is the best way to convey a message and this is most certainly one of those times.

If it weren't for questions, I'd be happily living my quiet Christian life, in my little Christian community, in a beautiful red county in the heart of a blue state. But then those f—ing questions bubbled. The questions that mutilated my happy life, the questions the divided me from my family, the questions that drove a stake through my business. Questions. *Gah.*

The madness began back in elementary school.

Why, oh why did I go to school that fateful day, the day that would ignite a process that would forever plague my existence?

It was sixth grade, Whittier Elementary, Kandiyohi, Minnesota. A harried reporter visited our classroom and presented me with the key that would screw up my happy little world.

"They're the five Ws and H," she announced. "Apply them to any story and you've got something solid to publish. Apply them to any situation and you can better separate the wheat from the chaff."

I'd never heard of such magic. Answer five tiny questions and you could not only examine situations, but you could build nearly any fact-based article. It felt like pure wizardry. The magic words were:

Who, what, when, where, why, how.

It couldn't be that simple. How can six tiny words cut through bullshit like a laser, plus help create papers that would maintain my 4.0? I had to give it a whirl.

I took to that formula like a fish to water, applying it to everything I wrote, eventually using it to sort my complicated pre-teen life. It worked wonders as my English grades skyrocketed, I was invited to write for my little school's newspaper, and my reputation as a writer rose.

But my new skills didn't bode well in one area of my life: religion. As my confidence soared as an ace reporter, I evolved into the terror of Sunday school teachers. In discussing a story like Noah and the Great Flood (Genesis 6–9) the conversation generally went something like this:

Who: So, we've got Noah, his family, a loving deity, lucky animals, evil people, and unlucky animals.

What: A global flood that would wipe out everything on earth except for the lucky creatures (including humans) on the ark. I was supposed to be comforted because God used a rainbow to promise that he would never destroy the earth with water again because the next time he destroyed the planet, he'd use fire.

When: Sometime after the creation, which supposedly happened around 10k years ago. This means that sometime during the Neolithic age, we had a global flood. There should be some archaeological evidence of that, right?

Where: While Noah lived somewhere in the middle-east, the flood was global. Don't try to call it a regional event, you'll get corrected faster than you can say, "Yeah, but..."

Why: Because God's creation, evidently the humans, were such an abomination and an affront to God that humanity was unredeemable. Because of this horrific evil in the world, God felt the need to destroy everything except Noah, his family, two of every creature, for various reasons.

How: Lots of rain. Water blew up from the ground, from what I hear. The animals came to Noah (Genesis 6:20) so evidently penguins hobbled over from Antarctica, kangaroos jumped over large bodies of water from Australia. Deer from America evidently could could make the Atlantic trek, like endurance swimmers. Of course, insects just buzzed on in. I suppose they didn't bunk near the snakes and other insect-eaters, though. As for the dinosaurs, they must have missed the boat.

Of course, Noah had a lot of building to do. Also a whole lot of people drowned along with every animal not lucky enough to get on board.

Finally, I assume Noah's family had a fair bit of clean up after the water evaporated. Imagine all the bloated, dead bodies. The stench must have been horrific. Of course, scientifically, this global flood has not been verified.

"Sooooo," I'd ask, "if everyone during Noah's day was evil, does that mean that the little kids were evil as well? How about the fetuses? What about the animals, especially the herbivores? What did they do wrong? And the plants, were they evil too?"

The Sunday school teachers weren't impressed with my questions. But I wasn't deterred, assuming everyone in each Bible class was as quizzical and accuracy driven as I was. After all, I had my reporter questions and had a burning desire to get to the root of the story. But my inquisitiveness was just the beginning of my church troubles.

Living in small town Minnesota had many perks. I recall endless summer nights running through town barefoot, weaving between houses, hiding in corn fields. The downside is that while my small town friendships flourished, I was viewed as an outsider in church.

All my church classmates lived in the larger town where the building was located. They went to school together, they were part of the same sports teams, plus they were nearly all male. When this small town female filled with questions joined ranks, they were less than impressed. The fact that females are commanded to keep their mouths shut while in the house of the Lord, didn't help matters.

So, week after week, day after day, my family hauled me to church where I sat voicing my questions, never receiving adequate answers, supremely uncomfortable under the glaring glaze of my classmates, wishing I were any place but at church.

As a family, we attended Sunday school, main church services (eating up the entire Sunday morning and much of the dinner hour). Church services on Sunday evenings often consisted of Vesper services. Morning Tuesday school was always interesting. We were back on Wednesday morning for Wednesday School.

Sometimes we were lucky and got to go on a Lock-In overnight event on Friday/Saturday. I attended week long church camps each summer as well as weekly Bible studies. Through it all, those questions plagued me and I struggled to keep believing, often turning off my mind to simply fit in. Church was my life, it was all I knew... until I met *him*.

"Don't date him. He's trouble."

I met him just prior to my sister's wedding. Untamed, with a disarming demeanor, he fascinated me. Even more interesting, I was pretty sure he wasn't saved. He drank alcohol, he didn't go to church, he was everything I could fix. I fantasized bringing him to the Lord, turning his life around, and for years he could present an incredible testimony meriting me (and the Lord) for his magnificent conversion. After an obscene amount of teen-aged flirting, he finally asked me out.

Within minutes I was in his car and we were chatting up a storm. We discussed my questions without reservation. At last, I had a fellow questioner, someone with whom I could discuss all these thorny issues without judgment. I'd never experienced that before. I couldn't stop. We talked for hours, every spare moment. We'd drive for miles, going nowhere, just to be together and talk.

One afternoon, I studied his face, really looked at him. That moment, I realized I didn't want to change anything about him. As we spoke I began to see my religion through his eyes. What I glimpsed caused discomfort. Here was the first person I'd ever met who, without an ounce of judgment, listened to my questions, didn't answer them, and instead discussed them.

Within a few weeks, I was engaged. Before six months passed, we were married.

251

Outside my family's influence, we began sincerely searching for God. Armed with my questions, I asked without hesitation, always knowing my long-suffering husband would "have my back" if things got ugly, which they often did.

When, at an Assemblies of God church, I heard the Triple Trio ladies were granting blow jobs to the bass section of the choir, I asked what part of the Bible condoned that behavior. He supported me. When they answered that "all sins are under the blood of Christ and he doesn't even see sin when believers sin" and I whispered, "bullshit," my dear husband just chuckled.

When he smirked while signing the "declaration of faith" needed to join a particular church and asked for the correct words the council needed so he could join me in "the faith," I knew he was joining simply to be with me. When we later left that church, hoping to find a real, living god somewhere, anywhere, I knew he'd stick with me, even though I suspected he didn't believe a word of it.

We traveled from my childhood church to an Assemblies of God, to the Church of God, back to my childhood church, then on to an Evangelical Lutheran church. Our child was both dedicated to God (Church of God) and baptized (childhood church). But, we never found god.

Toward the end of our church days, I began to get a bit punchier and bold with my questions. While discussing transubstantiation, I asked the minister, "OK. If the bread and blood turn into the literal body and blood of our Lord, does the act of partaking raise our blood cholesterol? If so, is the "blood and body" lean? What part of Jesus' body are we consuming... did he have a lot of body fat? Plus, if a vegetarian partakes of communion, will they have evidence of meat eating in their body or fecal matter?"

The minister never answered my questions.

A broken heart

Around 2002 my husband had a heart attack. Long story short, after much research, we decided that adopting a vegetarian lifestyle was the easiest way to control his blood numbers. It was a simple decision based on some solid research by the likes of Dr. Dean Ornish, Dr. Caldwell Esselstyn, and such. These researchers have not only arrested heart disease, but have had success in reversing it using a low fat vegetarian diet. The fact that Medicare, as well as our own cardiologists endorsed the practice made the decision a no-brainer. In fact, after ten years, my dear husband is the only person in his Cardiac Rehab class that hasn't experienced a second "event" or died. We're more than pleased.

Except for one thing: I didn't expect Christians to possess such a vehemently angry attitude towards vegetarianism.

Now, just to clarify things, I'm treading lightly because these past ten years, I've noted that people get pretty defensive when it comes to diet. It's for that reason that I rarely mention it. I'm not a vegetarian evangelist. Diet is a personal decision and I have not, and will not, push my views on anybody.

Judging from the reaction of our local congregation, however, you'd think we had turned into a family of demons. Bible verses magically made their way into my inbox. Seems St. Paul was quite an anti-vegetarian.

Meanwhile, over at the Christian Vegetarian Association, they were spouting verses supporting our lifestyle, the Genesis story, Daniel's fast, etc.

This was the first time I realized that the Bible was not only filled with unbelievable stories, it was terribly contradictory and could be used to support basically any point of view. At the time, I didn't appreciate the knowledge that the "good book" was so deeply flawed. The questions in my mind began screaming for answers.

True disillusionment began to set in. It wasn't long before we quietly quit attending church. Unfortunately, this action caused a rift between me and my parents that I'm not sure can ever heal. By rejecting their deity, I'd evidently committed an unpardonable sin.

At that point, I'd given up on religion, but not on God. So, the next logical step was to move on to metaphysics.

The wacky New Age world

Throughout our marriage, I worked as a freelance writer and my career was blossoming. As a stringer for the largest regional newspaper in Minnesota, I thoroughly enjoyed whipping out my questions as I covered each new story. I found a publisher for my first novel, I had a nice cache of copywriting clients, was published in nationally distributed magazines, and I was in the middle of expanding my own publishing company. To fund my publishing expansion, I ratcheted up my copywriting business which meant landing some larger clients. I decided to network with some successful copywriters, one of whom was a Jewish Rabbi.

This is how I, and my myriad of questions, entered the whacky world of metaphysics. After all, god had to be somewhere, right? My Rabbi co-writer was deep into metaphysics. Because his was an opinion I admired, I figured after searching high and low for God in the Christian church, why not see if my writing partner was onto something? What could possibly go wrong?

I'm not one to mess around. If I research a topic, I become a near-expert fast. This means I jump into a new topic with both feet, no net, I want to find out sooner rather than later if it's a scam.

Armed with my trusty questions, this is precisely what I did with metaphysics. I took a course from one of the largest metaphysical "universities" on the Internet, became a "spiritual counselor," and landed a position working for said "university." Excited with what I had discovered, I made plans to publish metaphysical books with the aid of said "university."

Through it all, my husband was the soul of patience. He listened as I incessantly processed the flood of zany, new information heading my way. He smiled as I talked about channeling, angels, energy, and quantum physics. Simply hearing the juxtaposition of this crazy world with reality resulted in very bizarre conversation starters:

"The Galactic Federation today announced that the grid of love surrounding the planet is strengthening and will soon jettison us into a new dimension."

"Abraham, the group of nonphysical entities channeled by Esther Hicks, are going on an Alaskan cruise. For only 5k each, we can join them."

"The 'university' is sponsoring a satsang. We're invited. It's clothing optional."

"The 'university' is moving to Ecuador in preparation for the 2012 apocalypse. They want us to join them. Do you think we should, or should we stay here and hold down the fort when the atomic bombs start hitting the USA?"

The longer I worked with them, the stronger the reality of the situation became: God didn't exist here either. All I found was one bizarre situation melting into the next. My publishing plans dissolved in a pile of disillusionment. So much for that expansion.

We stayed in the USA as the fearless founder of the "university" moved to South America. I didn't work for them much longer.

But worse yet? I still hadn't found any deities whatsoever. Plus, Abraham, the Galactic Federation, and every other "nonphysical being" were dead wrong in the vast majority of their predictions. The predictions they had somewhat gotten correct were so vague, they could have applied to any situation. I didn't know where to look next.

The Crystalline Moment

I remember the exact moment. I was on one of our daily walks, yammering about my latest search for the Almighty. It was in at that moment that a most terrifying thought occurred to me.

What if it's all made up, a sincere scam. What if deities didn't exist?

I quickly brushed the thought aside as we continued trudging along our path. My husband eventually asked, "What 'cha thinking?"

A dangerous question to say the least. I paused a moment, then whispered, "I think I don't believe in god."

He waited a moment and said, "I don't think there's a god."

He was so nonchalant, I half expected a lightning bolt to strike him dead. But all I heard were (literally) crickets. Dominoes fell in my mind as every spiritual question I harbored was immediately answered.

"Why would God kill everyone on earth with a flood?" Because it's a made up story.

"Why is the Bible so contradictory?" Because it's fiction, written by humans, cobbled together, and evidently didn't have a good editor.

"How come Christians tend to be cantankerous and difficult to work with when they're supposed to represent a loving deity?" Because Christianity is based on a myth and they're no different than any of us other tribal people.

"Why doesn't the Bible square with science?" Because it's a myth written by a superstitious, ancient people.

With nearly every one of my spiritual questions resolved in (basically) one fell swoop, I felt a huge burden lift from my shoulders. I didn't have to search for an elusive god anymore. All the time I spent in prayer and reading could be spent doing something productive. I could now focus on what was important: Living.

Now all I had to do was learn how to navigate life without a deity. Good thing I have my six dangerous words to help guide my way and separate fact from fiction.

AFTERWORD

TRISTAN VICK

BELIEFS ARE FUNNY THINGS. SOME BELIEFS ARE INHERITED, others are acquired over long periods of time, and still others seem to be innate within us. Almost everyone believes that their own beliefs are more correct than the next person's. Indeed, when our beliefs are challenged, we often feel a sense of indignation. Interestingly, this appears to be just one of our natural responses to the insecurity of not knowing. It's never easy finding out what we thought we knew is, more often than not, wrong. The only problem is that when confronted with differing beliefs and new worldviews we are often reluctant to give these alternatives fair consideration because we are equally as reluctant to change our own beliefs. Indeed, sometimes beliefs can be thoroughly irrational things.

After the New Atheist movement kicked off, in what could only be called a revitalization of secular values in America, I was in the middle of undergoing my own deconversion process. As I began making friends with other atheists and nonbelievers in the secular community (most of whom I found to be entirely amiable and surprisingly intelligent people) I began to notice that our stories were eerily similar. It was no surprise, then, that we all shared many of the same experiences. Our journeys from faith to the absence of faith paralleled each other in uncanny ways, but at the same time there were enough minute differences to make each experience uniquely interesting.

As I soon learned, unlike myself, some people went through living hell to gain their freedom from religion while others simply had a faith which evaporated into thin air almost on its own. Each and every one of these personal stories were fascinating to me and I wanted to collect them and put them into a book so that they might be shared. This compendium is the fruits of this labor.

You may be wondering: why compose a book collecting anecdotal stories rather than dealing hard hitting philosophical blows to religion? A couple of reasons, actually.

First, I felt a book like this would give those who might be experiencing their own personal struggles with religion, who might be having doubts, or who have questions but don't know who to talk to about them, a place to hear others who have experienced the exact same thing. A place to see that they aren't alone and that there are others who have gone through the same process of doubting and questioning of their religious faith, and some who are still doing so as they try to make heads or tails of it all.

Knowing that you're not alone in the struggle to regain yourself is half the battle. Surely, it's a comfort many of us didn't have the luxury of receiving as there were no such books like this available when many of us made the scary, sometimes painful, journey toward a life beyond the absence of faith.

Secondly, I felt this book would be important as a sort of metaphorical olive branch. The atheist and nonbelieving, non-religious community grows larger every single day, and I thought it was necessary to get our voices out there. Not as apologists for any one particular belief system, because atheism could hardly be considered a belief system, but as a means to reach out to the religious and explain, in our own words, what atheists commonly believe (aside from our obvious lack of belief in any God or gods). By explaining our position and views we will be able to find common ground with believers by seizing upon agreed upon opinions and start working toward bridging the vast misunderstandings that divide us.

This transparency, I feel, will also make it easier for believers to approach nonbelievers by striking up conversations about things we may have in common instead of always bickering about what we might disagree on, as so often seems to be the case.

Needless to say, I think you'll be pleased to find that this book is not an attack on religion. It's not a polemic against any world faith. It is simply a collection of personal stories by those who have undergone the transformation from religious believer to irreligious nonbeliever.

This isn't to say there aren't challenging or trying statements or ideas made within these pages, since many of those who come out of the fierce grip of religion will oftentimes lean toward a more anti-theistic disposition than others. But this is understandable. Not only as a form of psychological coping, but also because these personal reflections recount a common experience shared among all apostates, the experience of how religion and faith have so epically failed us. It is no wonder then, that some are still a little bit resentful when it comes to their own past experiences with religion.

Ultimately, this book isn't designed to convince anyone of anything. Even when the atheists' comments are *ipse dixit*, such phrasing reflects the personal outlook of the individual and does not reflect any overarching dogma shared among all atheists. Knowing this, I hope others will be fair in their response to, and treatment of, the personal stories contained within these pages. Those with compassionate understanding will realize just how much courage it took for every contributor in this anthology to come out as nonbelievers and atheists, let alone share their most personal traumas and hardships with others. Believe me, that's not an easy task for anyone.

We're not asking for your sympathy but we could use a little bit of your empathy. Atheists and nonbelievers are the third largest worldview on the planet, and yet we still are marginalized in nearly every society in the world today (minus a few extremely open-minded and liberated cultures). This book is to help open the hearts and minds of others who might scoff at the idea of living life without God.

Living a life without faith doesn't mean we have given up believing in things. To the contrary, many of us atheists believe in nearly everything the devout person of faith does. We believe in family values, we believe in helping others, we believe in good educations for our children, and we believe in things like science and better cultural awareness, too. We believe in all these things, and more, minus any supernatural suppositions which many believers seem to take for granted. So although we may not be perfect, we aren't godless heathens, loathsome nihilists, or degenerate moral monsters. All these libelous pejoratives are hasty generalizations at best, and reflect little to nothing of the truth of what atheists believe or who we are as people.

Hopefully, you the reader might find something value within these pages, something worth taking from these personal reflections that might benefit you in some small way. Something which you might find as a valuable insight or even just the comfort of knowing that you're not alone in having the same doubts or fears as others.

If anyone takes away anything from this book, I would hope that it is the sheer joy and sense of liberation that comes with living life without religion and certainly without faith in God or gods. What's more, my wish is that these personal "deconversion testimonies" might allow others to see that it's possible to live a good and wholesome life without the invocation, or even the desire, to fall back into the old superstitious habits of our religious past. By sharing these most personal stories and experiences with you, we hope you will come to understand us better as atheists, agnostics, humanists, freethinkers, nonbelievers, and as people.

Tristan Vick, 10 January 2014

BEYOND

AN ABSENCE OF

FAITH

About the Contributors

JONATHAN MS PEARCE IS THE FOUNDER OF PUBLISHING imprint Onus Books, which seeks to give a voice to (religious) skepticism and skeptics, scientists and philosophers. He is the author of several philosophical works about religion, including *The Little Book of Unholy Questions, Free Will?* and *The Nativity: A Critical Examination*, as well as editing *13 Reasons To Doubt* for JREF, and writing a chapter on morality for John W. Loftus' forthcoming book *Christianity is Not Great* (Prometheus). He can also be found on Skeptic Ink Network (SIN) where he writes the philosophical blog *A Tippling Philosophe*. Find it online at:

www.skepticink.com/tippling/

Jonathan MS Pearce is also an avid vlogger on YouTube. To learn more about Jonathan MS Pearce and see his videos go to:

http://www.youtube.com/user/johnnyp76

SARAH SABELLA IS A LAB ASSISTANT AND ASPIRING Biotechnology major. Sarah lives with her life partner in the northeast United States and is currently learning how to balance work and play, while daily fighting a rather serious procrastination addiction. In her spare time she enjoys engaging others in meaningful conversation, getting lost in a good story, lucid dreaming, and fantasy play over the Internet. Her strongest passion is simply learning and growing as much and as freely as possible. You can become a procrastination enabler by following and connecting with Sarah at:

http://www.mmgasms.tumblr.com.

Any questions or comments, onymous and anonymous alike, are welcome and encouraged.

BUD UZORAS WAS BORN AND RAISED IN CHICAGO, AND earned his bachelor's degree in theology from Lincoln Christian College in Lincoln, Illinois. During the day Bud is a martial arts instructor and by night he is a blogger. Bud began his blog, Dead-Logic.com, so that he could document his exodus from faith and his journey toward a life of reason. Bud is also founder of the *Carl Sagan Google Doodle campaign*. You can support the Carl Sagan Google Doodle campaign by liking the Facebook page at:

https://www.facebook.com/SaganGoogleDoodle

SALEHA M. IS CURRENTLY A SENIOR IN WOODBRIDGE SENIOR High School. She is planning to major in Creative Writing in college, Saleha spends most of her free time reading, writing original or fan-based works, or gathering inspiration from the world around her. Or crying over fictional characters in anime.

SERGIO PAULO SIDER IS A FIFTY YEAR OLD ELECTRONIC ENGINEER living in Brazil who specialized in the design of embedded microcontroller systems. He's also extremely passionate about his Mac (how about dem' Apples?). Married and the proud father of two godless boys, his current goal is to live his remaining years on earth joyfully and peacefully. Feel free to respectfully contact him on Facebook at:

https://www.facebook.com/sergio.sider

ALICIA NORMAN IS PROBABLY BETTER KNOWN BY HER popular vlogger noms de plume SepiaSiren and The Sistah Atheist. Her YouTube videos and blog podcasts draw a sizeable audience and her stats and online persona are quickly gaining in popularity. She also has an amazing singing voice. You can find her online at:

http://www.youtube.com/user/sepiasiren

ARSALAN IS A 23 YEAR OLD FORMER SERVICEMAN WHO WAS INJured in the line of duty and is now pursuing a Masters degree in International Relations whilst working as a freelance writer. He is an avid reader and keeps a close eye on foreign affairs, with a particular interest in geopolitics. His other interests include watching/playing various sports. In the near future, he hopes to become a lecturer of International Relations and hopefully contribute to state policy over engagement with foreign and domestic parties in a secular fashion.

VYCKIE GARRISON WAS ONCE A PROMINENT MEMBER OF THE Quiverfull community, a rapidly growing Christian fundamentalist movement that bans birth control and encourages huge, "Biblical families" such as the Duggar Family of TLCs *19 and Counting* fame. Garrison edited and published a Christian "pro-life, pro-family" newspaper for 16+ years in northeast Nebraska while home-churching, home birthing, and home schooling seven children. She made waves when she left the Quiverfull movement and began speaking out against the lifestyle. Vyckie has appeared on *The Joy Behar Show*, *The Secret Lives of Women*, *The Story with Dick Gordon*, as well as numerous podcasts and radio programs including *Thom Hartmann*, *Living After Faith* and *Godless Bitches*. She is a well-respected adversary of Biblical patriarchy and the damages that it can inflict. She started the blog "No Longer Qivering" to provide support to women and children who are escaping abusive religious movements and to provide the public with accurate and compassionate information on the unique challenges faced by the spiritually abused.

COUNTER APOLOGIST: FOR VARIOUS PERSONAL AND professional reasons he is regretfully writing this under the pseudonym of "Counter Apologist". If he had to describe myself to a stranger he'd start with being a husband and father snd next a engineer. He holds a Bachelor's of science in Computer Engineering and a Master's degree Information Systems. If he were to go further still he'd identify as a geek and a gamer. It's only if he was in the company of people he was reasonably sure were like-minded that he would identify as an atheist and Christian apostate. In the past few years that last bit has grown into a passion of his, probably as a reaction to how religious he was before he "deconverted". He has found an interest in philosophy and has made a hobby of debunking Christian apologetics. This hobby consists of a blog and YouTube Channel at:

http://counterapologist.blogspot.com

and

http://www.youtube.com/user/counterapologist

WILLIAM LUCAS WAS BORN TO DUTCH IMMIGRANTS IN NEW Zealand, but has worked in the Punjab, India, and now lives in Japan. It would be not too far off the mark to think of him as a writer, reader, teacher and learner. He has taken part in ultra-marathons, composed haiku, created tapestry kit-sets by digitizing images, and conducted medical research to list a few of his interests. But perhaps his longest-lasting preoccupation is with the nature of the universe, reality, existence and consciousness *not necessarily in that order.*

TRISTAN VICK IS THE AUTHOR AND EDITOR OF A HALF DOZEN works, including both fiction and nonfiction. He is author of popular novels like *Bitten the Resurrection Virus* zombie series, the comedic noir *The Scarecrow & Lady Kingston: Rough Justice*, as well as the bestselling non-fiction work *Ignosticism: A Philosophical*

Justification for Atheism. In addition to these publications has collected and edited the blasphemy trials of G.W. Foote and Robert G. Ingersoll in the compendium *Reason Against Blasphemy*, as well as the entire Freethought works of G.W. Foote in *Seasons of Freethought.* You can learn more about Tristan Vick and his upcoming publishing projects by going to www.tristanvick.com. You can also read his blog at::

www.advocatusatheist.blogspot.jp.

MINDI ROSSER IS THE WIFE AND MOTHER OF A beautiful family of five: husband, tween daughter, baby girl on-the-way and an English bulldog. Mindi's natural inclination towards marketing has led her to promote causes that deeply matter to her including health and physical fitness and sharing her inspiring story with others. Mindi writes psychological thriller novels, competes in physique competitions, and enjoys blogging and vlogging. You can find her at:

www.mindizone.com

NO CROSS NO CRESCENT IS A MIDDLE-AGED GUY, BORN AND raised in the Middle East//North Africa region with an Islamic upbringing. Moving to the US, what he learned in his own reseach about the truth claims of the Koran (which would go universally challenged in his place of birth) made him feel bitter about the decades of l lies. Adding to this was exposure to US Chrstian fundamentalism which helped move him into the ranks of New Atheism, and blogging for the Skeptic Ink Network, something which he has profoundly enjoyed.

http://www.skepticink.com/nocrossnocrescent/

REBECCA BRADLEY IS A NATURAL-BORN ATHEIST WITH A fundamentalist Christian background who has a PhD in Archaeology from Cambridge University, and has worked as a field archaeologist and ethnoarchaeologist in Egypt and the Sudan. She has also published four novels and numerous short stories, and currently blogs as The Lateral Truth for the Skeptic Ink Network. Her special interests are pseudoarchaeology, the anthropology of religion, and cult messiahs, both political and religious. You can find her at:

http://www.skepticink.com/lateraltruth/

MIKE DOOLITTLE IS AN AUDIOPHILE, HEAVY METAL JUNKIE, and avid guitar player. He is also the prominent blogger of the well-known A-Unicornist blog. When he's not bleeding from his fingertips or debating Christian apologists online he spends his time helping others get fit as a personal trainer in the Tulsa area, Oklahoma. You can visit him at:

www.tulsatrainer.com

and

www.theaunicornist.com

BRUCE GERENCSER IS A FORMER EVANGELICAL PASTOR WHO pastored churches in Ohio, Michigan, and Texas for 25 years. Bruce left the ministry in 2003 and left the Christian faith in 2008. Writer and avid blogger, Bruce is the author of the popular blog *The Way Forward* which discusses current issues in the religious climate. He currently resides in rural NW Ohio with his wife of 35 years. Visit Bruce and read his excellent blog at:

http://brucegerencser.net/

BETH ANN ERICKSON IS THE QUEEN BEE OF THE SMALL publishing press Filbert Publishing, located in Central Minnesota; and is the publisher/editor of *Writing Etc.*, one of the longest running free e-zines for freelance writers. She is the author of ten titles and hundreds of articles; frequently writes advertising copy and works with her authors to help them achieve their publishing goals. A recent cancer statistic, Beth lives in small town Minnesota with her husband, son, and two rescue dogs. You can find her on Skeptic Ink Network (SIN) at *Incongruent Elements*. You can visit Beth Ann Erickson at the following websites:

http://filbertpublishing.com/

and

http://www.skepticink.com/incongruentelements/

Lightning Source UK Ltd.
Milton Keynes UK
UKHW021018040619
343800UK00008B/2561/P